DATE D

CASS LIBRARY OF AFRICAN STUDIES

AFRICANA MODERN LIBRARY

No. 5

General Editor: PROFESSOR E. U. ESSIEN-UDOM
University of Ibadan, Nigeria

FANTI
CUSTOMARY LAWS

A BRIEF INTRODUCTION TO THE PRINCIPLES
OF THE
NATIVE LAWS AND CUSTOMS OF THE
FANTI AND AKAN DISTRICTS OF THE GOLD COAST

WITH

A REPORT OF SOME CASES THEREON DECIDED
IN THE LAW COURTS

JOHN MENSAH SARBAH

THIRD EDITION

WITH A NEW INTRODUCTION BY

HOLLIS R. LYNCH

FRANK CASS & CO. LTD.
1968

Published by
FRANK CASS AND COMPANY LIMITED
67 Great Russell Street, London WC1

First edition   1897
Second edition   1904
Third edition   1968

Printed in Great Britain by
Thomas Nelson (Printers) Ltd., London and Edinburgh

INTRODUCTION TO THE
THIRD EDITION

JOHN MENSAH SARBAH, 1864—1910, the first indigenous
barrister of the then Gold Coast, now Ghana, and an early
member of its Legislative Council was undoubtedly one of the
most distinguished African scholars and nationalists of his
time. His first major work, *Fanti Customary Law*, was first
published in 1897, and is one of the most important pioneer
legal and sociological work on an African people, but was
clearly intended to serve nationalist ends: to combat the
heedless obtrusiveness of the British administration by seeking
to educate the imperialist overlords to an understanding of
and respect for traditional Fanti culture; more particularly, it
was intended to bolster the campaign of the Fantis against
two proposed Land Bills which sought to vest ownership and/or
administration of lands in the Crown—measures which
represented the most serious threat thus far to Fanti integrity.
Merely as a treatise on the Akan people, [1] Sarbah's work has
been superseded by the works of such scholars as J. B.
Danquah, R. S. Rattray and Eva Meyerowitz. [2] It is, therefore,
primarily as the product of a nationalist that this introduction
seeks to illumine Sarbah's work, and it seems best to do so by
setting the author and his work in historical perspective. [3]

John Mensah Sarbah was born at Cape Coast on June 3,
1864, the son of John Sarbah, a devoted father and a wealthy
and civic-minded merchant who served on the Gold Coast
Legislative Council from 1888 until his death in 1892. In 1876,

---

[1] The Akans include the Ashantis as well as the Fantis.

[2] See J. B. Danquah, *Akan Laws and Customs* (London, 1928);
R. S. Rattray, *Ashanti Law and Constitution* (London, 1929); Eva L. R.
Meyerowitz, *The Sacred State of the Akan* (London, 1951).

[3] The two major sources, apart from Sarbah's own works, which
provided materials for this were: J. Magnus Sampson, *Gold Coast Men
of Affairs* (London, 1937) and David Kimble, *A Political History of
Ghana*, 1850–1928 (London, 1962).

at the age of twelve, Mensah Sarbah attended the newly opened Wesleyan High School, Cape Coast, but completed his secondary education in England at Wesleyan College, Taunton, Somerset. He went on to study law at Lincoln's Inn and was called to the Bar in 1887 at twenty-three, thus becoming the youngest West African barrister.

In the same year that he graduated he began taking an active interest in Gold Coast affairs: in February 1887, he wrote a letter to the Colonial Secretary protesting against the growing tendency of European, officials to ignore or scorn African customs and institutions and advised that the jurisdiction of chiefs should be restored. This indiscriminate encroachment of the British into the affairs of the Akan peoples of the Gold Coast was a relatively new development and was resented both by the educated élite and the traditional rulers. For most of the almost 400 years that Europeans—the Portuguese, British, Danes and Dutch—were on the Gold Coast, they had been there as tenants and on the sufferance of African chiefs and their jurisdiction had been strictly confined to their forts. But from early in the nineteenth century the British (who later controlled the entire coast by taking over the Danish and Dutch forts in 1850 and 1872 respectively), as allies of the Fantis against the powerful inland kingdom of the Ashantis, gradually extended an informal jurisdiction over them. This policy of informal protection was assiduously and effectively pursued by George Maclean, President of the Cape Coast Council of Merchants (1830–1843) and Judicial Assessor under the Crown (1843–1847), who acted as defender of the Fantis against the Ashantis, as well as an adjudicator among the chiefs and advisor to them. This relationship was formalized by the Bond of 1844 between the traditional Fanti chiefs and the British Government in which the former gave the latter authority to remove " barbarous practices " and to help " mould the country to the general principles of British law." As Gold Coast nationalists, including Sarbah, were later to emphasize, the Bond was an agreement between political equals, and had in no way diminished Fanti sovereignty. Fanti-British relationship took a new turn in 1874 when, just after the expensive Ashanti War, the British Government annexed Fantiland as a defensive measure. This act was of doubtful legality, for here again, as their spokesmen were quick to point out, the Fantis had not been conquered by the British, nor had they relinquished their sovereignty.

The period between the Bond of 1844 and the promulgation of a Protectorate in 1874 was characterized for the Fantis, alternatively, by hope in British good intentions and by growing mistrust, the result of a feckless, vacillating and at times seemingly treacherous British policy. This period began hopefully enough. In 1852, for instance, the British persuaded the Fantis to constitute a Council of Chiefs with legislative powers. Proceedings were to be superintended by the Governor and decisions could become binding only with his consent. The Assembly agreed to levy a poll tax, the proceeds from which were to be " devoted to the public good." But these experiments ended in failure. The tax was inefficiently collected and the Fantis did not derive any benefits from it. Nor were the Fanti Chiefs paid their promised stipends. Understandably, Fanti opposition to the tax grew, and the whole scheme finally collapsed in 1862.

New Fanti hope for constructive British help came with the recommendation of the Select Parliamentary Committee of 1865 that the British should withdraw from the West African Coast but should prepare Africans under its jurisdiction for self-government before doing so. But the fact is that nowhere, least of all in the Gold Coast, did the British Government find it convenient to implement this policy. Thus, when John Aggrey, the intelligent King of the Cape Coast (1865–67), acting in concert with educated Fantis sought to exercise his constitutional rights, instead of receiving British encouragement he was charged with insubordination, deposed and deported to Sierra Leone, thus becoming one of the first African political martyrs of British imperialism.

It was this increasing lack of confidence in the British Government together with fear of the Ashantis which prompted united action to an unprecedented degree on the part of the Fantis whose leaders met at the town of Mankessim in 1868 and formed the Fanti Confederation. Conceived primarily as a defensive alliance, the Confederation assumed a political nature in October 1871 with the promulgation of the Mankessim Constitution which provided for a Legislative Assembly in which both the traditional and educated elements would be represented. Indeed, the Constitution was the product of close co-operation between the traditional rulers and the educated élite; in particular, it was based on the blueprint set out by Dr. James Africanus Beale Horton in his *Letters on the Political Condition of the Gold Coast* published in London in

1870. But the British officials on the Gold Coast, heedless of the recommendations of the 1865 Parliamentary Committee, were, on the whole, unsympathetic to the Confederation. Thus, the announcement of the Mankessim Constitution was viewed as the crowning act of conspiracy against the British Government, and several leaders were arrested and imprisoned. Although the Fanti leaders were quickly released on the instructions of the Colonial Office, the hasty action of the local British officials had seriously prejudiced the Confederation's chances of success, and it collapsed in 1873. However, later Gold Coast nationalist leaders, including Sarbah, applauded and drew inspiration from this early effort at unity, and correspondingly, were critical of obstructive and seemingly treacherous British tactics.

The establishment of a formal protectorate over Fantiland, beginning in 1874, a year after the collapse of the Fanti Confederation, brought a further rapid decline in the authority of the Fanti Chiefs and dimmed the hopes of all Gold Coast nationalists. To the latter a retrograde step was taken when the Gold Coast Government was reorganized to exclude unofficial representation—which meant that there was not a single African voice on the Legislative Council. (It took twelve years of agitation led by James Brew, the foremost nationalist figure of this period, before unofficial African representation was resumed). The first act of the Gold Coast Government was to emancipate all slaves and abolish slave-dealing. The Supreme Court Ordinance of 1876 introduced a judicial system based on the English model and served greatly to widen the sphere of influence of English law. In 1878 the first Native Jurisdiction Ordinance was enacted and for the first time the Government was given the power to dismiss chiefs, albeit with the consent of the Secretary of State. Although this ordinance was never implemented, its main features were incorporated into the 1883 Native Jurisdiction Ordinance which was to form the basis of native jurisdiction until 1927.

The traditional rulers, often supported by the educated élite, continued to resent systematic whittling down of their power and influence, and especially the British assumption of the right to dismiss them—a right which traditionally belonged to the Oman Council of Chiefs or the people. Indeed the 1883 Ordinance led the educated élite to see the need to study and interpret the traditional institutions and customs for the purpose of defending them effectively against British encroachment. Thus it helped further to foster co-operation between the Chiefs and the educated élite.

On his return to the Gold Coast in the late 1880's, Sarbah quickly established himself as one of the leading defenders of African interests. His first major political act was to lead the fight against the draft Municipal Ordinance of 1888. In the previous year (1887) Africans in the Cape Coast had sought to institute Municipal Government as part of a campaign for greater African representation in the Gold Coast. The British Government (though not the local administrators) were sympathetic and prepared a draft Municipal Ordinance but insisted that the proposed new institution should not be granted Government funds; instead it was to be given powers of taxation. Africans for their part insisted that direct taxation was alien to traditional African society, and argued that an annual Government grant was initially necessary if the scheme was to succeed. In a petition with about 170 signatures of June 5, 1889, to the Secretary of State, Sarbah presented the African case. He asserted that " The Principle that Representation means taxation cannot be applied to this Colony. For from time immemorial we have enjoyed representative institutions without such direct taxation as is contemplated." He wanted " a Municipality built on our native institutions so adapted, reorganized and reformed as to satisfy our modern wants." Sarbah complained that " Today we are being ruled as if we had no indigenous institutions, no language, no national characteristics, no homes." The result of the recent British administration, he asserted, was " a great disorganization of society." The Ordinance was enacted but in protest Cape Coast Africans refused to implement it. This was replaced by the even more objectionable—from the African point of view—1894 Towns Council Bill which retained the principle of direct taxation and also sought to bring the proposed Municipal Councils under central control by giving the Governor powers to nominate half the number of officials and making the District Commissioner President with a casting vote. Mensah Sarbah later described this Bill as " a monument of faulty and unsympathetic statecraft." He especially deprecated the fact that the Bill did not permit effective African participation in their own affairs. It was not until 1898 that some attempt was made to implement the Bill, but because of lack of African co-operation it never worked well.

In an attempt to halt " the demoralising effect of certain European influences " and to " stop further encroachment into . . . (African) nationality," Sarbah played the leading role in organizing in 1889 the Mfantsi Amanbuhu Fékuw (Fanti National Political Society) in the Cape Coast. The Society undertook to study all aspects of traditional life. Its activities, which was much publicized in the Gold Coast papers, succeeded in stimulating pride among Africans in their culture; in particular Fanti names, dress and music came into vogue.

To help sustain the new cultural nationalism, Sarbah in 1891 founded his own newspaper *The Gold Coast People* (1891–1898). A typical report in the *People* was the following in the issue of November 30, 1893. " I failed not to be present at the . . . concert presided over by Mr. J. Mensah Sarbah, who in his native cloth looked like a Roman in toga garb at the Forum. Let us be thankful Fantis are proud to be Fantis and are not ashamed to be known by their native names, heard speaking their liquid language, and seen arrayed in their flowing robes . . . I am sorry I did not wear my cloth on that warm night. I had the misfortune to wear the alien badge of Coat and trousers." Later, Sarbah himself, partly in reply to attempted European ridicule that educated Gold Coast Africans had ' gone Fantee ' wrote thus: " I am fully convinced that it be better to be called one's own name than be known by a foreign one, that it is possible to acquire Western learning and be expert in scientific attainments without neglecting one's mother tongue, that the African's dress had a closer resemblance to the garb of the Grecian and Roman . . . and should not be thrown aside."

But what was really to unite Gold Coast Africans and catapult Mensah Sarbah into national prominence was the dispute over land. It had been understood by both sides that the British protectorate over the Fantis did not in any way impair their right to the land. However, the rise of the gold-mining industry after 1874, and the rapid expansion of the timber trade, had been accompanied by uncontrolled land concessions and speculations, with resultant disputes. To regulate further exploitation of the timber and mineral resources, the Government wished to bring all lands, not already privately owned, under its control. Accordingly, the Crown Lands Bill of 1894 was enacted to " Vest Waste Lands, Forest Lands and Minerals in the Queen." This far-reaching measure threatened the very fabric of Fanti society, but it is doubtful that the British then realized its implication. However, among the Fantis, it quickly created " a fiery indignation ": they objected to it on the grounds that it would violate native law and custom and would be tantamount to an illegal seizure of the country; and they saw it as another attempt to weaken further the authority of their Chiefs.

As a result of strong and widespread Fanti protest, the Bill was dropped in October 1895. But the Government felt committed to its principle. And so in March 1897 a new Lands Bill was introduced in the Legislative Council designed to give the Crown powers of administration though not of owner-ship of all " public lands." But Africans could see no significant difference in the two bills, and kept up their agitation. Mensah Sarbah and other leaders of the Fékuw took the lead in organizing a movement of protest against the new Land Bill. Indeed, finding Fékwu—primarily a social organization—inadequate for their new political purpose, they formed in its stead the Gold Coast Aborigines Right Protection Society. On New Years Day 1898 the Society started its own newspaper—*The Gold Coast Aborigines*—with the motto " for the safety of the Public and the welfare of the Race."

Because of the great public outcry, Governor William Maxwell agreed that Mensah Sarbah and P. Awooner Renner should appear at the bar of the Legislative Council on behalf of petitioners from Abura, Cape Coast and Anomabu during the second reading of the Bill. Sarbah expressed the popular view that the Bill would " deprive the aborigines of their rights in the soil of their native land," making them mere settlers of the Government with disastrous social consequences: the already waning authority of the Chiefs would be further greatly undermined, " the bonds of society " would be " snapped," " family ties . . . broken and family relationships destroyed." Concerned more with expressing his conviction than with cash, Sarbah turned down his retainer's fee of £400—a sum which went towards the founding of the *Gold Coast Aborigines*. The partiotic role played by Mensah Sarbah during the Land Bill dispute greatly enhanced his reputation among West Africans.

But despite vigorous opposition to it, a slightly amended version of the Lands Bill became law in 1897. For Gold Coast Africans the next step was to appeal against it to the British Government through the Secretary of States for the colonies.

Selected by the Aborigines Protection Society to do so were J. W. Sey, T. E. Jones and George Hughes—three wealthy Cape Coast merchants who sailed for London May 24, 1898. The delegates were successful beyond their expectations: Joseph Chamberlain, the Colonial Secretary, after an interview with them on August 5, 1898, conceded their two demands that " native law shall remain and prevail . . . with regard to the devolution of land," and that a Judicial Court should decide land questions. This decision led to a withdrawal of the recently passed Lands Bill: Sarbah and the A.R.P.S. had triumphed.

But although the Government had yielded to African objections to the Lands Bills, it still wished to regulate the granting of concessions so as to protect owners from fraud and give security of title to concession holders. To this end a Concessions Bill was passed in 1900. Although the Government was careful not to include anything which might be interpreted as disputing the absolute ownership of Africans to their land some Africans were still suspicious. To allay their fears the Governor appointed four Africans, among them, Mensah Sarbah, as extraordinary members to the Legislative Council for the debate on the Bill. The fact that Mensah Sarbah himself seconded the final version of the Bill was for most Africans evidence that it contained nothing inimical to their interests.

It is against this background of the struggle of Gold Coast Africans to maintain the identity and integrity of their culture, and more particularly their fight against the Lands Bills that we must view Sarbah's *Fanti Customary Law* published in 1897. It took its first form as a series of articles based on Cape Coast records written on the suggestion of Fékuw. But the decision to elaborate on it and publish it as a book, thus making it available to a much wider audience, was prompted by the desire to obviate the worse aspects of an increasingly felt British administration. In his book he was concerned to show that " The African social system . . . has been built up gradually . . . so as to meet its own special requirements." The first part of the book is a sociological analysis of Fanti society, the second is a compilation of decided cases grouped and classified in such a way to establish " the general Customary Law." An appendix of nine documents, among them the Bond of 1844 and the Protectorate Proclamation of 1874, seemed designed to show that the Gold Coast had never been conquered and hence its lands had never been alienated. Sarbah's work is undoubtedly an important pioneer legal and sociological work on the Akan people and attracted the sympathetic attention of his fellow educated West Africans, as well as of Europeans interested in West Africa. Among those who welcomed his work was Miss Mary Kingsley, the most important contemporary European writer on West Africa. To him she wrote: " It is exceedingly necessary . . . to demonstrate the existence of the African state . . . . You have done more than any one by your valuable *Fanti Customary Law*—which I continually advertise—to help. . . . " Sarbah's book has been in sufficient demand to necessitate the printing of two further editions.

Although Sarbah in his *Fanti Customary Law* and elsewhere was highly critical of the Gold Coast administration, he was no anti-British revolutionary: he recognised and admitted that the British could be a force for good, the more so if they respected the indigenous Fanti culture, and co-operated fully with the traditional rulers and the educated élite whom he believed would together govern the independent Gold Coast nation that he envisaged.

Until his sudden death in 1910 Sarbah, active as author, journalist, educator and legislator, remained the most prominent Gold Coast nationalist. In 1901 he was appointed one of two African members to the Legislative Council—a position he held for the remainder of his life. Both in the Legislative Council and out he continued strenuously to defend African rights and interests. In 1901 when the *Gold Coast Aborigines* temporarily ceased publication he once again started his own newspaper the *Gold Coast Weekly*. In 1906 he published his second major work *Fanti National Constitution* in which he sought to explain " the principles controlling and regulating the Akan state," but which was again partly designed to facilitate the kind of British rule which would most benefit Africans. In these years Sarbah also sought to establish independent schools which he hoped would foster the study and understanding of indigenous institutions and initiate an indigenous literature.

January, 1967   HOLLIS R. LYNCH

TO

THE MEMORY

OF

The Honourable John Sarbah,

MERCHANT, CAPE COAST CASTLE, SOMETIME MEMBER OF

THE LEGISLATIVE COUNCIL OF THE GOLD COAST COLONY, AND

CAPTAIN COMMANDING THE GOLD COAST RIFLE CORPS

DURING ASANTI EXPEDITION, 1873–1875. A MERCHANT ENTERPRISING

AND HONOURABLE, A STATESMAN LOYAL AND FEARLESS,

A PATRIOT CHIVALROUS AND TRUE, A PARENT

PIOUS AND MOST AFFECTIONATE,

THIS BOOK

IS

DEDICATED BY HIS SON,

THE AUTHOR.

ADVERTISEMENT TO THE SECOND EDITION.

THIS small contribution to the study of an aboriginal
system of West African Customary Laws has met with
an acceptance and appreciation wholly unexpected.

No labour, therefore, has been spared to secure accuracy,
and still striving after quality in this edition, every statement of the Law has been closely scrutinized and carefully
reconsidered; and without forgetting this is but a brief
introduction to the principles of the Customary Laws,
some new matter has been added to several chapters.
Guided by the experience derived from the use of this
book in Court practice, it is hoped, the cases in footnotes
will be found useful.

The work of 1665, relating to the "Golden Coast of
Guinney," referred to in this edition, is substantially com-
piled from de Faria da Sousa, the Portuguese author, the
travels of John Lok in 1553 and 1554, Towrson in 1555 to
1557, published in Hakluyt, and Artus who wrote in 1625.
A study of these ancient authors abundantly proves that
when, in 1481, Portuguese navigators and other European
trading adventurers first appeared on the Gold Coast, they
found an organized society having kings, rulers, institutions,
and a system of customary laws, most of which remain to
this day.

Suggestions and criticisms from whatever source emanating have been carefully examined, weighed, considered, and dealt with accordingly.

Reference to the decided cases has been made easy by the full index prepared by Sir W. Brandford Griffith, Kt., Chief Justice of the Gold Coast Colony, by whose kind permission it is inserted. Thanks are due to the learned Chief Justice for this useful index; and to Mr. Justice Francis Smith, through whose courtesy appears the information on certain Accra Customary Laws by the late Mr. Edmund Bannerman.

The *Times* newspaper review of the first edition of this work is here reproduced, in compliance with the urgent request of many West African readers, who are anxious to read it.

I am much indebted to my friend Mr. J. E. Biney of the Inner Temple for his assistance in passing this edition through the press.

J. M. S.

The Library, Lincoln's Inn,
Michaelmas Term, 1903.

FANTI CUSTOMARY LAWS.

(WM. CLOWES AND SONS, LIMITED.)

Mr. Sarbah has in this interesting volume done excellent work. He has collected so much that is instructive to the student of ethnology and comparative jurisprudence that it is to be hoped he will give further extracts from the judicial archives of the Gold Coast relating to the customs of the Fantis. He has examined, evidently with care and a desire to ascertain the truth, the legal proceedings in our regular Courts, and before those extremely anomalous functionaries our judicial assessors, relating to the family, marriage, divorce, property, tenure of land, suretyship, slander, and mode of enforcing payment of debts; and very curious are some of the customs. For some reason not explained, and apparently difficult to explain, permission to continue the examination of the archives of the Court at Cape Coast Castle was withdrawn before Mr. Sarbah's search was complete. It is to be hoped that the permission will be promptly renewed. The origin of the jurisdiction of the English Courts, and especially that of judicial assessors, on the African West Coast is peculiar, and more than one Secretary of State has been embarrassed in justifying a useful institution. Until recently English jurisdiction did not extend beyond the range of the guns of our forts; and on the Gold Coast the powers of our assessors were first derived, not from any statute or Order in Council, but from the assent of the native kings and chiefs; in particular, from the bond signed in 1844 by Cudjee Chibboe, King of Denkerah, Quashie Ottoo, chief of Abrah, and other magnates among the Fantis. Very wisely, our Government have respected, so far as possible, the local customs, and it was the duty of the judicial assessor to sit as a sort of head chief along with the local chief and hear and decide the disputes of the natives. This collection furnishes ample evidence of the good sense with which a difficult task was performed. While human sacrifices, and such barbarous customs repugnant to civilized ideas as "panyarring," or kidnapping, were repressed, the assessors gave to the Customary Law the flexibility necessary to meet new circumstances and to satisfy the rising standard of justice. Among the Fantis, descent is traced through the female, and a Fanti family consists of all persons lineally descended from a common ancestry through females. One peculiarity of the Customary Law is that the members of a family are jointly and severally liable for the debts, etc., of a member of it; all must pay, or the delinquent member must be given up to the claimant. A valid marriage is contracted when the husband has given his wife's family certain presents, usually called "head rum." The phrase does injustice to the Fantis.

The term "head rum" so-called, often used in the case of marriage, is an instance of erroneous and deplorable interpretation of Fanti into English. Rum was unknown to the people until brought to them by those engaged in the slave trade, and before then, surely, marriage was not unknown. The beverages made from maize and extracted from the date and palm trees were common, but instead of nuptial wine an ignorant clerk said "head rum" for *etsir ensa*. The term *etsir ensa* is evidently a contraction for *etsir nsa nkredzi*—literally, tokens or prices of the head, etc.

According to a rule, the existence of which we should have doubted but for Mr. Sarbah's explicit statement on the point, there are many contracts of surety under native law; and in the first instance the remedy is against the surety, and not the debtor. Mr. Sarbah's collection of cases contains more than one action for breach of promise of marriage. The faithless swain is, apparently, not mulcted in what counsel call "exemplary damages." One case tried before the Judicial Assessor and Chief Chiboo, Thompson and Robertson, resulted in a verdict for £5. In an action for *crim. con.*, tried in 1844, the defendant was ordered to pay 2 oz. of gold, a sheep, and a case of rum. Sometimes the native kings were called to account by our Courts; and in one case reported in this volume the ruler

of Eastern Wassah, charged with cruelty and extortion practised upon
his nephew, was condemned to refund treasure which he had obtained,
and to pay 5 oz. of gold for the barbarous treatment inflicted on his
relative. Evidently there is no superabundance of technicalities in the
procedure of justice in some of the Courts of which Mr. Sarbah is the
reporter, as witness the judgment attributed to Bailey, C.J., in 1884 :—

> There was a monkey who wanted to get some nuts that were hot and afire ; he
> got a cat and used her hands to pull the nuts out of the fire.   The monkey got the
> nuts and the cat burnt her fingers.   And they and the three chiefs are the monkeys,
> and you are the cats, and you have burnt your fingers to the extent of £1 each.
> Judgment : £3 and costs.

Times, Feb. 4, 1897.

PREFACE.

To George Emil Eminsang, Esquire, Elmina.

MY DEAR MR. EMINSANG,—Pardon the liberty I take in sending you this open letter, with this my first attempt in the thorny paths of literature. I dare do so, for not only are you a native of the soil and one of my father's friends, but you are also the senior member of the Bar of the Western Province of the Supreme Court of the Gold Coast, having commenced to practise when we, who are now members thereof, were but schoolboys. Your patriotism is well known, and your loyalty is undoubted, and as one who, in former years, served his country in his office as Chief Magistrate at Elmina—what time the Dutch held sway over a portion of the Gold Coast—and afterwards took a prominent part in executing the treaty under which British jurisdiction was extended on the Gold Coast, you have no idea, how often you have encouraged me to go on with, and persevere in, the task I had set myself, to reduce into writing the Customary Laws and Usages of the Fanti, Asanti, and other Akan inhabitants of the Gold Coast. I know that you have often given the first correct idea on Customary Laws to newly arrived European officials, who, having no intelligent person to explain things to them, would fain say there were no Customary Laws. I know how it has constantly pained and grieved you to notice any local Customary Law or Usage distorted by any practitioner from beyond seas solely bent on snatching a verdict.

Thanks, however, to Sir Joseph Turner Hutchinson, Knt., sometime Chief Justice of the Gold Coast, who readily gave permission when I applied to him to take notes from the records of the Court at Cape Coast Castle, I have made a selection of cases bearing on the local Customary Laws, and I hope that by grouping and classifying the decisions together, facilities will be afforded for ascertaining what is really the general Customary Law with respect to most matters to which, it is well known, the natives are tenaciously attached, the principles underlying it, and how far it is qualified by any special local or tribal custom. And now that comparison is rendered possible, and the lines of inquiry as it were placed before them, this is a field of investigation which should engage the close and studious attention of every educated native.

Unfortunately, not only was the expert evidence of the Chiefs on points of Customary Law carelessly and sometimes inefficiently translated to the Court, but no attempt had been made to test their accuracy by comparison with similar cases in other districts affecting the same class of persons. In spite of this, however, there is a remarkable uniformity and consistency in the decisions on the Customary Law in regard to certain matters, several recent decisions agreeing with old cases, the existence of which could not possibly have been known by the judges of the Supreme Court.

To wade through a mass of matter for the purpose of finding what was worth copying was no light task, and I would have been more satisfied had I been able to verify with care all the decisions reported in this book. But beggars cannot be choosers; wherefore, when I suddenly received an intimation from the Registrar that the Chief Justice had withdrawn his permission, I had to stop. If, therefore, any errors are detected in the reported cases, you will understand how they crept in, and this in spite of the special care I took when copying them in the first instance.

I have endeavoured in some instances to state the Customary Law in a few simply worded propositions, embodying what a careful analytical study proves to be the principles running through it. I am quite alive to the danger of reducing Customary Law to a condition of fixity in a semi-developed state of society, the effect of which may hinder the gradually operating innate generation of law by a process of natural development, independent of accident and individual will, which best accords with the varying needs and spirit of a people so circumstanced as the inhabitants of the Gold Coast.

A great thinker has said, "The value of a custom is its flexibility, in that it adapts itself to all the circumstances of the moment as of the locality. Customs may not be wise as laws, but they are always more popular." You will not be surprised, therefore, to find I have not attempted to write on every imaginable point of the Customary Law; to do that were to write an account of the everyday existence of the people, thus following the footsteps of Bosman and Cruickshank, whose works I have consulted at all times during the progress of this work. I have aimed, not so much at quantity as quality; and, as often as opportunity offered, I have tested the accuracy of what is here set down, by comparing the same with information gathered from all classes and conditions of men, from all parts of the Gold Coast, with whom I have come in contact, professionally or otherwise. At the same time, I am perfectly conscious how I have been

unable to attain the high standard I had set before me ; but
if by my efforts other natives of the Gold Coast, acquainted
with the several local dialects, and trained in the English
Inns of Court, are induced and stimulated to enter the
hitherto unexplored fields of our Customary Law, I shall
not have laboured in vain, for I am certain, that it is only
by patient investigation and intelligent study, that the
Customary Law can be well defined and consolidated.
Customary Law and other Usages recorded by Bosman, as
existing two centuries ago, have not altered to any extent
up to the present day, although one knows that, as the
mind of a community becomes enlightened, its legal convictions will change, and this will constitute a change in
its Customary Law, as that law is, from time to time,
recognized and enforced in the local tribunals.   It is a
universal truism that Usage generates the Customary Law,
as, in the long run, a sense of fitness becomes a sense of
necessity and obligation.   When Sir J. Smalman Smith,
in the Full Court held at Cape Coast Castle, on October
24, 1887, and presided over by Chief Justice Macleod,
stated, "I have found the native laws and customs always·
founded on very good and intelligible reasons, which are
perfectly rational and consistent," he expressed the conviction of every person who has any intelligent knowledge
of the Customary Laws of the Gold Coast, and although I
dare not claim to be he that shall come, I have endeavoured
to be the voice of one crying in the wilderness, while
preparing, perhaps imperfectly, the way before him.

I must now express my thanks, in addition to Sir
Joseph Turner Hutchinson, Knt., to His Honour Francis
Smith, Esq., Acting Chief Justice of the Gold Coast Colony ;
to King Amonoo of Anamaboe, King Otoo of Abura, Mr.
T. F. E. Jones, and other headmen and persons whom I
have often consulted, and from whom I have learnt

much on the Customary Law and Usage ; to Rev. J. B. Anaman, F.R.G.S., for his assistance in the compilation of the table of principal dates and events; to Mr. Registrar Bernasko and Mr. Coulon, for assisting me to discover the old records; to Mr. J. W. D. Johnson, for lending me his rare copy of Bosman's work ; to Mr. Adolf Neubauer, M.A., Senior Sub-Librarian, Oxford University, for allowing me to consult some rare old books in the Bodleian Library for this work; and finally to my friend Mr. Samuel E. Kaye, of Lincoln's Inn, whose unremitting assistance, in correcting the proofs and verifying many quotations and extracts herein referred to, has been simply invaluable.

I remain, yours very truly,

JNO. M. SARBAH.

The Library, Lincoln's Inn.
August, 1896.

TABLE OF CONTENTS.

———◦◦◦———

INDEX OF REPORTED CASES.

———◆◇———

LIST OF CASES.

The Family.

MISCELLANEOUS CASES.

GOVERNORS OF THE BRITISH SETTLEMENTS ON THE GOLD COAST SINCE THE YEAR 1750.

*Died on the Coast marked † ; acting ***

NAME.	YEAR OF APPOINTMENT.	NAME.	YEAR OF APPOINTMENT.
†Thomas Melvil	June 23, 1751	*James Lilly	1845
†William Tymewell	Jan. 23, 1756	William Winniett... ...	1846
*Charles Bell ...	.Feb. 17, 1756	Judge J. C. Fitzpatrick ...	1849
*Nassau Senior ...	Oct. 15, 1757	†*William Winniett ...	1850
Charles Bell ...	May 10, 1761	James Bannerman ...	1850
William Mutter	Aug. 15, 1763	Stephen John Hill ...	1851
†John Hippersley	Mar. 1, 1766	*Judge J. C. Fitzpatrick ...	1853
Gilbert Petrie ...	Aug. 11, 1766	*Brodie G. Cruickshank ...	1853
John Grossle ...	Apr. 21, 1769	Stephen John Hill ...	1854
David Mill ...	Aug. 11, 1770	*Judge Henry Conror ...	1854
Richard Miles ...	Jan. 20, 1777	Sir Benj. Chilly Campbell	
†John Roberts ...	Mar. 25, 1780	Pine	1857
*J. B. Weuves ...	May 20, 1781	Major Henry Bird ...	1858
Richard Miles ...	Apr. 29, 1782	Edward Bullock Andrews	1860
James Morgue ...	Jan. 29, 1784	William A. Ross	1862
†Thomas Price ...	Jan. 24, 1787	Richard Pine ...	1862
Thomas Norris	Apr. 27, 1787	William Hackett	1864
William Fielde	June 20, 1789	†Brevet-Major Rokeby S. W.	
John Gordon ...	Nov. 15, 1791	Jones	1865
A. Dalzell ...	Mar. 31, 1792	*W. E. Mockler ...	1865
Jacob Mould ...	Dec. 16, 1798	*Col. Edward Conran ...	1865
John Gordon ...	Jan. 4, 1799	Herbert Taylor Ussher ...	1867
A. Dalzell ...	Apr. 28, 1800	W. H. Simpson	1868
Jacob Mould ...	Sept. 30, 1802	Herbert Taylor Ussher ...	1869
†Col. G. Torrane	Feb. 8, 1805	*Charles Spencer Salmon ...	1871
E. W. White ...	Dec. 4, 1807	John Pope Hennessey ...	1872
Joseph Dawson	Apr. 21, 1816	Herbert Tayl r Ussher ...	1872
John Hope Smith	Jan. 19, 1817	Col. R. W. Harley ...	1872
†Brig.-Gen. Sir Charles Mac-		Sir Garnet Wolseley ...	1873
Carthy ...	Nov. 28, 1822	*Lieut.-Col. Maxwell ...	1874
†Major Chisholm	Jan. 21, 1824	*Charles C. Lees ...	1874
Major Purdon ...	July 1, 1824	*Col. Johnston ...	1874
Major-Gen. Charles Turner		Captain George C. Strahan	1874
	Mar. 22, 1825	Sauford Freeling	1876
Major-Gen. Sir Neil Campbell		†Herbert Taylor Ussher ...	1878
	Apr. 7, 1825	*William Brandford Griffith	1880
Captain Ricketts	Nov. 15, 1826	Sir Samuel Rowe ...	1881
Lieut.-Col. Lumley	Oct. 15, 1827	†W. A. G. Young	1884
Captain Hingston	Mar. 10, 1828	William Brandford Griffith	1885
Major Ricketts	May 18, 1828	*Col. F. B. P. White ...	1887
John Jackson ...	June 30, 1828	Sir Wm. Brandford Griffith	1887,
Captain Maclean	Feb. 19, 1830		1890, 1892, 1894
William Topp ...	June 26, 1836	†Sir Wm. Edward Maxwell	1895
Captain Maclean	Aug. 15, 1838	Frederick Mitchell Hodgson	1898
Commander Hill, R.N.	Apr. 5, 1843	Major Sir Matthew Nathan	1900

NOTABLE EVENTS.

Civil War between Agyiman and Atta, Chiefs of Akyim, 1860.
Akai War or Appolonian Expedition (1), 1835.
Akai War or Appolonian Expedition (2), 1849.
Asanti War (1), 1807-8.
Asanti War (2), 1811-12.
Asanti War (3), 1817.
Asanti War (4), 1824-26.
Asanti War (5), 1863-64.
Asanti War (6), 1873-74.
Asanti (Kumasi) Expedition, Dec. 7, 1895 ; Jan. 17, 1896.
Bobikuma battle, May 9, 1863.
Donasi and Abura Tribal War, 1851.
Dunkwa and Abura, 1859.
Dodowa battle, 1826.
Elmina War, 1868-70.
Insimakow battle, 1824.
Mansue expedition, 1864.
Tchibu and Gabir, 1853.

1807. Anamaboe attacked by Asantis; siege, defeat; first Asanti
        invasion, June 14.
1808. Hoogenboon Dutch Governor murdered by the natives of Elmina.
1812. J. Meredith, commandant of Winneba, arrested by the people,
        Feb. 6; d. Feb. 12.
1816. Rev. Phillip Quacoe, M.A., Oxon., d. Oct. 17; first native received
        Holy Orders, 1765.
1817. First Treaty with Asanti, Mar. 5.
1820. Second Treaty with Asanti, Feb. 28.
1821. Chief Paintsir and other princes of Abura fell at Mouree, Feb. 10.
1822. Sir Chas. McCarthy arrived, Feb 28.
1824. Sir Chas. McCarthy killed in battle at Insimakow, Jan. 21.
   ,,   Asanti forces defeated by the Fantis at Effutu, May 21.
   ,,   Siege of Cape Coast Castle, the Asantis repulsed, July 14.
1826. Battle of Dodowa in the plains of Accra, Asantis defeated, Aug. 26.
1830. De Graft and Sam imprisoned by Gov. Maclean, Feb. 1.
1831. De Graft and Sam open a night-school at Cape Coast Castle, Sept. 5.

1832.   Akremansah, Chief of Cape Coast Castle, d. July 10.
1834.   Kwofi Ekem committed suicide by gunpowder explosion, Sept. 6.
  ,,   Rev. Dunwell, first Wesleyan Missionary, arrived and landed at
          C.C.C., Dec. 31; d. C.C.C., June 25, 1835.
1837.   Amonoo, King of Anamaboe, d. Jan. 27.
  ,,   Amonoo, merchant, d. by gunpowder explosion at Anamaboe,
          July 20.
  ,,   Two Dutch officers killed at Boutry, Oct. 23.
1838.   De Graft, Wm., the elder, d. at C.C.C., Jan. 1.
  ,,   Thomas Birch Freeman arrived at C.C.C., Jan. 3.
  ,,   Foundation stone of the first Anamaboe chapel laid, Aug. 14.
  ,,   L.E.L. (Mrs. Maclean) landed at C.C.C., Aug. 15; d. at C.C.C.,
          Oct. 15.
1840.   Great fire at Anamaboe caused by Attarhū, Jan. 17.
1841.   Rev. Thackery, Wes. Miss., d. at Dominasi, July 4.
  ,,   Rev. T. B. Freeman started from C.C.C. for Kumasi the second
          time, Nov. 6.
1843.   Appointment of Judicial Assessor, Capt. Hill, R.N., Governor, landed,
          April 5.
1846.   Rev. John Martin embarked for Badagry, Feb. 14.
1847.   Governor Maclean d. at C.C.C., Dec. 13.
1849.   Kweku Akai, King of Appolonia, taken captive and brought to
          C.C.C., Nov. 29.
1850.   Kudwo Tchibbu, King of Assin, d. Nov. 11.
1851.   Kweku Akai, King of Appolonia, d. at C.C.C., Dec. 28.
  ,,   Joe Aggrey (Brupu), King of C.C.C., d. Aug. 31.
  ,,   Nanāmu god's grove deserted, Aug. 31.
  ,,   Kwesi Anka, King of Donassi, fought Akobina Amoah, King of
          Abura, Oct. 21.
1852.   Poll-tax introduced on the Gold Coast, April 1.
  ,,   First Wesleyan Ordination service, Rev. J. Martin ordained, Sept. 27.
1853.   Tchibbu and Gabir sentenced, April 16; beheaded for treason at
          Dunkwa, April 18.
  ,,   Peace established between Dutch and British Commenda, Sept. 22.
1854.   Christiansborg, Teshie, and Labodie towns bombarded by H.M.S.
          Scourge, Sept. 13.
1856.   Revs. Daniel and William West arrived at C.C.C., Nov. 18.
  ,,   C.C.C. inhabitants fought and revolted against King Kwofi Amissa.
          Jan. 23; and deposed him, Jan. 28.
  ,,   Major Orde interviews native kings and chiefs, Feb. 25; sails for
          England, March 7.
  ,,   Kweku Atta made King of C.C.C., Mar. 12.
  ,,   Samuel Bannerman the elder, d. Mar. 27.
1857.   Kwofi Affale proclaimed King of Anamaboe, Oct. 31.
1858.   Mons Regis Factory plundered by Accra people, Jan. 24.
  ,,   Kweku Attah, King of C.C.C, d. Feb. 20.

1858. Essien, proclaimed King of C.C.C., Mar. 6.
,, Governor Sir Benjamin Pine returned to England, May 11.
1859. Prince W. O. Quantabissa of Asanti, d. Jan. 8.
,, Ordination of Solomon, Laing, and Ansah, Jan. 16.
,, Christ Church foundation stone laid, April 11.
1860. Gov. Ed. B. Andrews landed, April 19.
,, Bentir and Intsin fight at C.C.C., Nov. 25.
1861. Accra market opened by Major Brownell, July 18.
,, Tuafu and Piranko companies fight, Anamaboe, Aug. 18.
,, John Aggrey, prince C.C.C., d. Oct. 5.
,, Wm. Hackett, Q.A., arrived, Oct. 19.
1862. Mutiny of Gold Coast Artillery Corps at the garrison, C.C.C.,
        Jan. 17.
,, Earthquake on the Gold Coast, July 10; Accra nearly destroyed.
,, Lagos made a British settlement, Feb. 8.
1863. Battle of Bobikuma, May 9.
,, Royal African Gold Coast Artillery disbanded, Aug. 19.
1864. Asanti expedition, ammunition thrown into the river Pra; West
        Indian troops returned to C.C.C. much reduced in numbers
        by sickness, July 2.
,, Riot at Commenda, 18 men killed, Oct. 30.
1865. Kwofi Affale, Amonoo II., King of Anamaboe, d. Oct. 25.
,, Kwa Saman, Amonoo III., of Anamaboe, proclaimed king, Dec. 5.
,, Col. Conran landed at C.C.C., Aug. 19.
1866. Christ Church, C.C.C., consecrated, Jan. 19.
,, Essien (Crentsil), King of C.C.C., exiled to Sierra Leone by the
        British authorities, Dec. 8.
1867. Anglo-Dutch Treaty signed, first exchange of territories, Feb. 5.
,, Kweku Dua, King of Asanti, d. April 7.
1868. Great Britain takes possession of Dutch Accra, Jan. 4; exchange
        of Dutch territories completed, Jan. 13.
,, The natives of British Commenda object to exchange of territories,
        refuse the Dutch flag, and evacuate the town, Jan. 31.
,, The Dutch bombard British Commenda, Feb. 1.
,, Elmina War, commencement of; Kwaprow people attacked,
        April 4.
,, Kweku Atta and Kwofi Amoa, chiefs of C.C.C., outlawed on sus-
        picion of treason, April 5.
,, Elmina War: Fantis besiege Elmina, May 26.
1869. Amonoo III. of Anamaboe deposed, May 28.
,, Amonoo IV. proclaimed King of Anamaboe, July 3.
,, Essien (Crentsil) returns from exile in Sierra Leone, April 14.
,, Dutch sailors held captives by Fanti kings, redeemed by the
        Dutch Government, July 15.
,, Mankessim day-school opened, July 19.
,, Abbankrome destroyed by the King of Akumfie, Nov. 6.

1869. Gov. Simpson opened Anamaboe market, April 30.
1870. British Commenda fought the Dutch at Kwissi Krome, Jan. 10.
 „   Jos. Smith, d. C.C.C., May 25.
 „   Mrs. Moseley opened a female school at C.C.C., July 1 ; d. Dec. 22.
 „   Afu Acka beheaded by some natives of Ahanta at night, July 22.
 „   Amonoo IV., of Anamaboe, returned from Ahanta War, Sept. 17,
 „   Asanti war chief Akempon, and other captives, released at C.C.C.,
           Oct. 3.
1871. Major Brownell returned from Kumasi, Feb. 13.
 „   Sixty-two Fanti captives restored by King of Asanti, Mar. 13.
 „   Small-pox epidemic began at C.C.C., May 13, and spread over the
           whole country.
 „   Gov. Ussher left for England, July 18.
 „   Creation of Fanti confederation at Mankessim, Nov. 24.
1872. Small-pox epidemic raging everywhere.
 „   Ghartey IV., King of Winneba, June 11.
 „   Chief Kwow Appia, Anamaboe, d. Aug. 7.
1873. Ankwanda destroyed by Dixcove men, May 28.
 „   Elmina bombarded, June 13.
 „   Sir Garnet Wolseley arrived C.C.C. by ss. *Ambriz*, Oct. 7.
 „   Col. Festing defeated the Asantis at Dwukwa, Nov. 3.
 „   Asantis defeated at Abakrampa, Nov. 7.
1874. Asanti expedition, white troops arrived after the enemy had
           crossed the Pra, Jan. 1.
 „   Battle of Amoafur, Jan. 29.
 „   Slavery abolished on the Gold Coast.
1876. Rev. T. R Picot visited Kumasi, Feb. 23.
 „   Accra new Wesleyan Chapel foundation-stone laid, Sept. 7.
1878. First Wesleyan camp meeting, Akrofur, Jan. 13.
 „   Mankessim Wesleyan Chapel opened, April 14.
 „   Adooah's religious excitement at Mankessim.
 „   Winneba Chapel opened, Sept. 14.
1879. Otu Ansah, King of Abura, d. Jan. 14.
 „   Fatal riots and fight between Bentir and Anaffu, C.C.C., Sept. 9–11.
1880. Judge W. B. Collyer arrived, Feb. 2.
 „   Imbia and Bentoom, two of the Bentir rioters, hanged at Elmina,
           the rope breaking thrice, Mar. 10.
 „   Wm. Thompson, Court interpreter, d. at C.C.C., June 28.
 „   W. S. Swatson, d. Winneba, Nov. 29.
 „   Gov. Ussher, d. Accra, Dec. 1.
 „   Capt. Davies, of Lagos, tried and acquitted at Accra.
1881. Asanti mission ; Buakye Tsintsin, special messenger ; golden axe
           sent to Queen Victoria by Sir Samuel Rowe ; threatened Asanti
           War, May 16.
 „   Buakye Tsintsin visits Anamaboe on his way to Asanti, Sept. 14.
 „   Saltpond Wesleyan Chapel opened, Oct. 2.

1881. Rev. T. Laing, C.C.C., d. Oct. 23.
,,   Capt. Lonsdale visits Kumasi on a special political mission, Nov. 7.
,,   Woodcock, Q.A., drowned at Accra, Nov. 4.
,,   Roman Catholic Missions started on the Gold Coast, first station Elmina.
1882. Chief Justice Sir James Marshall, K.C.M.G., retired on pension, Aug. 1.
,,   Comet: superstitious public commotion on its first appearance, Sept. 25.
1883. Acting Chief Justice Bridgman, d. Accra, May 6.
,,   Judge Stubbins arrived, Aug. 16.
,,   Miss Eliz. Waldron, C.C.C., d. Aug. 22.
,,   1st Elmina Wesleyan camp meeting, Nov. 11.
,,   Abaadzi and Kromantsi fatal riots, Dec. 22.
1884. Blai, a notorious burglar in C.C.C., killed, Mar. 12.
,,   Birwa Wesleyan chapel built, Mar. 16.
,,   Chief Asimaku (Jas Idun) of Kwaman, d. April 14.
,,   Chief Jos. Martin, Amanfur, near C.C.C., d. Oct. 23.
,,   Kudwo Edukuma of Anamaboe, chief, d. Nov. 9.
,,   Prince John Ossu Ansah of Asanti, C.C.C., d. Nov. 13.
1885. Beginning of Wesleyan Jubilee Memorial services, Feb. 15.
,,   Gov. W. A. G. Young, d. Accra, April 24.
,,   Awusie, chief of Dominasi, d. May 9.
,,   Rev. Hayfron with Coppin visited Kumasi, May 29.
,,   Isaac Robertson, Chief Kweku Twim, C.C.C., d. June 8.
,,   Putubiw and Ekrofur fight, Nov. 9.
,,   Akwasi Kaye, King of Denkira, d. Dwukwa, Dec. 3.
,,   Joseph Dawson of Takwa and Wassaw districts, d. Aug. 10.
,,   Ten Winneba rioters executed at Accra, Feb. 5.
1886. Okum (Joseph Green), chief of Egyaa, d. Sept. 27.
,,   Jacob (Akai) Williams, d. Axim, Aug. 2.
,,   The king and people of Adansi, defeated by the Kumasi and Bekwai forces, come into the protectorate for shelter, June 15.
,,   Assafu Egay, King of Dwabin, d. April 10.
,,   Chief Justice N. Lesingham Bailey, d. Accra, May 29.
,,   The great Accra disturbance, when a serious collision between the inhabitants and the Houssa constabulary under Capt. Freeman was narrowly averted, Oct. 10.
,,   Telegraph cable landed at Accra, July 12; telegraphic communication with Great Britain completed, July 28.
,,   Hector Wm. Macleod appointed Chief Justice of the Gold Coast, Oct. 21.
,,   Akinnie, King of Akunfie, subpœnaed all the Fanti kings and chiefs to meet at Saltpond, April 21.
,,   King of Akwamu visits Accra, July 15.
1887. Kwesi Atta, chief of C.C.C., d. Jan. 3.

1887. Overland telegraphs opened on the Gold Coast, May 24.

,,   Gov. Col. White visited C.C.C., June 11, and Anamaboe, June 23.

,,   Queen Victoria's Jubilee celebrations on the Gold Coast.

,,   Arrival at C.C.C. of J. M. Sarbah, the first native of the Gold Coast called to the English Bar, Sept. 4.

,,   Hon. G. F. Cleland, d. Accra, Nov. 26.

1888. Return of F. Egyer Asaam and S. R. B. Solomon from Richmond College to C.C.C., Sept. 9.

,,   Kwesi Atta of Nanaam fame, d. Assāfa, Aug. 10.

1889. Gov. Sir W. Brandford Griffith visited C.C.C., and at a public meeting about Kudwo Imbra's election became the object of much dissatisfaction, Jan.

,,   Mouree fight: Inkoom and Bentir companies, Feb. 7.

,,   Roman Catholic mission started, C.C.C., June 4.

,,   Over 700 people of Tavievie killed by Houssas, June 24.

,,   Saltpond Hospital opened, July 8.

,,   Kwofi Amissa, ex-king C.C.C., d. Aug. 29.

1890. The great Rev. Father Freeman, d. Accra, Aug. 13.

1891. West India troops removed from the Gold Coast, June.

,,   Fosu pond at C.C.C. opened into the sea for the last time, July.

,,   Commencement of the influenza epidemic, Dec. 1.

1892. Rev. R. J. Hayfron, Wesleyan Mission, d. Feb. 1.

,,   Hon. J. Sarbah, d. July 4.

,,   Rev. David Asante, Basel Mission, d. Akropong, Oct. 14.

1893. Great fire at Chama, when the chapel and half the town were burnt down, Mar. 30.

,,   Yow Antoo, chief of Sefwhi, left for Cape Coast, where he was tried and convicted of murder and sentenced, about Feb. 4.

1894. Kobina Gyan, King of Elmina, returned home from exile, May 17; d. Feb., 1896.

,,   Messrs. C. J. Bannerman and T. H. Mills, of Accra, called to the English Bar, June 6.

,,   Hon. Francis Chapman Grant, d. Oct. 4.

,,   Asanti messengers to England, under J. O. Ansah, reached C.C.C., Dec. 10.

1895. General commotion over proposed Crown Lands Ordinance, Feb.

,,   Asanti messengers leave C.C.C. for England, April 3.

,,   Gov. Maxwell relieves Sir W. B. Griffith, reaching Axim, C.C.C., and Accra, April 3, 6, and 8 respectively.

,,   Gov. Griffith leaves finally for England by *Bonny*, April 15.

,,   Elliott, a European agent, and Johnson found guilty of conspiracy to steal, and sentenced at Axim, May.

,,   Enimil Kwow, King of Wassaw, d. Sept.

,,   Beginning of Prempe-Asanti expedition; arrival of Col. Sir Francis Scott with Prince Christian Victor, Prince Henry of Battenberg, officers, and European troops, Nov.—Dec.

1895. Adansi king and people return to Adansi after signing treaty, Dec.

1896. Prempe-Asanti expedition. Invasion of Kumasi. Prempe made, prisoner with his chiefs and others.

" Prempe arrived at C.C.C., and conveyed to Elmina by H.M.S. *Racoon*, Feb. 2.

1897. Geo. E. Ferguson, killed at Wa, April 6.

" Public agitation against Lands Bill, May.

" Divisional Court established at Axim, June.

" Sir W. E. Maxwell, d. Dec. 14.

1898. Rev. J. A. Solomon, d. Aug. 17.

" Land Bill Deputation returned from England, Oct. 14.

1899. Abura and Paidu civil riot, Oct.

" J. C. Clinton, d. at Axim, Nov.

1900. Otoo Brebu, King of Abura, d.

" Siege of Kumasi through quest of the "golden stool" by Governor Hodgson.

" Gold Mining boom commenced, Oct.

" Amonoo IV. of Anamabu, d. Nov. 23.

1901. Queen Victoria, d. Jan. 22.

" Mutiny by Mendi soldiers from Kumasi, arrival at C.C.C., &c., Easter.

" Small-pox epidemic at Axim, May to November.

" Kofi Kayi, Chief of Himan, d.

1902. Kwamina Faibir, Chief of Tarkwa, deposed.

" Coronation of King Edward VII., Aug. 9.

" J. W. Sey, d. at C.C.C.; wreck of s.s. *Stanleyville.*

" Railway reached Obbuasi.

" Hearing of Concession, inquiries at Tarkwa.

" King Tackie of Accra, d.

1903. Edmund Bannerman, solicitor, d. May 19.

" Train first arrived at Kumasi, Oct. 1.

THE PRINCIPLES OF
FANTI CUSTOMARY LAWS.

PART I.

INTRODUCTION.

THE Gold Coast Colony is situate on the Western Coast of Africa, and is supposed to extend from Half Assinie on the west to the river Volta on the east. •No one knows precisely what the boundaries of the Colony are, or how far the so-called Protected Territories extend. Having applied to the Colonial Office for information, Her Majesty's Secretary of State for the Colonies expressed his regret that he could not undertake to supply the information which was desired.

There is every reason to believe, that in very ancient times, the original inhabitants of this country were not Fantis but a different people. It is a well-established fact that Cape Coast, the Cabocors of Bosman and other ancient writers, is situate in the Fetu country—a place formerly governed by a Dey. When that state fell, the people were obliged to submit to the laws, regulations, and customs of the Fantis.

Meredith, the unfortunate Governor of Winnebah, thus expresses himself concerning the Fanti people: "The Asantis are threatening to pay us another visit, and it is the current opinion, that the Fantis must be either subdued by the

Asantis, or means devised to restrain their ungovernable
conduct before the country is tranquillized, or before much
improvement is effected.   The Fantis are now to be considered a large body; they have brought under their subjection, either by threats or favourable promises, a number
of small estates; so that from Cape Coast to the extremity
of the Agoona country may be put down as governed by
the Fantis.   To say that such and such places bear distinct
names is now merely to signify that they were formerly
inhabited by a distinct people."

Fanti, properly so called, begins from the Sweet River
on the east of Elmina, and ends at the river Volta, according
to Cruickshank.   But the Fantis are so connected with the
other inhabitants of the whole country, from Assinee to the
river Volta on the seaboard, and inland to and beyond Asanti,
wherever the Akan dialect is spoken, that, for the purposes
of this work, we are not far wrong in designating all the
inhabitants of the Protectorate, except Accra and district,
as Akan Fanti, or, shortly, Fanti.   The language of the
country is undoubtedly Fanti—this is the language spoken
for general purposes and in everyday transactions;—and it
is a fact worthy of notice that Fanti is the *lingua franca*
of the Gold Coast and adjacent countries.

Nearly a century ago the aforesaid Meredith remarked:
" The Fanti language is understood in all parts of the Coast
from Apollonia to Accra, and to a considerable distance
inland.   It is understood in Ashanti, where the language
differs very little from Fantee.   This is probably the effect
of the Fantees being great traders and travelling over so
many parts of the country. . . . To behold a Fantee to
advantage, he must be seen pleading his cause; his words
are accompanied with action by no means ungraceful nor
unsuitable to the subject; and his attitudes and energy of
expression are by no means contemptible, but on the contrary, we will venture to say, highly interesting."

The Fanti people seem to be one of the tribes inhabiting
the country from very remote times.   In a rare book

published in the year 1665, in which appears an interesting account of the first voyage from England to the *Golden Coast of Guinney* in August, 1553, prepared probably for " The Adventurers of Guinney," the anonymous author, (Speeding ?) writes * : " Sailing a mile lower we come to the chief place of traffick, called Mourre, and a mile below that is Infantin, and not far from that is the Castle of Cormantin." There is not the least doubt that the ancient sea coast town of Anamaboe, the leading Fanti state, is what our ancient author called Infantin—a correct expression, when one remembers that even now, according to one's dialect or inclination, so he says Mfantsi, Nfanti, or Fanti.

The Akan language is nevertheless the parent language —the language of diplomacy and courtiers.

The people of Wassaw, Denkera, Fanti Assin, Akim, Akwapim, Asanti, Elmina, and those of the adjacent provinces and districts, speak dialects of the same language, more or less corrupt. This fact favours the belief, and is one of the facts adduced to prove the assertion, that the inhabitants of these districts, provinces, and kingdoms are sprung from the same source, and are branches of the same family.

But when one compares their customs, usages, and domestic as well as political institutions, and finds them in the main identical, one does not hesitate to say these inhabitants had a common origin. Well-established tradition has it, that the people were originally living in the regions of the Kong Mountains, and somewhere in Central Africa. Unwilling to turn Moslems, and driven from their homes, they founded a state Takieman; but, through some reason or other, a portion of Takieman betook themselves towards the coast. This portion came to be referred to as *Takieman fa atsiwfu*—that is, that portion of the Takiemans who have gone from the main body. In process of time this

* See extracts from several ancient works in " Fanti National Constitution," by the author; the new set of decided cases published in which is hereinafter referred to as 2 Fanti Law Report.

long, round-about designation became contracted into Mfantsi, or Fanti.

The Asanti people were so called on account of their stubborn and obstinate nature. We cannot find out what name was borne by these people of Takieman before the general splitting up. The words "Akan" (Akanfu) arose probably from the way the Mfantsifu referred to those who remained at Takieman. The word Akan to our mind means a remnant; we have heard these people speak of themselves as Kanye, a contraction of Kānnyimpa, that is, a person who has remained behind.

Another circumstance tending to strengthen the theory of a common origin is the division of tribes or clans.

The whole of these peoples are divided into twelve tribes or clans, wholly irrespective of their several and distinct nationalities. Individuals belong to one or the other without natural distinctions, and it is a characteristic of each tribe or clan, that the members thereof call each other brothers and sisters, father and mother. And when the persons are free (Dihi) it is unusual for them to intermarry. Cruickshank, writing on this institution, says (vol. i. 49), " A feeling of attachment to each other exists between individuals belonging to these clans, even although of different nations, and we have known instances of inheritances claimed and obtained upon the plea of this relationship, to the prejudice of a blood relation, where there has been no male to come to the succession."

The people of each clan have their own separate burial-place, unite in funeral rites and customs, and when a great liability is to be met, these clansmen have been known cheerfully and readily to contribute each according to his means. And often doth the way-lost weary sojourner in a most unexpected place, through this relationship, become the recipient of free hospitality. As an instance in point, Beecham records a statement of Mr. William de Graft to the effect that the "chiefs of the several families (clans) are distinguished by certain significant emblems, equivalent to the heraldic signs used in European countries. Mr. De Graft himself is of the Twidan or 'tiger' family, and he distinctly recollects old Baffu, a chief of the same family at Anamaboe, whose sign of office (his umbrella) was surmounted by a figure of the tiger. The emblems of the other families are in like manner figurative representations of the names which they respectively bear; wherever the distinction between the families is still preserved or is supposed to exist the brotherhood is uniformly recognized. De Graft has known his own father attend the funerals of individuals for the sole reason that they were members of the same original or patriarchal family with himself; and when he resided, a few years since, at Dixcove, he was informed that, some time previous to his going thither, the King of Appollonia sent a present of rice to the inhabitants, when they were suffering from scarcity, as an acknowledgment that he and they were all members of the Ntwa or 'dog' family. On another occasion, De Graft, being sent by the Governor to publish and explain a proclamation to the natives, was received with the greatest kindness by the chiefs of the Twidan or 'tiger' family, who invariably, wherever he met with them during his journey, which occupied three months, claimed him as one of their own relatives."

As far as can be relied on, these are the principal clans, divided sometimes into three principal classes: Akonna, Abrotu, Aburadi, Nsonna, Annona, Yoko, Ntwa, Abadzie, Appiadie, Twidan, Kwonna, and Dwimina. It goes without saying that the Akanfu have a different name to some of these clans.

Perhaps it is not a vain dream to hope a time is coming when the several nationalities, united under a beneficent and enlightened Government, will develop and foster the clan feeling and instincts, which in times past have been as free from the impulses, which have degraded the African nature, as great in the qualities, which have ever graced manhood in all ages and under all climes.

Others, who have studied this interesting subject, say the

various tribes above mentioned were comprehended in seven great families, in which the members still class themselves and recognize each other, without regard to national distinctions, viz.:

1. *Nsonna*, in some localities known as Dwimina.
2. *Annona*, Yoko, Aguna, or Eguana.
3. *Twidan*, Eburotuw.
4. *Kwonna*, Ebiradzi, or Odumna.
5. *Aburadzi*, Eduana, Ofurna, or Egyirna.
6. *Ntwa*, Abadzi.
7. *Adwinadzi*, Aowin.

In this country the system known amongst jurists as the patriarchal system prevails. The (Egya or Penin) father is the head of his family. Within his compound he reigns supreme over his younger brothers and sisters, his wives and children, his nephews and nieces, and his grandchildren; and if he be a man of wealth, his servants, pawns and slaves. So long as a father who is free lives, all his children and grandchildren, by a free woman, not residing with their uncle, are under his authority and power. Married people here have no community of goods, but each has his or her particular property: the man and his wives generally adjust the matter together, so that they are able to bear the charge of housekeeping, while the clothing of the whole family is at his sole expense.

Bosman, who wrote in 1700 his "Description of the Gold Coast of Guinea," says, "On the death of either the man or the wife, the respective relations come and immediately sweep away all, not leaving the widow or widower the least part thereof, though they are frequently obliged to help to pay the funeral charges."

We mean by servants persons who are being trained or brought up in the house, as well as persons who are working in the house for their living. Among the people, one often sees persons in the same position as Jacob held in the house of his uncle Laban.

Slaves.—On proper analysis of the incidents of this

condition, one is quite reluctant to give the name "slave" to persons in bondage. The word "slave," to the European ear, conjures up horrible atrocities—kidnapping, murder, bloodshed, fire, plague, pestilence, famine, whips and shackles, ruined and desolated villages, and all that debases and makes man worse than the brute beasts.

The Fanti terms for a person in a state of bondage are—

1. *Ténni*, that is, native of the Intar country.

2. *Donkor*, said to be corruption of words meaning captive of an army.

It has been already stated the Fanti*fu* and Akan*fu* have one origin, and as such were free persons.

As wars take place and war captives increase, slavery bears a recognized state, and the issue of a female slave continue slaves.

The terms Ténni and Donkor are reserved exclusively for foreigners who are in bondage. There is another term, Akuwaa (feminine, Afunaba), meaning a dependent. Like the Hebrews of old, there is a distinction between bondmen captured in war or purchased from another distinct tribe, and bondmen of the same tribe. Great numbers of the former were annually imported from districts outside Asanti, where these persons were either captured in war, or were received by way of tribute from conquered states by the Asantifu. These, on being sold, are they who can be properly called *slaves*. When the iniquitous and accursed slave trade stirred up the cupidity and all the degrading passions of men, it became highly expedient for every person to be under the protection of a powerful neighbour ; it became absolutely necessary for every individual to belong to a household. At this period, clan feeling and clan hospitality becoming weakened began to decay, because cupidity and blighting avarice were supreme. The solitary traveller was no longer safe. The hunter who had wandered too far from home in pursuit of game, the farmer on his secluded farm, women going to market or to the spring, were ruthlessly captured and sold into foreign slavery.

Then it was that parents, spurning all holy impulses, and dead to natural love and affection, sold their very offspring into foreign bondage. But through all these horrors, through fire and sword and bloodshed, which desolated many a prosperous village, amid all the wailings of the unhappy captives, the distinction between the alien slaves and native bondmen was well marked, and never once do we hear any native in bondage called a slave, a Donkor. It is only misfortune that has brought him into that condition, and though such person cannot interfere in the affairs of his own family, being regarded for the time as dead, nevertheless as soon as he regains his freedom, whether by his own exertions or by the aid of his family, or by the favour of his master, at that very instant he is reclothed with his family rights, and he returns to the same position in his own family as though he had never been in servitude to another, and as completely as the Roman Law, by *Jus postliminii,* restored to the original owners, property taken in war and retaken from the enemy, and re-established in all their former rights, all captives who had returned to their own country.

Consulted by Judicial Assessor Chalmers, in the case of *Kendall* v. *Quabina Abakan,* August 25, 1871, Mayan and Amoah, Chiefs, said: "According to custom, when a man is married and the woman dies, he is never entitled to the property of the woman, and in all cases that a man took a woman without marrying her properly, and the woman had a child by him, the woman dying, the man would not be entitled to keep the child, but the mistress would. The child must live in the father's house. In case of son of slave, he lives in his mistress's house, but visits his father's house.

"By the Court: Do persons who have been made free retain any relationship to the family of which they were members?

"They call themselves family. If the slaves all belonged to one country and they happened to be with one master, and the master set them free, they retain relationship to one another because they all belonged to one country; though the master had made them free, they retain relationship to their master, because they did not belong to the place where they were freed. We speak of the sixteen girls of Mr. Hutton. If a slave was a Fanti, when he was freed by his master he goes to his relations; but if not a Fanti, but Donkor, he retains his relationship to the master because he knew no one else and would not find his way to his country, and if his master had any relations he sticks to them. Persons freed have right to go where they like, but their master looks after them that they may not be molested." And judgment was given in accordance with what was so laid down by the two chiefs. And as recently as August 2, 1895, Assistant Puisne Judge Hayes Redwar followed Judicial Assessor Chalmers, and accepted the correctness of the custom in *Cromwell* v. *Arba* and *Krabba*, Insarkun claimant.

The freeborn inhabitant enters into a state of bondage from several and various causes. As in feudal Europe, unprotected peasants commended themselves to a powerful or influential neighbour, even so in former days on the Gold Coast, persons and whole families, threatened with danger or pressed by hunger in a time of famine, were accustomed to throw themselves at the feet of one who could protect them from the foe, give them sustenance, or employ them. Persons like these become members of the family they have appealed to, and become merged therein in process of time by marriage and other ways.

Others, pressed with debt, give up themselves and all their possessions in pledge to the man who would pay the whole. Persons of this class do not lose their clan distinction, even though they remain in bondage for many years. They are members of the master's household, but not of his family.

There is another class of persons, who, for some great service rendered to them, their relations or ancestors, are bound to serve their benefactor and his family. These persons, whose services are transferable from master to master, and who may be said to be a species of mercenary soldiers, swell their master's retinue, defend his person, and magnify his importance. In some places these persons are bound to help their master at the season of tillage, sowing, and harvest.

Standing between the slave and the bondmen is the Pawn, whose lot is the hardest.

Before pawning was abolished, a person in embarrassed circumstances wishing to obtain a loan, usually placed one or more of his family or slaves in temporary bondage to another. Says Cruickshank, "The terms of this contract are that the pawn shall serve his new master until such time as the person pawning him shall make good the sum lent, with fifty per cent. interest; the services of the pawn, even if they should extend over a great number of years, counting for nothing in the liquidation of the debt. If a woman has been pawned, her new master has the right to make her his concubine, and her children continue to serve him also."

It must be remarked here, that Cruickshank is in error as to the master's right to concubinage. As a matter of fact, unless it was distinctly stipulated at the time of giving the pawn, that the master or his successor may so treat the female pawn, any improper behaviour of this nature by the master or any of his blood relatives or any of his servants invariably cancelled the debt, and discharged the pawn and her family from all liabilities.

"A father cannot pawn his child without the concurrence of the mother's relations, unless the mother herself be his slave. Neither can a mother pawn her child without the father's consent; but if he cannot advance the sum required, then she can do so. We have always regarded this system of pawning as much worse than actual slavery, and we have seen but too many of its victims irrecoverably reduced to perpetual bondage."

There are many instances where slaves have succeeded to their master's property, but a pawn is always considered a stranger, and never do we hear of one so succeeding to his master.

Bosman, the Dutchman writing in the year 1700, makes mention of the several social degrees which he had observed, namely :—

(1) Kings or Captains.
(2) Caboceros.
(3) Rich men.
(4) The common people ; and, lastly,
(5) Slaves.

What he wrote is so accurate, and is in the main so true now as then, that it claims attention, since it shows the conservative nature of native institutions. Says Bosman, " I have observed five degrees of men amongst the negroes, the first of which are their kings or captains, for the word is here synonymous.

" The second, their caboceros or chief men, which, reducing to our manner of expression, we should be at a job to call them civil fathers, whose province is only to take care of the welfare of the city or village, and to appease any tumult.

" The third sort are those who have acquired a great reputation by their riches, either devolved on them by inheritance or gotten by trade.

" The fourth are the common people employed in the tillage of wines, agriculture, and fishing.

" The fifth, and last, are the slaves, either sold by their relations, taken in war, or come so by poverty.

" The dignity of king or captain in most of these countries descends hereditarily from father to son, and, in defect of issue, to the next male heir, though sometimes so much regard is had to his riches in slaves and money, that he who is plentifully stored with these is often preferred to the right heir."

King is not synonymous with captain. Ohin means

chief; Oman-hin, king; Safu-hin, a captain. The confusion which exists in many of these things, arises solely
through the faulty interpretation of incompetent, ill-taught,
and stupid interpreters. The headman of a village, merely
as such, is not, and can be only slovenly called Ohin, a
king. If he is a captain under some king, he is called so-
and-so's Safu-hin; but his usual and most correct appella-
tion is Odzi-kro.

The foreign term Caboceer has fallen into disuse, and
the ordinary term Omanfu is not so often used in these
days as Penyin, Penyinfu. The persons holding this office
are commonly limited in number, and are elected thereto.
See Cruickshank, vol. i. ch. 9.

A person reputed rich by inheritance or trade is called
Brempon. But unless such a person is successor to a stool,
his wealth alone cannot make him the occupant of a stool.
The king of a district, with his town councillors, can create
a stool, and thus confer on the occupant a political position.

Slavery has been abolished as from December 17, 1874,
by Ordinances 1 and 2 of 1874, but it is provided that
"nothing shall be construed to diminish or derogate from
the rights and obligations, not being repugnant to the law
of England, arising out of the family and tribal relations
customarily used and observed in the Protected Territories;" and this clause received judicial interpretation in
Bimba v. *Mansa*, 1 F. L. R. 137.

Along the coast are towns, which, for martial purposes,
are divided into companies. The one at Cape Coast Castle
is fully described in the letter written by the Mayor of
Cape Coast Castle to the Chief Justice, dated November
29, 1859.

"SIR,—I consider it my duty to forward, for the
information of your Honour and of the Executive Government, the following circumstantial account of the events
leading to and connected with the recent unhappy dis-
turbances in the town of Cape Coast.

" 2. Your Honour will better understand the statement
I am about to lay before you, if I preface that statement
by a brief account of the nature and organization of those
bodies known as town companies.

" 3. The town of Cape Coast is divided into seven
companies or quarters.

" These are : No. 1, Bentil ; No. 2, Anafu ; No. 3, Intin ;
No. 4, Inkoom ; No. 5, Brofu-mba (artificers) ; No. 6,
Volunteers ; No. 7, Amanful.

" Each company occupies its own part of the town, and
although some persons properly belonging to one quarter
sometimes happen to reside in another, yet, on the occasion
of any outbreak, these go up to that quarter to which they
originally belong.

" 4. The companies are commanded by Saphohins, or
chief captains. The chiefs have nothing to do with them,
nor indeed has the king himself. The companies may be
described as so many little republics, each independent of
the rest, and having its own officers, laws, and customs.
Over every company there is a Saphohin, and he (called
Supi) has under him subordinate captains, who are elected
by the companies. These captaincies may be said to be
hereditary in some sort, more from custom than by law ;
the companies generally preferring to elect the sons of
deceased captains to succeed their fathers. When a
company makes any new law, it is done in a public
assembly of themselves, and communicated to the other
companies, who, if they have any objections to raise, do so
at once, when the matter is discussed.

" 5. The Saphohin, or chief captain (*Supi*), holds
supreme authority in every company. He is the sole
depositary of the power of the company, and the ex-
ponent of their wishes.

" 6. Each company has its flag ; but besides its regular
' company flag,' each company has in addition a variety
of fanciful flags with devices on them, intended to represent some event or circumstance connected with the

history of the company that carries them, or of some rival company.

" 7. When making their grand customs, each company, if it has no quarrel with any others, passes through the various quarters of the town with its original ' company flag,' but when there is a desire to convey defiance or insult, a company, in passing through the quarter inhabited by the company whom it is desired to annoy, will there display a flag having some device ostentatiously offensive.

" 8. In the same way, whilst each company has its war-songs, which, without being offensive to other companies, are, of course, self-laudatory, each has also a habit of exciting rival companies by singing insulting songs at the same time that the objectionable flags are paraded.

" 9. From time immemorial these flags and songs have been the cause of ill-feeling, strife, and bloodshed, as has unfortunately been the case in the present instance."

This letter was written at the time of a serious civil fight at Cape Coast Castle, which resulted in the case of the *Queen* v. *the Captains of Bentil and Intin Companies*, wherein the Chief Justice delivered the following judgment :—

" The Court also requires that all the companies of the town shall, within one month, send into the fort such flags as they wish to use in future, for the approval of the Governor, who, if he disapproved, will substitute some other in its place ; and the patterns and colours of all that may be approved will be registered in the secretary's office in the fort, and the exhibiting of any other flag by any company will be rendered and proclaimed to be utterly unlawful, subjecting the persons doing so to heavy penalties.   In the mean time, the use of any new flag or flags not now in use is hereby strictly prohibited.

" The king's authority while it remains must in all lawful matters be obeyed, but there are ample means of appealing against any unjust or oppressive exercise of it."

This judgment clearly shows how often laws are enacted

in these days in absolute and entire ignorance of what has been done in times past. And viewing events since then, one is drawn to the conclusion that, had this judgment been enforced, many a fatal civil fight would have been averted, many lives saved, and the new ordinance about flags and tribal emblems, which has not yet made civil fights impossible, better drafted in every respect.

CHAPTER I.

FANTI CUSTOMARY LAWS.

FANTI laws and customs apply to all Akans and Fantis, and to all persons whose mothers are of Akan or Fanti race.

If a person travel to or reside in a foreign country, he does not lose the benefit of the laws and customs of his native country, province, or district.

As a general rule, the right or property of a Fanti is in no way forfeited, diminished, impaired, or affected by change of religious opinions. But where the persons entitled to the immediate succession of an ancestral property do not acquiesce in, and the dependants raise an objection to, a change of religious opinion or belief, an absolute bar is thus raised to succession to stool property. Where a person, head of the family, changes his religious belief and becomes a Christian, he thereby becomes liable to be removed. For instance—

Kudwo, the eldest nephew of his uncle, who is possessed of a large ancestral stool property, forsakes heathenism for Christianity. In his family, ancestor worship is practised, and at the stool festival every year, the head of the family goes through the necessary sacrifices and makes the libations to the spirits of those departed this life. In such a case, the other nephews are preferred to Kudwo, who is passed over.

But where Kudwo, while on the stool, changes his religious belief, he must depute some one to perform the necessary stool ceremonies, and if he neglect so to do, his negligence will be a good ground for removing him from the stool.

Colour is no bar to the right of succession by the native laws and customs (*Hutton* v. *Kutah*).

By the Supreme Court Ordinance, 1876, sect. 19, native laws and customs are to be enforced in certain specified class of cases, and sect. 92 provides for calling in the aid· of Referees on native laws and customs.

A learned writer has recently said, in discussing Indian topics, it cannot be too strongly asserted that there is great danger in too indiscriminately applying the technicalities of the English Law to a country like India, whose institutions, popular traditions, and prejudices are so entirely different from those of England. Indian customs are not to be tested by the arbitrary rules peculiar to English law, but rather, as Sir Erskine Perry, Chief Justice, well remarked, by the rules of universal applicability.*

If such caution is still necessary in discussing Indian customary laws, much more is it essential when investigating any customary law, or custom, or usage, or local institution in any part of the Gold Coast. We justify all references to India and Indian decisions in this work by pointing out the remarkable resemblance and similarity between the customs and usages of some parts of India and

---

* "This custom has not only been attacked on the score of unreasonableness, but it has been tested by every one of the seven requisites which Blackstone has laid down for the validity of an English custom. It may be asked, however, and I did ask why the various special rules which have been laid down in any particular system, and some of which clearly have no general applicability, should be transferred to a state of things to which they have no relation. . . . I apprehend that the true rules to govern such a custom are rules of universal applicability, and that it is simply absurd to test a Mohammedan custom by considerations whether it existed when Richard I. returned from the Holy Land, which is the English epoch for dating the commencement of time immemorial" (Perry's Oriental Cases, p. 120).

those which are herein treated. To give only one instance : the rule of succession in Malaba and among the Canarese is through the female line, and almost identical with the Fanti Customary Law of succession. Moreover, it was in India that the eminent jurist Sir Henry Maine pursued his researches and studies in jurisprudence ; and there, for a longer period of time, Indian judges, afterwards members of the Queen's Privy Council, had been administering Customary Law and testing the usages of several semi-civilized communities.

It has been said that to the great and eminent judge and profound scholar Sir William Jones belong the renown and credit of first having directed the attention of the British Government to the vital importance, nay, the imperative duty of allowing the natives of India the benefit of their own laws and customs.* Outside India and the great East,

* "In a letter of 19th March, 1785, addressed to Lord Cornwallis, the then Governor-General of India, he said nothing could be more obviously just than to determine private contests according to those laws which the parties themselves had ever considered as the rules of their conduct and engagements in civil life, nor could anything be wiser than by a Legislative Act to assure the Hindu and Mussulman subjects of Great Britain that the private laws which they severally hold sacred, and the violation of which they would have thought the most grievous oppression, should not be suppressed by a new system of which they could have no knowledge, and which they must have considered as imposed on them by a spirit of rigour and intolerance."

As a result of his great efforts in India as well as in England, the British Parliament, by 21 Geo. III. cap. 70, and the Indian Legislature, by Regulation IV. of 1793, enacted that in suits regarding inheritance and succession to lands, rents and goods, marriage caste, and all matters of contract, and dealing between party and party, the laws and usages of Mohammedans in the case of Mohammedans, and the laws and usages of Hindus in the case of Hindus, should constitute the general rules by which the judges were to form their decision. This principle has ever since con-trolled Indian legislation; thus the Punjab Code Act IV., 1872, directs in sect. 5, "in questions regarding succession, special property of females, betrothal, marriage, divorce, dower, adoption, guardianship, minority, bastardy, family relations, wills, legacies, gifts, partition or any religious usage or institution, the rule of decision shall be :—

(a) Any custom applicable to the parties concerned, which is not

the Gold Coast, which formerly included Lagos, is the only
Crown colony in the British Empire to which this beneficent
Indian principle has been extended, for neither for Sierra
Leone nor the Gambia was any provision made for the
recognition of native law or custom or any local usages.
The Supreme Court Ordinance, having noticed the existence
of native laws and customs, practically imposes a duty on
the courts to give effect to them, in the class of cases therein
specified, and, to enable the courts so to do effectually, by
sect. 92 above mentioned provides for the assistance of
referees. It cannot, therefore, be correct to say, as it has
been sometimes said, that the native laws and customs are
foreign matters which, unless proved, cannot be recognized
or noticed by a judge. For if that view be correct, then
what can be the necessity or effect of the concluding
sentence of sect. 19, " that no party shall be entitled to claim
the benefit of any local law or custom if it shall appear . . .
that such party agreed that his obligations . . . should be

contrary to justice, equity, or good conscience, and has not been by this or
any other enactment altered or abolished, and has not been decreed to be
void by any competent authority;

(b) The Mohammedan law, in cases where the parties are Mohammedans, and the Hindu law, in cases where the parties are Hindus, except
in so far as such law has been altered ·or abolished by legislative enactment, or is opposed to the provision of this Act, or has been modified by
any such custom as is above referred to.

" Sect. 6. In cases not otherwise provided for, the judges shall decide
according to justice, equity, and good conscience.

" Sect. 7. All local customs and mercantile usages shall be regarded
as valid, unless they are contrary to justice, equity, or good conscience,
or have before the passing of this Act been declared to be void by any
competent authority." Among many decisions bearing on this matter may
be noted that of Mr. Justice Lindsay: " I think the courts are bound to
inquire whether a custom existed even when not specifically pleaded; and
only when the parties specifically declare they desire to abide by Mohammedan or Hindu law, can the courts in my opinion set aside the question
of custom. It is the intention of the Legislature that the courts shall
find out by oral examination the points in issue between the parties,
whether they consider law or custom applies to their case and frame issue
accordingly."

regulated EXCLUSIVELY by English law " ? * Applying the
method of Mr. Justice Lindsay, perhaps the court should find
out the native law or custom, if any, bearing on the matter in
dispute before it; next, discover whether the parties agreed
to be bound by English law, and whether such English law
was to bind them exclusively or partially.

The comparatively modern practice of parties to a suit
calling experts as witnesses to prove what is the custom, is
of doubtful value, and has been the means of some erroneous
opinions finding their way into the records of the court as
native laws and customs. Having learnt the history of some
of them, care has been taken to exclude the same from the
cases reported in this work. It is always safer and better
for the court, after the parties have stated the native laws
or customs they rely upon, to seek the assistance of others
who may be versed in the native laws and customs, and to
do so in the way known to the judicial assessors and the
person who framed rule 92, who knew the practice, subsequently followed by Mr. Justice Hector Macleod.

But the question that demands an answer arises : what
is meant by the terms "any law or custom," "such laws
and customs," "local law or custom" in the said sect. 19;
and "native law or custom" in sect. 92. As far as can be
ascertained by research in the records at Cape Coast
Castle, and by inquiry at every available source, only
once has the court endeavoured to throw light on the subject, and this was in *Welbeck* v. *Brown* † before the Full
Court of Appeal. Unfortunately that court was not unanimous, for Mr. Justice Macleod, an eminent and most pains-
taking judge, who had a varied experience in the courts
at Lagos, Accra, and Cape Coast Castle, and whose knowledge of native customary laws and the customs and usages
of the people was certainly equal to, if not greater than,
that possessed by the two other judges of the Court, being
of contrary opinion, distinctly said, "I do not find it necessary to give any opinion as to the meaning of the words

* *Longdon* v. *Sagoe*, 2 F. L. R. 97. † 1 F. L. R. 185.

native custom, and I must not be understood as coinciding
on that point with the Chief Justice."

It will be noticed that the judges, who essayed to discuss the point, confined their remarks to *native customs;*
they said nothing about native law. The reason may be
that the point was not raised or was not before the court ;
but jurists, however, have always felt a difficulty in so
defining the term Law, as would make it comprehend not
only express enactments by a sovereign legislature, which
Austin and his disciples alone admit to be law properly
so-called, but also those rules regulating conduct and
usages, which are habitually acted upon in the ordinary
affairs of everyday life, in communities having no regular
political organization, without at the same time confusing
mere notions of abstract morality which do not even possess
the essentials of what Austin calls positive morality.

It is universally admitted that wherever there is an
assemblage of persons united together for common purposes
or ends, there must be some notion of law; for mankind
have, as Cicero observed, a genius for law. "That there
must be a supreme power in every state or in every
self-dependent community," says Paterson, "is an axiom
which cannot be explained, but which must nevertheless be assumed. Even in the rudest forms of state there
is a similar power, whether lodged in the patriarch or the
elders of the tribe, and it is usually found to assume by
turns a legislative, a judicial, and an executive phrase. This
supreme power is only a synonym for that human voice,
which cannot be resisted by any one individual or by any
minor combination of them short of the majority ; for whenever one resists it, all the other individuals readily combine
consciously or unconsciously to uphold it."

The family group being the unit of society among the
peoples on the Gold Coast, Asanti, and neighbouring states,
in the head or patriarch of the family resides the supreme
power. The towns scattered over the country have grown
from villages originally founded and occupied by single

family groups, the members whereof, bound together by ties of kindred, possessed rules of life naturally simple, which were observed more because they were in accordance with the general notions, views, 'and convictions obtaining or current among them, than from any undesirable results their violation or breach may cause. As the family group gets larger, and the village community grows, and the households increase in number, the public or general affairs of the community are guided by the patriarch of the family, now the headman of the village, who acts with the assistance of the village council composed of the heads of the other family groups or households and others, usually old men. The village council thus represents the fountain-head of the common life, and its determination finds expression in the popular voice.*

There exists in such community much of those positive rights and obligations constituting that Austinian Positive Morality, which may be called the Customary Law, and which each person can enforce against his neighbour, either by means of the village council sitting and acting judicially as a local tribunal, or by invoking, as already stated, the silent force of the popular sanction according to an usage long established or well known, all of which, more or less, possess an imperative attribute, and therefore rightly partake of the character of law. "To restrict the term law," says Mr. Rattigan, "to statutory law would be to throw all early or semi-civilized communities into an absolutely lawless condition, which is not inconceivable but diametrically opposed to all we know concerning them, and especially of a large and typical class still existing in India. While on the other hand, to attempt to make a definition sufficiently flexible to include statutory as well as Customary Law, is to be reminded of the Roman jurist, *omnis definitio in iure civile periculosa est*. It may, however, be said that law in the earliest stage of its existence represents nothing more

---

* *Amfoo* v. *Yardonuah*, 1 F. L. R. 198; *Ghambra* v. *Ewea*, 2 F. L. R. 64; and Fanti Customary Laws, p. 244, 1st Edition.

than the will or conviction of a community, whereby a given rule is adopted by common consent to govern the conduct of its members in their relations with each other." We take consent to mean, not one of necessity formally given at a particular time or place, or promulgated by a person or body of persons having power, or whose duty it is so to do, but a common consent which prompts the repetition of a single action by others, or which is evidenced by that tacit acquiescence in the existence of a rule, which commending itself to the individuals composing the community, is found to be of the greatest utility by such individuals shaping their conduct or guiding their transactions in consonance with or within its scope. As by repeated course of action a habit is acquired, so from isolated instances an usage springs up, which in process of time comes to be the Customary Law ; or as Professor Newman hath it somewhere, "Law is everywhere built on usage," an opinion perhaps identical with the train of thought suggested by Herbert Spencer when he speaks of the "gradual establishment of law by the consolidation of custom. Every new member of the family or village community at his birth, or admission by purchase before the abolition of slavery, or by commendation or any method, finds existing general usages which regulate his rights and obligations, and to which, under pressure of circumstances or the popular sanction, as already stated, he must submit. Submission or war to the knife is the substratum of all human companionships, and the new comer, on his arrival, must submit to what he finds already existing. As the original community gets larger, as aforesaid, many of the rules formerly observed within a small circle of persons gradually acquire a wider operation, moulding and controlling the habits of the people within its sphere. By such process, say some writers, arose that large body of undigested Customary Law, which, although evidenced by long usage, is founded really on a pre-existing rule sanctioned by the will of the community, and which in the history of every

nation is found to be long anterior to the more formal
written law. This process is still going on throughout the
Gold Coast, and the regions over which the Asanti sway
once extended. As law is said to derive its force by publication, so is it correct to say that Customary Law exists
by usage. The Customary Laws on the Gold Coast are not
written laws, by oral tradition they have been handed
down, and they are developed by usage. It will be found
in the native tribunals, that whenever there is any new
case, the like of which had not been known previously, the
difficulty is got over by making a new rule, concealed
under a fiction that it is only an old pre-existing custom,
perhaps fallen to the background, that is being applied,
restated, and made prominent.

Besides this more general source of the formation of the
Customary Law, are the comparatively few orders or commands issuing from the chief or headman of a tribe, which
on examination will be found to be negative in character.
Such laws usually forbid the commission of certain specified acts or the pursuit of a certain line of conduct under
penalty, and state that a person contravening such command shall be considered to have broken or taken in vain
the great oath of the native tribe, village community, or
ruling power, as the case may be, and so subject to all
the pains and penalties issuing therefrom. In the same
manner, the headman of a clan, or the senior members
thereof, can make an order, which has the force of law
binding on the clan, and which the members are bound to
obey. If such law is against the interest of the clan, or is
considered oppressive, it can be only repealed by the headman and senior members, or, on their being lawfully
removed, by a new headman with other senior members
repealing such obnoxious law. So also are laws made
for a company by the head captain, acting with and by
the consent of the committee of captains having the
management of the company affairs. Persons offending
against or disobeying such laws are liable to be expelled

the clan or company as the highest punishment. Laws emanating from such an ascertainable or specific source must be published before they can have any force, and this must be done by the beating of a gong in the public streets, beginning at the public place of meeting and ending there, and in places where those to be affected are wont to assemble. Most of these laws have become merged in the Customary Law, while those dealing with matters covered by the English criminal law have in the protected territories ceased to exist since the Bond of 1844. The term Customary Law in this work means and embraces the general and fundamental principles of the Customary Law well known over the whole of the country, and which law has sprung from usage, as well as laws or commands made by chiefs or rulers, headmen, the village council, headmen of clans, and company captains. As such Customary Law is continually being generated among a people advancing in civilization as the inhabitants of the Gold Coast are and will continue to advance, and having regard, further, to the fact that it is nowhere forbidden any chief, headman, village council, head of clan, or company committee of captains, to make new laws as has been done from time immemorial, we know of no native laws other than those which have been described, and if the Supreme Court Ordinance does not refer to this kind of law, then it refers to what did not exist. It is also clear from sect. 92 that Customary Law or usage does not become native law by its having been judicially noticed in a suit.

Having endeavoured to state the sources of, and to explain what is the native law, to the question now remaining, what is *native custom*, the answer is, usage—which, developing into custom, becomes apparently crystallized and merged into native law. But from the standpoint of the natives, an usage is invariably the practical result of the application of some principles of the Customary Law, however much such usage may be influenced by the time when, and place where it first sprang up. In the

native tribunals there are no difficult problems produced
by a combination of circumstances, however novel or
intricate, which remain unsolved. The process of deduction may be unsatisfactory, but the result frequently
commends itself to the general public.

Assuming that the judges in *Welbeck* v. *Brown* meant
by the word " custom," and used it as a general term for
" native laws and customs," Chief Justice Bailey expressed
the opinion that he had no reason to suppose that when
the draughtsman of the Supreme Court Ordinance, 1876,
spoke of customs, he meant anything more or less than
that word imparts to legal ears; and Mr. Justice Smalman
Smith, concurring with the Chief Justice, said : " We must
of course conclude that the native customs to which the
Supreme Court Ordinance of 1876 requires us to give effect
in the administration of the law of this colony, must be
such as in the contemplation and according to the principles of English jurisprudence would be regarded as
customs, that is to say, such as have existed in the colony
from time immemorial, or ' to which the memory of man
runneth not to the contrary.' " The English law has
several rules by which the validity of any custom or usage
must be tested. When one studies the said English law,
he discovers one of such rules to be, that for a usage or
custom to be valid, it must be immemorial or ancient,
having existed " from the time whereof the memory of
man runneth not to the contrary." On further investigation it is found that before the Prescription Act, by
the statute of Westminster (3 Edw. I.), a period of legal
memory was established distinct from that of living
memory, whereby prescriptive claim was taken to be
indefeasible if existing before the reign of King Richard I.
in A.D. 1199. One need not fully go into the reasons
assigned by English lawyers, who say King Richard's
reign was taken as the limit, because from that reign only
exists a connected record of legislative enactments, the
laws of the realm prior to that reign having been merged

in the general custom. "In like manner," says a writer
on Indian institution, "with regard to India there was no
system of legislation in force at all prior to our rule, nor
has any authentic record of the law administered by native
Courts come down to us. Under former rulers *Might*
generally formed the standard of *Right*, and disputes
between private individuals were for the most part settled
by arbitration. Such a course of proceeding naturally
favoured the creation of Customary Law, handed down
traditionally, and acquiring its force according to the
frequency of its practical application and recognition.
Accordingly, if we take the analogy which the English law
affords, we should require every custom to be at least as
ancient as the commencement of our rule, which would in
fact constitute the limit of legal memory in this country.
And this was the principle which Sir Charles Grey, the
Chief Justice, actually affirmed in a case which came before
him in the late Supreme Court of Calcutta."

If such opinion be accepted for the Gold Coast, it
follows that as soon as any new district is brought under
the jurisdiction of the Supreme Court, the legal memory,
of which so much was made in *Welbeck* v. *Brown*, starts
into being from that day, and not from 1876, the date
of the Supreme Court Ordinance. The most important
question is, Did the judicial assessors act in accordance
with or under the English rules or tests at any time?
Certainly not. We know when and how that office was
created, and who filled the post from time to time. The
first Chief Justice and first puisne judge of the present
Supreme Court had been judicial assessors, and in the
Assessors' Court, which was the highest native Court
(*Buafoo* v. *Enimil*),* was administered not only the
general Customary Law, which the learned assessors
treated as the common law of the land, but mindful of her
Majesty's instructions to Mr. Hill, the then Governor of
the Gold Coast settlements, they gave to the general

* 1 F. L. R. 247.

Customary Law the desirable flexibility and adaptation by enforcing new customs and usages in the same way as the native tribunals were wont to do, and so keeping abreast of the times, their decisions satisfied that rising standard of justice which continues to grow and expand from age to age.

Eminent judges in India and the East are doing the same thing. Says West, J., in *Naikin* v. *Esu Naikin*, "in *Abraham* v. *Abraham*, 9 Moore's Indian Appeal, 195, the Privy Council say that customs and usages dealing with property, unless their continuance is enjoined by law, as they are adopted voluntarily, may be changed or lost by desuetude, and though race and blood are independent of volition, usage is not. . . . Custom can be entitled to recognition as a law, only in virtue of some power outside the court which has given it validity, and this must be the autonomy of the people in matters not withdrawn from their plastic power by positive legislation and the principles implied in its enactments."

The history of English law illustrates the true capacity of custom or usage, as a source of law, in a striking manner. On the one hand, we find it laid down by Tindal, C.J., in *Tyson* v. *Smith*, 9 A. and E., p. 421, that a custom is not invalid merely because it is contrary to a rule of the common law; while on the other, it is said by Abbot, C.J., in *R.* v. *Joliffe*, 2 B. & C., p. 59, that "if that custom be against any known rule or principle of law, it cannot stand, however great its antiquity." No doubt the apparent contradiction is explained by a consideration of the different scope and purpose of different parts of the general law, and of the rejection of desuetude as affecting English statutes. A custom cannot prevail against a recognized general interest of the community, more especially when this has been guarded by an explicit law ; but as to the merely regulative or subsidiary laws, "wherein the State has no immediate interest of its own," a divergence is not impossible. At what point this general

interest arises, or is considered to arise, is determined by
the Courts as the authorized expositors of the imperative
will of the Sovereign and the community, and varies at
each stage of the national development. In delivering
the judgment of the Exchequer Chamber in *Goodwin* v.
Robarts, L. R. 10 Exchequer 337, Cockburn, C.J., refers to
Williams v. *Williams*, wherein it was decided that the
custom of merchants was part of the common law. After
discussing a series of cases by which the negotiability
given to various instruments by usage had been ratified,
he says, at p. 352, " Usage adopted by the Courts having
been thus the origin of the whole of the so-called law
merchant as to negotiable securities, what is there to
prevent our acting upon the principle acted upon by our
predecessors, and followed in the precedents they have left
to us ? *Why is it to be said that a new usage which has
sprung up under altered circumstances is to be less admissible than the usages of past times ?* Why is the door
now to be shut to the admission and adoption of usage in
a matter altogether of cognate character, as though the
law had been finally stereotyped and settled by some
positive and peremptory enactment ? " In *Crouch* v. *The
Credit Foncier of England*, L. R. 8 Q. B. 374, it was held
that a recent custom could not have the effect of making
an instrument negotiable which was not already so, " because it formed no part of the ancient law merchant." On
this it is observed : " For the reasons we have already
given, we cannot concur in thinking the latter ground
conclusive. While we agree that the greater or less time
during which a custom has existed may be material in
determining how far it has generally prevailed, we cannot
think, that if a usage is once shown to be universal, it is
the less entitled to prevail, because it may not have formed
part of the law merchant as previously recognized and
adopted by the Courts. It is obvious that such reasoning
would have been fatal to the negotiability of foreign bonds,
which are of comparatively modern origin, and yet, according

to *Gorgier* v. *Mieville*, 3 B. and C. 45, are to be treated as negotiable. We think the judgment in *Crouch* v. *The Credit Foncier* may well be supported, on the ground that in that case there was substantially no proof whatever of general usage. We cannot concur in thinking that if proof of general usage had been established, it would have been sufficient ground for refusing to give effect to it, that it did not form part of what is called the ancient law merchant."

It is clear that a new usage which has sprung up under altered circumstances can be properly admitted and enforced by the Court when once it has been shown to be universal, or a fair and reasonable result of the development of a progressing community as the inhabitants of the Gold Coast. The law, however, " has laid down no rule as to the extent of the evidence necessary to establish a custom, or from which the inference of the fact of a custom may be drawn. It is the province of a jury to draw these inferences of fact " (*Hanmer* v. *Chance*, 4 De G. J. and S.).

Without pursuing this subject any further, it may be said the Legislature has stated the tests which are to be applied to native laws and customs; they must not be repugnant to natural justice, equity, and good conscience, nor incompatible either directly or by necessary implication with any enactment of the Legislature, *e.g.* if a law were to be passed to-morrow that tenants must pay their rents for gold mines not to their landlords direct, but through a specified channel, such law would prevail against the Customary Law relating to rents of that nature or description; so also, any custom recognizing the right of an illegitimate child by an adulterous intercourse, in the property of the putative father, is immoral, and therefore can have no effect. Westrop, C.J., and Melville, J., in the appeal case, *Bharthi* v. *Laving Bharthi*, say : " The alleged custom amongst the Gosavis to recognize a right of heirship in the son of a Gosavi, by a woman, who, in the lifetime of a previous husband and without his consent, has

married the Gosavi, would be a bad custom and such as
could not be treated by Courts of justice as valid."

There is one point which has not, perhaps, received the
attention which it deserves. When it does not appear to
the Court, either by express contract or from the nature
of the transactions out of which any suit or question has
arisen, that such party agreed to be bound exclusively by
English law, the Customary Law is to prevail, but if there
is no Customary Law on the point, the Court is not to be
governed by the doctrines of equity, but by the principles
of justice, equity, and good conscience. It can be argued
that the principles of equity so mentioned are not to be
interpreted by the light of English authorities, which are
necessarily unknown to the litigant parties. The Supreme
Court Ordinance was passed on the 31st of March, 1876,
about the time her Majesty's ministers in London were
directing their special attention to the laws in force in
India, and it is not unreasonable to think the result of the
study and researches then going on may have influenced
those who gave instructions for the making of the Supreme
Court Ordinance. Writing to the Governor-General of
India about the expediency of another code for India, Lord
Salisbury, on 20th January, 1876, said, *inter alia*, " I may,
however, observe that the need of such a code appears
to me to be even greater at this moment than when its
preparation was first resolved upon, because there is now
an additional agency at work which is already producing
embarrassing effects, and requires to be properly directed.
The amalgamation of the Presidency and Mufassal Courts
having taken place before the formation of the civil code
which they were intended to administer, it has been remarked that the general direction to follow the dictates
of equity which is alone given them for their guidance, is
apt to be interpreted by many of the judges of appeal by
the light of English authorities with which they are
familiar, but which are necessarily unknown to the litigant
parties. . . . Thus, it is said, many rules ill-suited for

Oriental habits and institutions, and which would never recommend themselves for adoption in the course of systematic law-making, are indirectly finding their way into India by means of that informal legislation which is gradually effected by judicial decisions."

In conclusion, the alien would-be-reformer, reckless and in haste, should ever remember in his dealings the common saying : " Wo-si, Ko man Ko tu ; wo-nsí, Ko man kasin "— the saying is : " Enter into a community and settle ; not, enter into a community to boast." Sir Richard Burton, the great West African traveller, correctly remarks : " This is addressed to those who leave their native land and settle in another ; they ought to join the people with whom they live, and not pride themselves upon retaining their own manners and customs, or attempt to set up new rules." This saying, in a sense a warning, is current throughout the Gold Coast, Asanti, and neighbouring states. For any reform to be permanent and enduring, it must be based on and rooted in the principles of the aboriginal institutions. The patient inquirer will discover there is very little that is new on the Gold Coast, if not in all West Africa ; persons administering justice may well bear in mind the words uttered by the late Judicial Assessor and first Puisne Judge of the Supreme Court, Sir James Marshall. Speaking at the Colonial Exhibition in London, 1886, he said : " The Gold Coast must remain the country of the natives, but with a handful of Europeans among them who have the power by which they rule these people and enforce obedience. And whenever this rule is carried out and enforced according to European ideas, without consideration of the ideas, equally ancient and equally deep rooted, which pervade the native mind, it may break and destroy, but without securing any real improvement. My own experience of the West Coast of Africa is that that Government has for the time succeeded best with the natives, which has treated them with consideration for their native laws, habits, and customs, instead of ordering all these to be suppressed as nonsense,

and insisting on the wondering negro at once submitting to
the British constitution, and adopting our ideas of life and
civilization. As Judicial Assessor I was a sort of head
chief, and sat with the local chiefs in Court, hearing causes
brought by natives among themselves.

"By this I learned that a complete system of laws connected with both land and personal property existed among
them, which had been handed down by oral tradition from
time immemorial, and was better suited for them than our
modern feudal elaborate and intricate laws of real and
personal property. The natives of the Gold Coast and West
Africa have a system of laws and customs which it would be
better to guide, modify, and amend, rather than to destroy
by ordinances and force. So they have their chiefs and
court forms and etiquette, their own customs and mode
of living, which will not be improved by ridicule or forced
abolition."

We have seen it stated somewhere that native laws
and custom know nothing of crimes; but we must differ
from that opinion. They do know of crimes, which are few
in number, and they invariably bring the death penalty.
At first by the decisions of Maclean, then by the famous
bond of 1844, the Fanti rulers agreed to the British Government having exclusive jurisdiction in matters criminal.
Maclean created the Gold Coast Protectorate, but the British
Government did not and does not own the soil of that
country beyond the actual sites of the forts and castles
in their possession.

It was in 1836 that the President in Cape Coast Castle
assumed power and tried Adoasi and Anumah for wilful
murder. When a full report of this trial reached England,
the Committee of African Merchants, in their despatch of
October 20, 1836, wrote: "Your proceedings in Council of
April 6, in reference to the trials of Adoasi and Anumah
for wilful murder, we observe were conducted in the Public
Hall of Cape Coast Castle in your presence and that of the
Caboceers and Peynins, and, found guilty upon their own

confession, these men were executed. It seems from your information to us, that there has been a very important departure from the proceedings of our Criminal Courts, inasmuch as the confessions of the prisoners had been admitted as the chief evidence against them, but of the justice of the sentence there can be no doubt. These remarks lead us to remark to you, which we feel bound to do, that WE HAVE BEEN INSTRUCTED EXPRESSLY BY LORD GLENEG, ' that the British Government pretends neither to territorial possession, nor to jurisdiction over any portion of the Gold Coast, excepting the actual site of the several forts and CASTLES.' It is, therefore, necessary that your authority should be exercised with very great caution." We have seen the original of this letter, which was published in the *Gold Coast People* newspaper of May 20, 1892. More light is thrown on this matter by the papers printed in the Appendix.

CHAPTER II.

PERSONS.

(i.) THE FAMILY.

A FANTI family consists of all the persons lineally descended through females from a common ancestress, provided, that neither they nor those through whom they claim to be the descendants of the common ancestress had severed their connection with that root by—

(i.) Cutting Ekar, also called Kahiré,

(ii.) Adoption,

(iii.) Partition, or

(iv.) Commendation.

(i.) *Cutting Ekar* is a particular mode of disowning any one's blood relation. When a man desires to disown a blood relative, he brings him before the elders of his town or village, and in their presence, as well as in the presence of the other members of his family, an ekar is cut in twain, and saying clearly, "We are now divided," he takes one-half and the disowned the other half. As soon as this ceremony is completed, the two persons have no more share or portion in the property of each other. Where a man is disowned, it affects him alone; but in the case of a woman, her issue is included, for the saying is, the children follow the mother's condition.

In *Welbeck* v. *Brown*, February 4, 1884, per Chief Robertson: "The cutting of the custom or ekar is a thing of the past in Cape Coast, as a sign of disownment. It was abolished by Governor Maclean."

(ii.) *Adoption* is practised by persons who have no next of kin to succeed to their property. The person adopted is usually of the same clan as the person adopting, but if of a different clan, he assumes the name given him and becomes a member of his clan. To make adoption valid, it must be done publicly, and the person who wishes to adopt must not only get the consent of the family and parents whose child is about to be adopted, but he must clearly state before witnesses his desire and intention. A person cannot adopt another outside his tribe. On account of the custom of descent, which is traced through the female line, it is more usual to adopt females in preference to males.

(iii.) *Partition* is of rare occurrence, where persons live in the same town or locality. It takes place frequently where two branches of one family, living in separate localities, agree to relinquish to the other, all claim to whatever family property that other has in its possession.

E.g.: The family of Anan is divided into two branches, one residing in the family house at Chama, and the other branch living on the family land at Siwdu. As soon as the two branches agree to give up all claim to the property in each other's possession and retain what each has, none of the members of the Chama branch is considered member of the Siwdu family. The successors to each property will be selected from each branch. If one branch get into family difficulties, and the members thereof decide to sell their possessions, the other branch cannot stop such sale. But if at any time the right person to succeed to one branch of the family be a minor, then the headman or senior member of the other branch is, by his position, guardian. On failure of the legal successors, the two branches merge, and the existing line succeeds to both. Partition does not cause an absolute severance from one's family. In fact it is usual for the headman of one branch to preside at the ceremony by himself or deputy, whenever a successor is about to be installed as headman of the other branch.

(iv.) *Commendation.* When a person is anxious to enter another man's family, so that he may share in the protection and privileges which the members thereof enjoy, he goes before the head of that family, and formally transfers himself and all his worldly possessions into the safe keeping of his new protector. Such is the ordinary commendation. This must not be confounded with that voluntary fellowship of a person in the retinue of some influential neighbour, or with that species of service whereby a man with his family, in town or village, voluntarily accepts a sum of money from an influential king or chief, in order to be counted among his subjects. The head of a family and the whole family can (and in days gone by did so) commend themselves to rich, powerful, or influential neighbours.

In former times, where, through straitened circumstances at home, or through a crushing family debt or calamity, a member of the family was sold or pawned, he ceased to be a member of his family; but whenever he was reclaimed, he regained all his rights, privileges, and position in the family. But when a person through misconduct was expelled the family,* or was sold and got rid of by the

---

* Derx, Governor of the Dutch possessions, in an official communication to Geo. Maclean, the Judicial Assessor, on November 30, 1846, writes: "The 9 ackies alluded to as subsequently borrowed from *Effoom*

family after due deliberation, he ceased to be a member of
the family, even if his master gave him his freedom.

The members of the family are termed Ebusuafu. The
normal condition of a Fanti family being joint, the law
throws the burden of proving that a person has ceased to
be joint, or that a person has ceased to be a member thereof, on the person asserting it. There is no limit to the
number of persons of whom a family may consist, or to the
remoteness of their descent from the common stock, and
consequently to the distance of their relationship from each
other. But the Fanti coparcenary, properly so called, con-
stitutes a much larger body. When we speak of a joint
family as constituting a coparcenary, we refer, not to the
entire number of persons who can trace descent from a
common female person, and among whom no cutting of the
ekar has ever taken place; we include only those persons
who, by virtue of relationship, have the right to enjoy and
hold the joint property, to restrain the acts of each other
in respect of it, and to burden it with their debts. Outside
this body there is a fringe of persons who possess inferior
rights, such as that of residence in the case of children, of
maintenance in the case of domestics, or who may under
certain contingencies hope to enter into the coparcenary.

The ordinary incidents of a family are—

(i.) Common clan ;

(ii.) A common penin ;

(iii.) Common liability to pay debts ;

(iv.) Common funeral rites ;

(v.) Common residence ;

(vi.) Common burial-place.

In the native courts, and with the experienced Judges
of the Supreme Court, these several incidents are most
carefully looked into in deciding contending claims, and for

by the father of the above-mentioned boy, *Quashie Kin*, which person,
through making of much debts, was publicly abandoned by the family, and
according to the black laws the debts are thereby null and void " as against
the family of the debtor.

any light which may be thrown upon the matter, the opinion of the neighbourhood, and the statements of domestics and friends and servants, are received in evidence. *Amonoo* v. *Ampima.**

(i.) Common clan: members of the family belong to the same clan, and to this rule there is no exception whatever. The slave becomes a member of his master's clan. The children of a freeborn woman belong to their mother's clan and not to that of the father: *e.g.* a man of the Nsonna clan whose father is an Annona clansman is not at all entitled to any Annona property, for he is not a member of his father's family. Nor can a man be a member of two clans.

(ii.) A common penin (elder), also called Egya, father.

The senior or other male member of a family who has control of the family, and is its representative, is called the penin, or egya. Such person must of necessity be a member of the same clan; he may be a freeborn person of the heritable class (Dihi) known as the head of the family, managing and directing its affairs; or he may be the person who first brought wealth into the family; or increased its importance by buying slaves or receiving several persons by way of commendation; or who, by some act or deed, had increased the family possessions. The penin has control over all the members of the family and the issue of such members. Where the founder of the family is deceased, then the senior male member in the line of descent is, in the absence of any direction to the contrary, the penin. As such, he is the natural guardian of every member within the family. He alone can sue and be sued,† as the representative of the family, respecting claims on the family possessions, and he is as much the guardian and representative for all purposes of property as the Roman father—Paterfamilias.

The members of the family are bound to obey the

* 1 F. L. R. 214.

† *Mensa* v. *Krakue,* 2 F. L. R. 86 ; *Asraidu* v. *Dadzie,* 1 F. L. R. 174.

lawful commands of the penin; he arranges the rooms in
the family residence to be allotted to each,* and what
portions of the family lands each is to cultivate or possess.
Rooms and lands so allotted continue in the possession of
such persons and their successors until the penin re-
arranges them.

When a member takes upon himself to take possession
of the family property or a part thereof without the permission of the penin, he can be removed at any time, and
another person placed in his stead. So also, a member of
the family making any additions to the family residence
or property cannot have an exclusive right thereto as
against the family, unless at the time of making the
addition the penin reserved to him the exclusive or special
enjoyment of the addition or improvement.

The penin is usually one whose fitness had been recommended by the immediate predecessor, and who had been
confirmed in his position by all, or by the majority of, the
principal members of the family.

The principal members of the family have the right to
pass over any person so recommended, and to elect another
member of the family instead. Where the penin suffers
from mental incapacity, or enters upon a course of conduct
which, unchecked, may end in the ruin of the family, or
persistently disregards the interests of the family, he can
be removed without notice by a majority of the other
members of the family, and a new person substituted for
him.

In the absence of the penin, the eldest male member of
the family acts as penin, for the long absence or incapacity
of the penin must not prejudice the interests of the family.

Like other members of the family, the penin has
but a life interest in the immoveable property of the
family.

(iii.) *Common liability to pay debts.*   Not only does the
Customary Law render the person or persons who defray

* *Barnes* v. *Mayan,* 1 F. L. R. 180; *Halmond* v. *Daniel,* 1 F. L. R. 182.

the burial expenses of any person *primâ facie* liable and responsible for the debts of the deceased, but, as Bosman states, the members of a family and the head thereof are jointly and severally responsible for any family liability. If a member of a family contract debt which benefits the family, or commit a wrong for which he is liable to pay damages or give satisfaction, the other members of his family are bound to pay, or such member must be given up by the family to the person making the claim. If the family do not wish to be held responsible for the future acts of a certain member, there must be a public notice of their decision to that effect, and such person must be expelled the family, thereby severing his connection with them. A person is liable for the debts and the consequences of the torts of his slaves and the members of his family under his control. While a husband is living with his wife, or is providing for and maintaining her, he is not liable for her contracts, debts, or liabilities, except for any medical expenses she may be put to for herself or child by him. For the wife, if freeborn or domestic of a different family, can acquire and hold property apart from the husband, and has her own family to fall back on. If the wife be a domestic and member of the same family as the husband, their common master's liability for them remains.

Children are liable for the debts of their mother.*

Not only is a father liable to maintain his child, but if he fail to obtain a wife for his son on reaching the age of puberty, he is liable for damages arising from the son's misconduct with any woman. On this point the Commissioners appointed by the Governor of the Gold Coast Colony in August, 1894, to inquire into various matters relating to Native Courts, suggest in their report that the question whether a father is liable for his sons' debts or wrongful acts, and whether the family or the head of the family is liable for one of its members, and whether a host is liable for his guest, should be left to be decided in each

---

* *Quacoom* v. *Ansa*, 2 F. L. R. 1.

case when it arises by evidence as to the custom of the particular district.*

(iv.) *Common funeral rites.* On the decease of a member, all persons who are members of the family take part in making the funeral custom and contribute in defraying its expenses, for which they are primarily liable. The members of the clan also take part in observing the funeral custom, and contribute collectively towards the payment of the same, but they are not liable at all. It is usual for the local senior member of the clan, with the head of the family of the deceased, to preside over the funeral custom, to receive the expressions of condolence from sympathizing neighbours, and to accept funeral donations. " It is customary for friends and acquaintances to bring presents to the relations of the deceased, to assist them in performing the funeral ceremonies in a becoming manner." (Cruickshank, vol. ii. 217.) Funeral donations are of two kinds, to wit: (*a*) *Insawa*, which are not repaid at all, being considered as gifts to the deceased; (*b*) *Esi-adzi*, which may be more correctly called funeral custom advances. Respecting *esi-adzi*, Cruickshank writes: " Considerable sums are received in presents at the time of the funeral. They are seldom a source of gain, as it is expected that the receiver will make similar presents to the donor upon the occasion of death in his family." On entering into the accounts of the funeral custom expenses, *esi-adzi* sums are set aside, and if the *Insawa* presents are found insufficient to defray the expenses, the immediate relatives of the deceased contribute for this purpose. Any sums received from the children or grandchildren of the deceased, or from his widows, are in the nature of *Insawa;* the liability to pay such sums by no means makes them members of his family, where such widow or widows are of a different family, since they are not entitled to be present when such accounts are being gone into, nor can

* *Gold Coast Government Gazette*, January 31, 1895, p. 34, reproduced in 2 F. L. R. 182.

they be compelled to contribute towards the liquidation of any deficiency.

(v.) *Common residence.* Persons who have a right to reside in the family house, or the right to dwell on the family possessions unconditionally, are members of the same family. " It was customary to regard the possession of a house as a common family fund in all the members of the family ; while they remained such, each had a share at the same time that the head or representative of the family had the direction and disposed of it." (Cruickshank, vol. i. 316.)

(vi.) *Common burial-place.* It is customary for the family to have a common burial-place, which may be either in the family dwelling-house, or a grove or a plot of land set apart for burial. Children by a woman, free-born or of a different family, can only be buried in the family burial-place of the father, by special leave of the head of the family. The members of a family have a right to burial in such burial-place, and it is here that libations are made on the special *Adai* seasons, or during the time of *Ahuba kuma.*

(ii.) MARRIAGE.

The customary law relating to marriage is very simple, but, by some inexplicable process, it is a stumbling-block to the foreigner, and to the native who considers himself better than his forefathers. The attention of those whose sole object on the Gold Coast is to discredit the Fanti marriage institution is respectfully directed to an accurate study of the English marriage system.* From the

* WOOINGS AND WEDDINGS IN MANY LANDS. By Annie Hyatt-Woolf.—Many of our own wedding customs are survivals of the days when marriage laws were of the laxest description, and it was the vogue for the would-be husband to seize and carry off by force the lady of his fancy. But later times, better manners. When Cæsar invaded Britain (52 B.C.) a suitor for a maiden addressed himself to her father, whose

English law point of view, a man's family is that of his father, and pedigree is generally traced in the male line.

property she was, and if the father consented the girl had not the power to say "No." But naturally a woman's lot would not be so beset with hardships if she were given away or sold as if she were stolen. The Anglo-Saxons regarded the bond of matrimony with all reverence, and no man could lawfully marry without first gaining the consent of the woman's father, or, should he be dead, of her nearest male relative. In acknowledgment for the permission thus granted he paid a price according to the rank of the lady. Practically the girl was sold, and it was therefore advantageous to a father that the "spindle side," or female part of the family—to use King Alfred's term—should outnumber the "spear side," or male members of the family. Marriage banns are said to have been established by the Synod of Westminster in 1200, which ordered that no marriage should be contracted without banns thrice published in the church, unless by the special authority of the bishop.

The "best man" is a survival of the time when marriage by capture was the mode of procedure. His office then was to carry sword or spear and assist in the seizure of the bride. Of course, if much difficulty were anticipated, the number would be multiplied to two or three, and, possibly, for a chief or king's daughter there would be a band of "best men." The honeymoon is distinctly a relic of the days when the newly wed couple deemed flight the better part of wisdom, and sought safety in refuge either from an irate father robbed of his daughter, or other too ardent suitor. To trace the bridal veil to its earliest origin we should have to go back to a very ancient period. Our Anglo-Saxon forbears received the nuptial benediction from the priest, sometimes under a veil or square piece of cloth, called the "care-cloth," held at each corner by a man to conceal the blushes of the bride ; but this little attention they deemed superfluous to bestow on a widow. A ring was used at the marriage as well as at the betrothal ceremony, and at the wedding both the man and woman were crowned with garlands of flowers. The custom of introducing orange blossoms into wedding wreaths and bouquets is a comparatively modern innovation, although orange trees were growing in England when bluff Hal was king, who, as every schoolboy knows, distinguished himself by marrying six wives. The fashion of adorning the bride with orange blossoms we have borrowed from the East. There it is regarded as a symbol of a prosperous and fruitful marriage. In indigenous countries orange trees bear fruit and flowers at one and the same time. With us, in the days that were earlier, a sprig of gorse was often introduced into the bridal bouquet, possibly because of the old saying that "When the furze is out of bloom kissing is out of fashion." Throwing a slipper after a bride is a somewhat doubtful compliment, for it is generally agreed among competent authorities that, at the marriages of the Anglo-Saxons, the father or nearest of male kin presented the bridegroom with one of the

The converse is the case with the inhabitants of the Gold
Coast, Asanti, and other neighbouring places.   In the

bride's shoes as a token of the transfer of his authority to his son-in-law,
who then and there, in appreciation of this mark of ownership, gave his
bride a blow on her head with her own shoe.   Yet the husband was
bound by oath to treat his wife kindly, and if he did not she was free to
leave him.   But he appears to have been allowed a very wide margin—
different times, different manners, and, to quote the words of an old author,
" he might bestow moderate castigation on her."

An interesting link with olden times is " Bidden Weddings," and in
Cumberland and Westmoreland and the North of England, about a hundred
years ago, this form of marriage was still celebrated.   A wedding in these
districts was not so much a private as a public affair, and called a " bride-
wain," or " bidden wedding."   A match being arranged, the parties gave
notice of its intended celebration to all and everybody, and to mark the
festive occasion " open house " was kept, and the guests congregated from
miles around.   A " bidding letter " sent as late as 1850 gives information
of the place and hour to the invited guests, and concludes with the words,
" and whatever donation you may be pleased to confer on us then will be
thankfully received, warmly acknowledged, and cheerfully repaid whenever
called for on a similar occasion."   Newspapers were also used as a medium
to advertise the coming wedding, and invite whoever would to attend.
Such an advertisement appeared so late as 1803.   Usually, in response to
this summons, hundreds of persons assembled at the bridegroom's house
or other place indicated, where they all joined in outdoor sports.   After
much feasting and drinking it was the custom to place a plate or bowl in
some conspicuous spot, and it was *de rigueur* for each visitor to contribute
something to its contents.   The relatives and near friends generally made
special gifts of household furniture, pewter plate, candlesticks, grain, and
money, several days after the wedding ceremony.   And in a lower, middle-
class wedding, the value of the total gifts were, we are told, " sometimes
as much as £200."   A servant girl who had been in one situation for seven
years was entitled upon her marriage to a copper kettle capable of holding
from four to six gallons.   Other weddings celebrated in the same public
fashion were called " bride-ales," " bride-bushes," or " bride-stakes."   On
these occasions the bride on her wedding-day sold ale to the guests, who
paid in either money or goods.   A bush at the end of a stake or pole was
the olden sign of a country ale-house, and around the pole the customers
congregated and often danced.   The term " bride-ale " was also applied to
the marriage procession.   In Queen Elizabeth's time a law was passed
limiting the quantity of " *weddyn-ale* " that any person or persons shall
" *brewe to sell*."   From this restriction we gather that " bride-ales " were
in early times conducted with much deep drinking.   A very quaint usage
prevailed in Essex until comparatively recent times.   " It is the common
custom there, when poor people marry, to make a kind of dog-hanging or

early days of the missionaries on the Gold Coast, a practice or usage arose amongst the converts of recognizing the English law, while native custom was retained. The wife, by matrimony, took the name of her husband, and at his death, his children and widow took a half of his moveable property, while his own family took the other half. This practice cannot be said to be unreasonable or against the principles of justice, equity, and good conscience.

money-gathering, which they call a wedding dinner, to which they invite tag and rag, all that will come ; where, after dinner, upon summons of the fiddler, who setteth forth his voice like a town crier, a table being set forth, and the bride sat simpering at the upper end of it, the bridegroom standing by with a white sheet athwart his shoulders, whilst the people march up to the bride, present their money, and wheel about. After this offering is over there is a pair of gloves laid upon the table most monstrously bedaubed about with ribbon, which, by way of auction, is set to sale at who gives most, and he whose hap it is to have them shall withal have a kiss of the bride." The history of the wedding-ring is so ancient that it is based upon fables, and who wore the first wedding-ring no man can say. In the long ago the ancients wore the betrothal ring, as we do to-day, on the third finger of the left hand, because they thought that a vein or nerve ran from that finger directly to the heart, and the outward sign of matrimony they considered ought to be placed in near connection with that seat of life. Another reason not so complimentary why women wear their wedding-rings upon their left hand is said to be because that hand is a sign of inferiority. In early times in England the date of a marriage was often fixed after a due consultation of the aspect of the heavens, and probably that is why there was a superstitious belief that there were lucky and unlucky seasons. As many popular sayings bear witness, " Marry in Lent, and you'll live to repent." The Romans regarded May as an ill-fated month for weddings, and our forbears were certainly of the same opinion. And an old couplet says, " From the marriages in May all the bairns die and decay." Another old saying was, " May never was ye month of love." " Who marries between the sickle and the scythe will never thrive." A popular rhyme gives the folklore relating to the days of the week on which weddings ought and ought not to take place—

> " Monday for wealth,
> Tuesday for health,
> Wednesday the best day of all ;
> Thursday for crosses,
> Friday for losses,
> Saturday no luck at all."

From *Lloyd's Weekly Newspaper*, by kind permission of the Proprietors.

Marriage is the union of a man to a woman to live as husband and wife for life. It is sometimes preceded by betrothals, which often take place long before a girl arrives at a marriageable age. This is done when a person desires to be connected with the family of a friend, or desires his child or relative to be so connected with a desirable family. The acceptance of any money or token, called *consawment* money or token, and a piece of cloth for this specific purpose, destines the girl to be the wife of the person for whom the alliance is sought. This betrothal is perfectly binding on the family of the girl, who is regarded as the wife of the person betrothing her. He narrowly watches her conduct, and frequently demands and receives compensation for any liberties she may allow other men to take with her.

According to the law of the country, every person is the member of some family, and all the other members of that family are answerable for him. In theory, the stranger belongs to the family of the person with whom he lodges, to whom he came, or who is his landlord. A father is entitled to all the earnings of his son before his marriage. It is the duty of the father to engage a wife for his son as soon after he reaches the age of puberty as possible ; and he is generally liable in damages, if his unmarried son, living with him, commits adultery with another's wife or any woman. This customary law is an old one, and is referred to by Artus in 1625. According to him : " Marriage being the foundation of Society, they keep their daughters in cloisters, when they are marriageable, and their sons leave themselves to their disposal, never wooing or looking on their wives before they marry them ; giving nothing with their sons but what they earn themselves. Only the father gives a peto and a half of gold, and the mother half a peto, *i.e.* half an ounce, and the richest no more." In very many parts of the Gold Coast, that is in the inland districts, this custom still exists, but where European influence has had its way, he thinks twice who desires to take a wife, what with sundry initial fees of eighteen shillings and upwards, besides other heavy expenses.

If the father be dead, his successor is entitled to the aforesaid earnings, and he is bound to provide the wife when the occasion arises.

He who desires a woman, whether maiden or widow, in marriage, must apply to her family, or person or persons, *in loco parentis*, for consent, and without such application and consent there can be no betrothal. Nor is there any remedy for breach of promise of marriage. If a man fail to marry a woman for whose hand he had applied, or if such woman refuse to marry him, or her family withdraw their consent, no action arises, and no damages are incurred by the person in default, who, however, forfeits any *consawment* or anything given to the other.* For instance, a man after giving *consawment* to the family of his intended wife, and money, trinkets, and other valuable presents to herself, cannot have any of them back should he improperly break off the engagement. But, if the breach is caused by the woman or her family, they are bound to return him the *consawment* and every present to herself and family, even though he may have received presents from them ; the only exception is, in the case of funeral custom donations, as to which accounts are entered into and the balance struck off.

In order to be valid, a marriage must not be in violation of any rule as to tribal relationship, in some districts, or consanguinity. A man may not marry his uterine sister, his father's sister, or mother's sister, or brother's daughter, or mother's sister's daughter. A man can marry his father's sister's child. The union, however, is not encouraged. An adopted son or daughter falls within the same rules both in his adoptive and natural families, and the same rule applies to their issue. In some districts, a marriage between freeborn persons of the same clan is very much discouraged,

* *Neizer* v. *Dontoh*, 1 F. L. R. 129.

but is not improper between a freeborn and a domestic, or between two domestics. To the question of the judicial assessor in *Penin* v. *Duncan*,* about the essential acts or ceremonies to constitute a valid marriage, according to the custom of the country, the chiefs replied : " When a man intends to have a certain woman for his wife, he applies to her family, asks her to be given in marriage by taking to the family according to his means, two flasks of rum, or two ackies of gold dust, or four or six ackies, according to his means. Upon this, if the family approve, they agree to give the woman. This request and consent with the first present alone make a valid marriage." The term "head rum," so often used in the case of marriage, is an instance of erroneous and deplorable interpretation of Fanti into English. Rum was unknown to the people until brought to them by those engaged in the slave trade, and before then, surely, marriage was not an unknown institution. The beverages made from maize, and extracted from the date and palm trees, were common, but instead of nuptial wine, an ignorant clerk said "head rum" for *Etsir ensa*. The term *Etsir ensa* is evidently a contraction of *Etsir nsa-nkredzi*, literally, tokens or price of the head; for in all primitive societies the idea of purchasing a wife underlies the institution of marriage, but rum, the curse of West Africa, is not essential at all in contracting marriage. Cruickshank, writing on marriage, says in his second volume, " native contracts of marriage are made by the payment of a certain sum to the relations of the bride. This sum varies according to the rank of the individual from 2 ounces gold = £8, to $4\frac{1}{2}$ ackies = 22s. 6d., but it is more frequently paid in goods than in gold." Gold or goods so given, for the hand of a woman in marriage, were called *Etsir nsa-nkredzi*, rendered, in the records of the old judicial assessors, *consawment money*. This word is also mentioned by Bowdich in his work on Asanti; and when one bears in mind that some of the *Etsir nsa-nkredzi* are distributed among the relatives

* 1 F. L. R. 118.

and more immediate friends of the woman, as proof of the honourable alliance, the absurdity of "head rum" becomes manifest.

After the *consawment* is accepted, follows the matter of dowry. "That depends on the family. If they tell the man that they require dowry to be paid, they state the amount they wish, sometimes one ounce, or nine ackies." If the woman's family do not wish for dowry, the man is not bound to pay anything. Among the poorer classes, the man and woman live together without any dowry having been paid at all, and yet such marriage is perfectly legal, and the husband can sue any one for satisfaction, that is, damages for misconduct with the wife.

If a man seduce an unmarried woman, he is liable to pay to her family damages for the wrong so done her and the disgrace brought on her family. When such seduction was under promise of marriage, the liability to damages is not extinguished by any *consawment* subsequently given by the seducer to her family, who can at any time hold it as satisfaction of the claim for damages for the wrong done their child. Where a married woman is seduced, her seducer is bound to pay to the husband as damages a fine or penalty called Brabbu, which is for the pacification of the injured husband, and is not less than the value of the *consawment* dowry and all the marriage expenses. If the marriage is continued, only pacification fine can be claimed, the amount of which is fixed according to the social standing of the injured husband, guided by the general character of the seduced woman. Moreover, where the conduct of the wife was brought about more or less by the husband's treatment, the seducer is liable to a nominal fine.* And if, on account of such seduction, the former marriage is dissolved, and he marries the woman, he cannot at any time recover from her family what he had so paid, even if the woman, without any cause whatever, refuse to live with him then or afterwards. Nor can he recover compensation

* *Penin* v. *Duncan*, 1 F. L. R. 118. See judgment by Chalmers.

from any one who may take this woman away from him, for, unless a man has given *consawment,* he cannot recover against anybody for seduction of a person who is nothing more than his mistress.

Where the consent of a woman's family cannot be gained, either because they improperly refuse to give such consent, or because they reside in such a distant place that it is impossible to obtain such consent, a man and woman, who voluntarily agree to live as man and wife for life, can contract a valid marriage; provided that such agreement is expressly made in the presence of credible and respectable witnesses, or in the presence of the chief or headman of the place, followed by the man and woman living as husband and wife.

When there has been a marriage in fact, the validity thereof is presumed, and where the caprice, avarice, or ambition of a parent has not been excited to force on a marriage, it will be found by careful study of the people and examination of the local marriage institution, that marriage entirely rests on the voluntary consent of a man and a woman to live together as man and wife; which intention, desire, consent, or agreement, is further evidenced by their living together as husband and wife. All other ceremonies and expenses attending marriage are superfluous, but are useful and taken account of in assessing damages in case of criminal conversation. Briefly stated, therefore, when a man desires to marry a woman, he goes personally or sends some one to her parents or family for her hand. If his proposal is agreeable to the family, and he receives their consent, the *consawment* money or token, valuing as much as he can afford, is sent to them. That is all that is necessary to constitute the marriage tie. The man may, according to his means, send to his bride some dresses, so that she may come to him properly attired. In marriages where one finds such expensive ceremonies, it is a notorious fact, there is no unity of interest, for the domestic arrangement is such that the wife rarely resides in the same house

with her husband, but only carries his food to him daily
and ministers to his desires.

On the death of the husband, his widows, him surviving, and their children by him, are entitled to reside
in any house built by him, and the children and their
issue have a life interest in such house, subject to good
behaviour.*

When there has been a betrothal, a man can claim his
wife on her reaching the age of puberty, and he is bound to
support and maintain her from the day of betrothal. A
man is bound to maintain his wife, and it is her duty to
obey his request to live with him, and to perform all his
lawful orders. A man can contract other marriages. By
courtesy, the first wife should be informed of the proposed
alliance; but the omission to do so is no cause for divorce
or termination of the marriage by the first wife. A woman
living in concubinage cannot sue the man with whom she is
so living for any maintenance, nor can her family or parents
sue the man for any satisfaction or maintenance. Whatever
is given or entrusted by a man or woman to the person
with whom he or she is living in concubinage, cannot be
reclaimed on any consideration whatsoever. This custom
of forfeiture is called *sarwie*. At first sight, this custom
may seem repugnant, but the grounds for it are not unreasonable. Although men of substance and the influential
classes will deny, or question, the existence of the custom
or usage known as *sarwie*, or at least endeavour to limit its
effect on account of its restraining influence on concubinal
and illicit intercourse, this salutary custom or usage undoubtedly exists, and is well known to the female community
(*Quassua* v. *Ward*).† In former times, this particular
custom placed a great check or restraint on the wealthy,
and those traders, European and native, who were in the
habit of keeping a host of women under their protection
as concubines, euphemistically called *friends*. Knowing

* *Barnes* v. *Mayan*, 1 F. L. R. 180 ; *Amamoo* v. *Clement*, 1 F. L. R.
180; *Swapim* v. *Ackuwa*, 1 F. L. R. 191.   † 1 F. L. R. 117.

perfectly well that the Customary Law compels no man to maintain his mistress, these "friends" had no claim for support or maintenance on their so-called protectors. But if such a woman has a child by her protector, he is bound to look after her during her illness only, and to pay any expenses attending her confinement. The sole or principal object of keeping these women, for whom no *consawment* had been given, and who had neither the status nor rights of a wife, was for their services. The protector lives on their services. A man having such a woman usually employed her without any pay or remuneration in selling goods, which he constantly, or at times, supplied her. Now and again the man may give to the woman money or clothing, with the object of inducing her to continue her services, and, with fair words, a woman is ever a prey to a designing man. The protector invariably manages to make the woman indebted to him, and whenever he fears she will transfer her affection to another in honourable marriage or otherwise, he endeavours to dissuade her by frightening her with false unfounded claims. A woman living with a man as concubine, mistress, or friend, is not encouraged in the eyes of the Customary Law, which stamps the relationship as immoral, to be remedied as quickly as possible. But women are frail, though the desire to have issue is keen in them, and men are deceivers ever. If a man therefore will not be properly and honourably married to a woman, but will for his own purposes keep her and live upon her labour, she is at liberty to terminate the immoral relation at any time she pleases, and she shall not be liable to return to him anything whatsoever he may have given or entrusted to her for safe keeping, sale, or any purpose whatsoever. Where a person living with a woman as his concubine wishes to marry her, he is bound to pay to the family of the woman satisfaction money, which can be waived, before giving the *consawment*, and if in consideration of the marriage the family of the woman or she herself be willing to return to the man whatever he

may have given her or entrusted her with, the amount
thereof is ascertained by the man and woman going into
detailed accounts, immediately before the *consawment* is
given and accepted.   Such a marriage legitimizes the
children of the man already born by the woman.   The
issue of an adulterous connection is illegitimate, and cannot
be made legitimate by the subsequent divorce of the woman
and her marriage with her paramour; *e.g.* Amba, wife of
Kwamina, during his absence at Akassa, bears a son, the
issue of an adulterous intercourse with Kwesi.   Such son
is illegitimate, and cannot have any interest whatsoever
in the house of his putative father, even if, on being
divorced by Kwamina or on his death, Amba is married
by Kwesi.

Although a man may lawfully marry several wives, a
woman cannot at the same time have more than one husband.
Adultery is a ground for divorce, and a wife's adultery
justifies her husband in expelling her from his house and
refusing her any maintenance.   Notwithstanding the vague
ideas in the coast towns about divorce of native marriage,
there is no doubt that, save and except the competency of
a native tribunal to decree the dissolution of a marriage,
the right of divorce is marital only.   The wife cannot
declare her marriage void, nor can her family give her
permission to remarry in the absence of the consent of her
husband, signified by his releasing her from her conjugal
obligation, either by chalking her, or saying so in the
presence of competent witnesses.   For adultery or witchcraft on the part of the wife, a man can divorce his wife
and claim from her family the *consawment* and other
expenses.   But the wife cannot enforce divorce or discontinue marriage on the ground of her husband's adultery,
or on his marrying more wives.

Change of religion is no ground for divorce; therefore,
if a married woman embrace Christianity and thereupon
deserts her husband, she does not cease to be his wife, and
whosoever weds her can be sued for damages.   By the term

"ground for divorce," is meant cause for which the husband could recover the *consawment* and all his expenses from the woman's family; or cause for which the wife and her family would not be compelled to return any portion of the *consawment* to the man.   If a husband is impotent, or neglect his wife or grossly ill-treat her, or absent himself for a long period of time, so that she commits adultery, he can divorce her, but cannot recover the *consawment;* for a wife has a right to the protection of her husband, and Customary Law does not countenance negligence of marital obligations.

There is no law on the Gold Coast similar to the Indian Act XXI., of 1866, the Native Converts Marriage Dissolution Act, under which, if a married person deserts his wife or her husband for six months or more, on the ground of change of religion, the Court can fix a year, on the expiration of which, if the defendant still refuses to continue the marriage, divorce is decreed.·   In our native tribunals a husband can bring an action against a man harbouring a wife, and against her family for her recovery.   This form of action is well known in India, and there the British Courts constantly enforce decrees to recover possession of wives by their husband.

A woman living with a man as concubine is always looked down upon, and is considered immoral, however wealthy she may be.

Where the marriage is discontinued through the fault of the husband, so found by arbitrators or a native tribunal on a complaint made against him, he cannot get the *consawment* or money or any of his expenses, and the wife goes away with all the property she possessed at the time of marriage, and, in addition, she is entitled to claim from him whatever she or her family may have expended on him.   When the marriage is at an end, the wife can demand from the man a return of all monies and goods of her own in his possession.*   If, on the other hand,

* *Fatimer* v. *Wellington*, March 5, 1872, *Cape Coast Court Record.*

it was through the fault of the wife or her family, the
consawment, and his trinkets and clothing, not worn out
in the service of the wife to her husband, are returned.
Moneys expended by the husband for the maintenance of
his wife are not recoverable.   An account of loans advanced
to each other, as well as of funeral donations, is gone into
and a balance struck, on paying which the woman is free
to contract another marriage.*   On the death of the
husband the wife is bound to contribute towards the
funeral expenses.   Children bear the cost of the coffin and
burial clothes of their father, but are not liable for the
expenses of the funeral custom.   They have the right to
live in their father's residence or rooms, provided they are
of good behaviour.†

A regrettable departure from the Customary Law relating to the recovery of the *consawment* on the determination
of the marriage is becoming somewhat frequent in proceedings before the District Commissioners.   In many cases
it is assumed that the mother-in-law is always liable,
whereas the person *primâ facie* liable is the head of the
family, or person who acted as such when the *consawment*
was paid.   When a woman deserts her husband the family
is liable for all the property supplied by the husband then
in her possession.‡

A child receives its name from its father or the head of
the father's family, eight days after its birth, and every
child bears as its first name the day of the week on which
it is born.   Be it noted that Saturday (Miminda) is the first

---

* *Karaba* v. *Quansima*, May 17, 1871, *Cape Coast Court Record*, p.
348. In answer to the Judicial Assessor, the Chiefs state that "it is a rule
that when a woman refuses to continue marriage her husband recovers his
expenses. If she leaves from her husband's misconduct and she makes
palaver, and gains her case, the husband would lose his claim for expenses."
And judgment accordingly.

† *Barnes* v. *Mayan*, 1 F. L. R. 180; *Swapim* v. *Acquuah*, 1 F. L. R.
191; *Amamoo* v. *Clement*, 1 F. L. R. 180.

‡ *Sackie* v. *Agawa*, 1 F. L. R. 126.

day of the week, and is considered as God's day. The natal
day names are—

	Male.	Female.
Saturday ...	Kwamina, Kwamin	Amba.
Sunday ...	Akwesi, Kwesi	{ Essi, Akosua.
Monday ...	Kudwo	Adwua.
Tuesday ...	Akobina, Kobina	{ Araba, Abina.
Wednesday ...	Kweku	Ekua.
Thursday ...	{ Ekuow, Kuow, Yow	Abba, Yā, Yawa.
Friday ...	Koﬁ	Eﬀua.

According to the order of the birth a child may receive an
additional name; the third male child is called Mensa, female
child Mansa.   Children of a woman bearing the same natal
name, being twins or otherwise, are distinguished by the
words Penin (elder), and Kakraba or Kakra (younger).
Some natal names have certain endearing synonyms or
complimentary salutations attached to them : *e.g* Adwua as
Adai ; to Kobina the salutation is " Ebo Kobina ye bremba "
(" thou art a brave man, Ebo Kobina ") ; he replies, " M'afe
na wosi " (" so say my comrades ") ; to a Mensa's salutation,
" Abur ampa " ("ingratitude still lurks "), the reply is, " Wo
oyimpa tsirim "(" in the head of man "); meaning, no doubt,
one does not easily forget an ungrateful conduct.

" What is most commendable among the negroes is that
we find no poor amongst them who beg : for though they
are never so wretchedly poor, they never beg. The reason
of which is, that when a negro finds he cannot subsist, he
binds himself for a certain sum of money, or his friends do
it for him ; and the master to whom he hath obliged himself, keeps him in all necessaries, setting him a sort of task
which is not in the least slavish, being chiefly to defend
his master on occasion, and in sowing time to work as
much as he himself pleases."   (Letter ix. p. 140.)

"Married people here have no community of goods; but each hath his or her particular property. The man and his wives generally adjust the matter together, so that they are to bear the charge of housekeeping, while the clothing of the whole family is at his sole expense.

"On the death of either the man or the wife, the respective relations come and immediately sweep away all, not leaving the widow or widower the least part thereof, though they are equally obliged to help to pay the funeral charges. Some negroes, besides wives, have also their concubines, which they several times prefer before their wives, and take more care of them; but their children are esteemed illegitimate, and not reckoned amongst the relations.

"If a negro has a child by his slave, whether married to her or not, his heir will look after it and keep it only as a slave, on which account those who love their slaves will take care to make their children free, with the usual ceremonies, before they die, after which they are in every particular treated as free persons.

*   *   *   *   *   *

"I have already told you how many wives the negroes marry; and herein they place the greatest glory and grandeur, as their riches consist in the multitude of slaves, though they frequently conduce to their ruin, because every man is obliged to make good the injury which his slave does; if he is guilty of theft or adultery his master is obliged to pay the fine imposed for his crime. The negroes are also responsible for their sons, nephews, and other relations, though in this case the relations help each other by a mutual contribution, each giving something towards it according to his circumstances; which if he should not do, the criminal would be condemned to death or slavery." (Bosman's letter xii. p. 202.)

CHAPTER III.

PROPERTY.

THINGS are divided into moveables and immoveables.

These two kinds are sub-divided into—

(1) Ancestral, including stool property.

(2) Family.

(3) Self-acquired or Private.

Moveables : *e.g.* sandals, cloth, a gold ring.

Immoveables : a house, land.

Moveable ancestral : a gold ring left by an ancestor or ancestress.

Moveable family : a gold ring purchased by general contribution of the members of a family.

Self-acquired : a gold ring purchased by a man with his own earnings.

Immoveable ancestral : a house or land which has descended from an ancestor or some relative.

Immoveable family : a house built or acquired by members of a family.

Self-acquired or private : a house or land purchased or gained by a person by his individual effort or exertion.

There are certain kinds of immoveable things which, either from their nature (as a fetish grove, public river or lake).or by reason of the uses to which they are put (as a burial grove), cannot be sold.

The acquisition of property is either original or derivative.

Original acquisition may be by—

(1) Appropriation of what has no owner, or of property whose owner has plainly expressed his intention of giving up and has, in fact, given up his ownership by leaving possession.

(2) Conquest or capture in war.

(3) Accession by means of the increase or development of a thing in one's possession : e.g. crops and fruits from one's land ; rent of property ; trees planted on one's land by any person whatsoever without the owner's permission ; lands gained from the sea or river, either by alluvion from the washing-up of mud, sand, or earth, or by the water gradually or imperceptibly receding.

An inundation effects no change of property in land.

Where treasure-trove is found on some one's land, the owner of the land is entitled to a moiety of such treasure, and the chief or headman of the district to the other moiety. If such treasure was there hidden by the owner of the land, the finder is bound to restore it to its owner without any deduction whatsoever.

If a hunter or any person kill game on another man's land, the owner of the land is entitled to the shoulder or a quarter of such game.

Derivative acquisition may be by—

(1) Transfer, as in gifts.

To complete a transfer, it is necessary that—

(a) The transfer be by the owner of the thing transferred, or by one duly authorized by him. Where the thing transferred is ancestral or family property, the transferor must act with the concurrence and full approval of the senior members of the family having an interest in the property.

(b) The transferee must be placed in possession of the thing.

(c) The nature of the estate, title, or interest therein transferred must be distinctly stated.

(d) The transferee must show his acceptance of such estate, title, or interest in the thing.

(e) The subject of transfer must be capable of ownership.

(f) There must be witnesses of the transaction.

(2) Contract: e.g. sale, mortgage, lease, or loan.

(3) Succession of another's property.

(4) Partition: on the division of ancestral, family or other property held or enjoyed in common.

Ancestral property is—

(i.) Any moveable or immoveable thing which has descended to a person from an ancestor or ancestress however remote.

All savings made out of such moveable or immoveable thing, and all purchases or profits made from the income or from the proceeds on the sale thereof, follow the character of ancestral property.

(ii.) Property acquired on partition of or in exchange for, ancestral property (*Mary Barnes* v. *John Mayan*, June 24, 1871). *Per* Chalmers :—

"The ground on which Mrs. Barnes bases her right is that the subject in question was given by Mr. De Graft to her mother, who was one of his wives, and was occupied by her as a dwelling-place. It appears that Mr. De Graft's family house stood formerly near the Castle; that it was removed as well as other houses by order of the Government, at a time when that part of the town was opened up, and that the tenement now in dispute was assigned by the Government to Mr. De Graft, in lieu of the one from which he had been dispossessed. He received also a money compensation for the building which it may be presumed he laid out in the construction of his new house. These things being so, I consider that the new tenement took all the incidents of the one for which it was substituted, and was therefore, in De Graft's lifetime, in the same position as if it had been land of inheritance to which he had actually succeeded."

(iii.) All accretions of any ancestral property. A person, whether member of the family or otherwise in possession of stool, ancestral, or family property, wishing to improve or make an addition thereto, must apply to or inform the stool-holder or head of the family for his permission so to do, and if no objection is raised, he acquires a right to the prior enjoyment of the improvement or addition so made, which is not liable to be sold for a stool or family debt so long as other property is available, otherwise not; for it is not lawful for persons to ignore the stool-holder or the head of the family and deal with the property as if it were their own absolutely.

(iv.) Property earned by a person with or by means of an ancestral property or its accretions.

(v.) Property which, belonging to a branch of a family, has come into the possession of another branch of the family on the failure of a successor.

Family property is any moveable or immoveable thing—

(a) Acquired by the joint labour of two or more of the members of a family;

(b) Or by contributions from the members of a family.

Property is designated self-acquired or private, where it is acquired by a person—

(a) Through his own personal exertions, without any help or assistance from his ancestral or family property;

(b) By gift to himself personally;

(c) By superior skill in business or intellectual pursuits.

Whatever a person acquires with the aid of his sister or their children or his brothers is family property. If his children by a free woman (Dihi) help him to acquire any property, they have no interest therein, and in the absence of any help from his own family, property so acquired is self-acquired or private. Whatever a wife helps her husband to acquire is the sole property of the husband.

If any property lost by the ancestor or any of his successors be recovered by a member of the family out of his own private resources, it is no longer considered as ancestral or family property, but is private property; unless such property had been recovered by the use of any part or portion of the ancestral or family patrimony; or it was acquired for the purpose of its forming part of the ancestral possessions, and this was made known to the members of the family. With the exception of the coast towns, where there is much contact with European ideas, private property in its strict sense does not exist. The family group is of the pure patriarchal type. The head of the family owns the whole of the property, and all acquisitions made by the members of the family are made for him, and fall into the common stock. This custom obtains in all parts of this country.

When the ancestral or family property is owned by a family, whether whole or divided, of which the headman sits on a stool, then the property is known as stool property, and is attached to the stool. As the family increases in prosperity and influence, the stool-holder creates junior stools, subordinate to the head stool, and any property, attached to the junior stool on its creation or subsequently acquired or possessed by the junior stool-holder and the people of that stool, is also called stool property.

In the coast towns a member of a family may make separate or private acquisitions and dispose of them as he pleases in his lifetime, provided none of his family nor any part or portion of his ancestral or family property contributed to the acquisition of such property. But any property of his that remains undisposed of at his death, descends to his successors as ancestral property.

As in India, even so in this country, the advance of civilization tends to break up the unity of the family.

Where the members of a family support themselves on the produce of a common land, the proceeds of their united labour must be necessarily small.

The family has a claim upon its constituent members for their assistance in the cultivation of the common land, or in the ordinary labours of the household; hence it is no matter of surprise to find the units breaking up, on the discovery of new industries requiring skill and producing great rewards, and giving scope to each individual unit for the exercise of his skill and ingenuity in the acquisition of wealth and private property.

In this country joint property is the rule, and must be

presumed to exist in each individual case until the contrary is proved. If an individual holds property in severalty— that is, as sole owner and possessor—it will in the next generation relapse into a state of joint tenancy.

Absolute, unrestricted, exclusive ownership, enabling the owner to do anything he likes with his immoveable property, is the exception.

The father is restrained by his brother, the brother by his nephew and sister's children, and the woman by her own issue. If land be free to-day in the hands of its acquirer, it will to-morrow resume its fetters in the hands of his heirs. In the English law, individual property is the rule, but corporate property is the rule on the Gold Coast and among the Akan and Fanti tribes. A careful comparison and analysis of the several kinds of systems commonly known here, show that there are but three forms of corporate system of property, to wit, the village community, joint family, and patriarchal family.

The Village community is a corporate body, of which the members are families, or family groups, residing in the several households, and including the joint as well as patriarchal families.

These village communities are scattered over the length and breadth of the whole of Guinea. The headman of the village is in some places so by hereditary right, in other places he is so by election. But in places, where the right is hereditary, the members of such village community have a right of veto.

The Joint family is a corporate body whose members are persons or individuals having a remote common ancestor, or who, though alien in blood, have become members of the same clan by commendation or otherwise.

Patriarchal family is defined by the great jurist Sir Henry Maine, to be a group of natural or adoptive descendants, held together by subjection to the eldest living ascendant uncle, father, or grandfather. Whatever be the formal prescriptions of the law, the head of such a group is always practically despotic ; and he is the object of respect, if not always of affection, which is probably seated deeper than any positive institution.

In the more extensive assemblies of kinsmen which constitute the joint family, the eldest male of the eldest line is never the parent of all the members, and not necessarily the first in age among them. To many of them he is merely a distant relative, and he may possibly be an infant. The sense of patriarchal right does not die out in such groups. Each father or grandfather has more power than anybody else over his wife, children, and descendants ; and there is always what may be called a belief that the blood of the collective brotherhood runs more truly and purely in some line than in any other. Among the Hindoos the eldest male of his line, if of full mental capacity, is generally placed at the head of the concerns of the joint family ; but where the institution survives in any completeness, he is not a paterfamilias, nor is he owner of the family property, but merely manager of its affairs and administrator of its possessions.

If he is not deemed fit for his duties, a worthier kinsman is substituted for him by election, and, in fact, the longer the joint family holds together, the more election gains ground at the expense of birth (" Early History of Institutions," 117).

According to the Fanti laws, a father has in subjection under him his son and his son's children. Whatever is acquired is acquired for the father, and this state of subjection doth only terminate on the father's death. In a patriarchal family, one finds the father having power over his sons and daughters and grandchildren, his wife, servants, and other dependents. If on his death his sons separate, this will be the setting up of several subordinate families, over which each son will be the head, but under the head of their mother's family.

Under the system of village community, the land belonging to the village is so held, that all the inhabitants of

the village have each of them a proportionate share in it
as common property, without any possession of, or title to,
distinct portions of it.   Each person is entitled to cultivate
any portion of it, and during such cultivation he has an
absolute right to his crops.

In the joint family all the holdings are enjoyed in
severalty, and each member manages his portion of land.

The extent of such holding is equal to the land originally brought under cultivation, or transferred on the day
of commendation, or is determined by long usage.

In the patriarchal family all the lands are under the
control of the patriarch, who alone directs how they are to
be cultivated. He is entitled to all the produce of the land,
and nothing can be done with anything belonging to the
family without his approval or confirmation.

There is a fourth kind of corporate system of property,
which may be called the " clan property."   Property of
this nature was originally acquired by the local clansmen
clearing the virgin forest and afterwards setting it aside
for the use of the clan, usually in the possession of one of
the principal clansmen, whose duty it is to look after it for
the benefit of all the clansmen in that locality in particular,
and for the fellow-clansmen in general.   Hence one hears
the expression, "The land (Asiasi) is the property of the
Okonor clan." Plots of such lands are granted to members
of the clan desirous of building thereon. The freehold is
always in the senior clansman for the time being of the
locality.   By no length of uninterrupted enjoyment can
any one acquire any title adverse to the title of the whole
clan. It is very doubtful whether the clansmen have any
power of sale over any part or portion whatsoever of such
clan property. Analogous to such clan property are burial
groves, or places set apart for the burial of the members of
each clan.

CHAPTER IV.

TENURES.

THE ordinary tenures of land are freehold, and the derivative tenure of leaseholds.

An estate of freehold is an estate either of inheritance or for life in lands of free tenure.

An estate in lands and tenements may be considered—

(i.) In reference to the quantity of interest, that is, whether freehold or less than freehold; or

(ii.) With regard to the time of enjoyment, as to whether the interest is in possession or expectancy; or

(iii.) With regard to the number and connection of the tenants.

The term "freehold" denotes the tenure of the property, and shows that the owner thereof has a life estate at least.

An estate of inheritance is where the tenant is not only entitled to enjoy the land for his own life, but where, after his death, it is cast by the law upon the persons who successively represent him *in perpetuum* in right of blood, according to an established order of descent.

With regard to the quantity or duration of interest, there are estates more or less similar to English estates of (i.) fee-simple, (ii.) for life, (iii.) for years.

An estate in fee-simple is the largest estate or interest which the English law allows any person to possess in landed property, and is that which a man has to him and his heirs. The holder of such property is called a tenant in fee-simple. Strictly speaking, the term "fee-simple," as used in English law, cannot be correctly applied or used when speaking of the highest kind of the tenures obtaining on the Gold Coast. Even in those parts, such as Wassaw Amenfi, where the king is the owner of all the lands in his district, the use of the term "fee-simple" is misleading. At the most the king or head chief is but a trustee, who is as much controlled in his enjoyment of the public lands by his subordinate chiefs and councillors as the head of a family by the senior members thereof. *Per* Chalmers, in *Barnes* v. *Attah*, July 17, 1871 : " I apprehend that not even the regular occupant " (of an Egua) " could alienate property without some concurrence by the people of the stool (Agua) who have an interest in it, and are usually consulted on such a matter."

The king, by the law of England, is the supreme lord of the whole soil. Whoever, therefore, holds lands must hold them mediately or immediately of him ; and while the subject enjoys the usufructory possession, the absolute and ultimate dominion remains in the king. (Co. Lit. 1a.)

As far as the Gold Coast is concerned, this portion of the English law does not apply, for it is a group of territories under native rulers taken under British protection ; it is British territory, but not so by conquest or cession ; as a matter of fact, the Colonial Office stated on the 11th day of March, 1887, as published in Parliamentary Blue Book of that year, that it is inaccurate to state that after the successful Asanti expedition of 1874, the Protectorate was annexed by Great Britain and became a colony, " inasmuch as the greater portion of the Gold Coast Colony still remains a Protectorate, the soil being in the hands of the natives and under the jurisdiction of the native chiefs."

According to native ideas there is no land without owners.* What is now a forest or unused land will, as years go on, come under cultivation by the subjects of the stool, or members of the village community, or other members of the family.

The granting of permission to others and outsiders to reside on or cultivate the lands of a family, a stool, or a village community, is a practice of the greatest antiquity, and was in times past more universal than sale of land, which is of comparatively modern growth. The chief or

* *Vide* Mr. Justice Smith and Mr. Bruce Hindle's opinions in Appendix.

king of a tribe, or headman of a family, can, with the consent of the whole or major part of the sub-chiefs, and councillors, village elders forming body of councillors or senior members of the family, as the case may be, allow strangers and foreigners to live on certain lands. In cases where the land is appurtenant to the stool of a king or head chief, the tenant becomes subjected to such stool, and he, with his people, is bound to perform such services, or pay such annual sums as may be declared to be performed or paid yearly. Plots of land in the actual and lawful possession of a subject of the stool, or a member of the village community, or a member of the family or company, cannot, unless with the express consent of the person in possession, be so granted. But where a person in possession of a portion of the public land abandons it, or his family have abandoned it for more than ten years at least, the village headman and elders can allow another person to occupy the same.

The making of grants to strangers, particularly to Europeans, of waste lands, that is, lands abandoned or never under cultivation by any one, and of minerals, and of concessions of forest land for a term of years, though said to be modern comparatively speaking, is not necessarily illegal, according to Customary Law. A person who desires to procure a grant of land or any concession from a local ruler, should make special inquiries, and inform himself who the members of his council are, and get them or the linguist of the council to join the head chief in making such grant. Where the concession is made by a subordinate chief, inquiries should be made to find out whether the concurrence of his paramount chief is necessary or no, for whatever lawful grant or permission is so given by a person *de facto* chief, with the concurrence of men *de facto* members of the village council or stool, is good and valid according to Customary Law, and the grantee by taking possession of the land and working thereon becomes a tenant of the stool, village council, or family, as the case may be, and not

of a specific individual. Among European communities the
title of a landlord, or vendor, or grantor of property, is
sought for by searching his muniments of title and making
an abstract of his title-deeds; on the Gold Coast one has
to make careful inquiries, which must be guided by the
Customary Law. The occupant of the stool, or head of
the village community or family, as trustee, has the right
to enforce performance of the conditions under which the
permission was given. If the tenant fails so to do, or
denies the right of the person who, or whose predecessors,
gave him title, or encourages some other person to contest
such right or title, he can be sent away from the land.

Conveyance of land is invariably made in the presence
of witnesses. The symbolic tokens and ceremonious per-
formances, taken in addition to the words expressed before
such witnesses, set forth the nature of the transaction, the
quality of the estate granted or transferred, and the conditions, if any, of such grant.

There are certain well-established usages in the enjoyment of lands, one of which is the practice of allowing
plots of land to lie fallow for a longer or lesser period of
time.

It must be borne in mind that no person can acquire
by long uninterrupted possession, an adverse title against
the owner of property, through whom or whose ancestors
possession was first acquired.

The simplest and most common kind of tenure is what
may be called " sowing tenure." Here, the owner of a plot
of land usually gives to a person, who has applied to him,
leave to have the use of his land for one sowing season.
In the absence of agreement, the owner of the land is
entitled to take 500 heads of corn, or a small proportion,
about one-tenth, of any other crops grown on such land.

If the tenant die before his crops are gathered, his heir
or successor is entitled to reap them, and the owner of the
land cannot appropriate such crops, without giving notice
to the representatives of the deceased, to the effect that the

crops must be removed before the end of the harvest season, or before the festival Ahuba Kessi. Having once sown his crops, the tenant cannot sow a second crop on any part of the grantor's land without his express permission, for as soon as the crops are gathered in the tenancy ceases.

Where, after notice, the tenant's crops are not removed, such crops become the property of the owner of the land.

There is also known what may be called an " annual tenure " running from year to year.

A person having once got the land has full right to cultivate it for any duration of time until the owner, by due notice, terminates the tenancy.

The rent usually reserved, in the absence of special or other agreement, is the help which the tenant is bound to render the landlord at the period or seasons of sowing and reaping, usually three days in the week.

Unlike the sowing tenure, the tenant has the right to build and reside on land so granted him. On his death, his heir or successor, after notifying the owner and after certain ceremonies, acquires the same rights and privileges until the landlord gives notice to terminate the tenancy, when the land goes back to the owner with all the improvements thereon. But the owner of the land is not entitled to such crops as are sown and reaped yearly, unless the tenant has failed to remove them after due notice. Where the owner of land gives to a person permission to cultivate a portion of his land, and this person and his heirs continue the cultivation of such land, for upwards of forty years, without paying any rent or giving any produce therefrom to the owner, such long possession does not destroy the title of the original owner and his representatives.

The original owner or his successor can at any time go upon and retake possession of the land as soon as the tenant asserts an adverse claim to it. In the absence of such adverse claim he cannot disturb the quiet enjoyment of the tenant, without prior notice to the tenant that he requires the land. Where, however, there are palm-trees on the land, whether planted by the owner of the land or by the tenant, the landowner has full right, at any time he pleases, to cut trees or gather any nuts therefrom. Custom does not permit any person to be improved out of his land, and palm-trees not only improve, but also enhance the value of, lands.

Where the nuts from a palm land are manufactured into oil, the owner of the land receives half of the oil, and the oil manufacturer the other half, and the expenses of preparing the oil is equally shared by them. If, instead of oil manufacture, there is extracted from the palm-trees palm-wine, then the owner of the palm-trees is entitled to one-fourth of the proceeds of such palm-wine, the person who fells the trees and prepares the wine is entitled to one-fourth of such proceeds, and the person who sells such palm-wine is entitled to half of such proceeds. According to a well-known practice of the Law Courts, each palm-tree is valued at twenty shillings.

Abehem tenure arises where a person is placed on palm land, and the only stipulation is for a specified quantity of oil to be delivered to the owner each year, whether the tenant makes any oil or not during the year.

In the absence of agreement, an owner of land, from persons having the use of his land, is entitled to claim when corn is planted 500 heads.

Grants of land for building purposes are very frequently made in the form of perpetual leases, either for some valuable consideration, or by way of reward for past services, or on the ground of mere affection or friendship. Lands so granted are resumable by the grantor and his successors on failure of successors in the grantee's family.*

Land so granted is inalienable, except with the express consent and concurrence of the grantor, if it be his self-acquired property; but if ancestral or family property, then the consent of the persons entitled to the reversion, and who have an interest in it, and who are usually consulted before any alienation is made, must be gained.

---

* *Boun* v. *Steele*, 2 F. L. R. 77.

The grantee of a building lease does not acquire any right in the soil.*

Grants of land for building purposes are generally made by members of a family to a junior member at the time of marriage. Thus a man takes in marriage a woman. The members of her family give or point out to the husband a plot of land to build on, and the only object of this is that the man may have somewhere to reside with his wife and any issue of the union.

The rule of the descent with regard to any erections on such lands is somewhat similar to what is known in English law as tenancy in tail special. The grant is invariably made to a man and his issue (not heirs)—say, on Essie, his wife begotten or to be begotten. Whatever is erected on such land goes to Essie and her children by him. For all practical purposes, the man has only a life interest, which he forfeits by wrongfully and improperly terminating the marriage.

The man's heir or successor has no title or interest in such premises, nor can he himself sell or mortgage them.

If the land was granted by the family of the man to him for building purposes, then neither his freeborn wife nor her issue has title or claim to the ownership of such premises, but his children by her have only a right of residence in the father's house, *i.e.* a life interest subject to good conduct.†

Land so granted for building purposes reverts to the grantor and his family—

(*a*) On the grantee quitting possession ;

(*b*) On the grantee denying the title of the grantor to the land by setting up his own title or the title of any other person ;

(*c*) On the building erected thereon, or the greater part of such building, falling into ruins ; ‡

(*d*) On the grantee leaving no issue by the woman on

* *Lyall* v. *Dougan*, 2 F. L. R. 56.
† *Swapim* v. *Ackuwa*, 1 F. L. R. 191.
‡ *Awortchie* v. *Aidgun*, 2 F. L. R. 56.

whose marriage with him or through whom the grant was originally made ;

(*e*) By purchase of the building erected thereon.

The woman is, however, entitled to live in such buildings as may have been erected by the husband.

The right of the grantor is lost by—

(*a*) Gift or sale of the freehold to the grantee ;

(*b*) Sale of the land by the grantor to any person ;

(*c*) Death of the grantor without heirs or any successor.

If the grantee erects any building on land so granted, and he desires to sell such building, there being failure of issue by his wife then deceased, the grantor or his successor has an absolute right of having the first offer.

Where the grantee has issue by the wife, through whom he came into possession, he cannot sell premises erected on land so granted without the concurrence of his wife and his children by her.

If such premises be sold without the consent of the grantor or his successor and family, but only with the concurrence of wife and children, the purchaser acquires, at the most, only a life interest, and can only enjoy the property during the life of the grantee, his wife, and their children, for as soon as they all die, the grantor or his successor is entitled without any interruption to take back the land, without paying any compensation whatsoever for any improvements made or for any buildings thereon erected.

And not only is the grantor or his successor entitled to the first offer, but he is entitled to demand from the purchaser an acknowledgment, that the land is not the property of the person who built the premises. This acknowledgment may be made by payment of money or by giving any token.

If the grantee or purchaser neglect or refuse to render the acknowledgment, or to pay any reserved rent, he must remove his buildings and quit the land. The creditors of the owner of the buildings can at any time pull down the buildings and remove the materials in satisfaction of their claim. Therefore, where the owner of land gives leave to a person to build, the maxim *quicquid plantatur solo, solo cedit,* doth not apply, and even if the materials were acquired from the land, and the occupier unsuccessfully contests the right of the owner, yet he can pull down the houses, when he is being turned out, or he is voluntarily leaving.*

It is a well-established custom that no one should be improved out of his land, and also that family and ancestral properties must not be alienated except for well-recognized reasons.

Where family or ancestral property has been alienated for value, the original owners, or those descended from them, can repurchase such property, provided the proper sacrifice is offered, the necessary libations are made, and the family or persons in possession are not residing on such property or using it. If a portion of the land has been set apart for a burial-place, that part need not be reconveyed to the family of the original owner at their request. The re-purchasing of such property is called Pŭn, that is Redemption.† A family owning or in possession of other lands as freeholders in the same neighbourhood, cannot compel this kind of redemption, and a long period of time does not bar the right to such recovery of ancestral property. This kind of redemption must not be confounded with the redemption of mortgaged or pawned lands.

Owners of lands where gold and other minerals are found give permission to miners to work thereon. These men open mines and sink several shafts, and the customary rent is what is known as Ebusã, which is a division into three parts of whatever the mines produce, whether gold, or quartz, or other minerals. To the landlord belongs one-third. But whenever gold nuggets are found in such mines the landlord takes one-half.

* *Wood* v. *Aisawa*, 2 F. L. R. 51.
† Compare Leviticus xxv. 23-27.

The owner of land covered with timber is entitled, in the absence of express agreement, to one-third of all logs, beams, and other timber felled or gotten of his land. And generally the owner of land is entitled to one-third of all produce gotten of his land by his tenants; this one-third is given him in kind, or its value paid in money, as the owner shall direct.

In the Wassaw Amenfi district *Tikororo* custom prevailed, that is, King Enimil was entitled every Saturday during the mining season to be paid from each mining shaft a measure of quartz, and this was collected on each Saturday by the king's servants.

Grantees or their successors asserting title to a land adverse to the grantor, or disputing his title, forfeit their possession, and may be ejected at once from the land by the grantor or his successors.

CHAPTER V.

SURETYSHIP.

SURETYSHIP, *Eginam-dzi* or *Aba-su-dzi*, is a collateral engagement by a person to be responsible for the debt or performance of the obligation of another. The person who undertakes to be so responsible is called the surety, *Eginam-dzi nympa* or *Aba-su-dzi nyi*. To constitute valid suretyship, it is essential to have the mutual assent of all the parties, namely, the creditor, the person secured, usually called the principal debtor, and the surety. These three parties must be persons competent to contract, and they must do so with the necessary formalities and ceremonies.

However much a person may like to stand surety for a principal debtor, he cannot do so against his approval, whether such person is related to him or not. The creditor also must assent to the suretyship, and, until his acceptance, the offer to be so liable is revocable. Where the creditor and his debtor are subjects of the same stool, or members of the same village community, under the same headman, chief, or king, such king, chief, or headman cannot be a surety, and any engagement on his part to be responsible to a person so under him for another person under him is void. Likewise, the head of a family cannot be surety to a member of the family for another member of the family. But where the creditor belongs to a different family, even though of the same clan, the head of the family can become surety for a member of the family to the creditor. Insane persons and lunatics cannot be sureties. If a person, through intoxication or by duress, become a surety, he can avoid his responsibility by acting promptly, and calling upon the creditor to release him from his obligation, otherwise his acquiescence will bar his release. A married woman cannot without the consent of her husband become surety for any person whatsoever, save and excepting her parents and children. Except with her mother or other immediate blood relatives, an infant can never become surety. The liability of a surety to answer for the debt of another, or for the consequences arising from failure of the performance of his principal's obligation, is a personal responsibility, and does not bind the surety's family or his successors. When a man becomes surety none of his children are bound by his contract, except such as joined in the contract with the consent of their mother or her family. Although there may be slight variations in some localities, there is always a promise made or oath taken by the principal debtor to the proposed surety, that on such and such a day he will hand to the surety the amount in question, or that before the expiration of the specified day the contract will be performed ; *e.g.* A requiring 2 ackies goes to B, who agrees to give it him on his finding a surety. C consents to guarantee the amount. To complete this contract there must be witnesses, in whose presence B counts the money and places it in the hands of C, who passes it to A. Immediately before or after the receipt of the money, A has to promise C, or take oath in the presence of these witnesses, that he, A, will repay C the loan on the day fixed, so that he, C, may pay B. If A has sureties, whether members of his family or otherwise, each of them makes the same promise or takes an oath to the same effect. After this C also promises B, or takes oath, that, on the day specified, he will see A repay B the loan, or he, C, will make it good. Where C also has sureties, each of them promises B, and takes oath to the same effect, each promissor in his turn calls the witnesses to take note of what is going on. The witnesses are usually invited by the creditor, debtor, and surety respectively, and in their presence the considerations must be distinctly stated. After the creditor has consented to accept C as surety for A, a sum of money or chattel is given to the witnesses as token of the contract. If there are persons who "*stand behind*" the surety to ensure the due performance of his guarantee, they do not always expressly make any promise or take any oath, the surety C merely saying to the creditor, "these stand behind me," *i.e.* they are my sureties. Money or token given to the witnesses is added to the debt of the debtor.

In default of payment, the remedy of the creditor is against the surety in the first instance, and not against the debtor. It is only where the surety cannot be found, or he fails to pay, that the creditor can sue the debtor, for then it is certain that the debtor had failed to keep his solemn promise to the surety. It is the duty of the debtor to perform his solemn stipulation, and to see that his surety does not fail in doing likewise, for the debtor should know more of his surety than the creditor. Where there are several sureties for one specific sum of money, they are jointly liable, and each cannot be made to pay more than a proportion of the debt. Where the creditor makes further arrangement with the debtor, unknown to the surety, or without his consent, or grants him more time, or instigates the debtor to run away or so deal with his property, that the surety's means of falling on it to recoup himself is lost, the surety is discharged. Where a creditor, by fraud, or misrepresentation, induces a man to become surety for a debtor, the contract is void. A person does not become a surety by merely interceding for a debtor. At the time of accepting the guarantee, the creditor is to give the surety some money, varying in amount from a takoo, or ninepence, to an ounce of gold (£3 12s.), to bind the contract of suretyship.

When the surety wishes to strengthen his claim on the debtor's relations, the debtor is usually joined by his brothers and nephews, the younger ones being preferred, as in the ordinary course of nature the younger ones may live longest. In order that the debtor may expeditiously fulfil his contract, it has long been customary for a child, relative, or servant of the debtor, to live with the surety, and in the event of the death of the debtor, the fact of such a person residing with the creditor, or surety, is a strong proof to the debtor's family of the existence of the debt.

This custom is quite distinct from pawning (*Ahuba*). A person placed in pawn is not personally liable for the debt, although in temporary bondage to the creditor, and as such he cannot acquire any property, which will belong to the creditor. The death of the pawn does not cancel the debt and he must be replaced. But in the case of *Eginam-dzi* (suretyship) the co-surety, *i.e.* the person " standing behind," is personally liable for the settlement, and while remaining with the creditor he can acquire property or earn means to liquidate the debt. The creditor may, though not bound, maintain him, and if he does maintain him he can add the expenses thereof to the debt, unless the co-surety gives his services in return.

The surety has a right to fall on the debtor to repay him all monies he may have paid to the creditor, together with any expenses and disbursements incident thereto. A surety is not entitled to the benefit of any set-off the principal debtor may have against the creditor, unless by express agreement.

CHAPTER VI.

ALIENATION.

ALIENATION of property may be by (i.) gift, (ii.) mortgage or pledge, (iii.) loan, (iv.) sale, or (v.) testamentary disposition, and any property about to be alienated should be so described and defined that there can be no reasonable doubt as to its identity.

The head of a family has greater powers of alienation over moveable ancestral property than he has over immoveable ancestral and family property.

He can alienate the former in gifts to any of the members of the family, or for their education, support, or relief from distress, or for starting in trade or business, or for getting a wife for any member.

Whenever there is a stool or family debt, the stool or family property, whether moveable or immoveable, can be taken and sold to pay such debt. And where the members under the stool or of the family refuse or are unable to pay such lawful liability, the stool-holder or head of the family can, after due notice to the senior members of the stool or family, with or without their concurrence, mortgage or pledge any stool or family property.*

Amid all the conflict of contradictory accounts which meet one at every turn, it is nearer the mark to say, that the head of the family has the moveable ancestral property in his absolute control; if, therefore, the family find he is misappropriating, wasting, or squandering the ancestral fund, it is to their interest to remove him at once and appoint another in his stead.

The head of a family cannot, without the consent of all the principal members of the family, or the greater part thereof, that is the Ebusuafu, alienate the immoveable ancestral or family property.

* *Aidoasi* v. *Abban*, 2 F. L. R. 90.

And although an alienation may be necessary for some family purpose, or for the discharge of a family obligation, nevertheless, unless confirmed by the senior or principal members of the family, such alienation is revocable.

Neither the head of the family acting alone, nor the senior members of a family acting alone, can make any valid alienation nor give title to any family property whatsoever.

Any person buying or advancing money on any property should carefully inquire whether the property is ancestral, or family, or private. If he find from his inquiries that it is not of the last description, he is bound to inquire into the necessity for the alienation, and find out whether all the beneficiaries are parties to the transaction; whether such alienation benefits the estate or family; and in cases where the property is in a stranger's possession, whether the senior members of the family have received notice of such transaction. *Pandy* v. *Koonwaree*, 6 Moore's Indian Appeals, 423 :—

" The court will consider whether the debt for the discharge of which the alienation is alleged to have taken place, has been incurred owing to misfortune, an income inadequate for the ordinary expenditure of a person in the position of the person incurring the debt, or antecedent mismanagement of other managers; or, on the other hand, whether it is owing to profligacy and wanton waste of the estate on the part of the alienor; and if the latter state of facts be proved, the court will scrutinize rigidly to see if the person advancing the money was in any way a party to such profligacy or wanton waste, and if it be shown that he was so cognizant of or a party to it, the court will not deem the alienation to have been lawful." Thus decided their lordships of the Queen's Privy Council, and it is worthy of remark, that in the native tribunals the purchaser of ancestral family or stool property must have clean hands, if he is to retain possession of such property.

Where money has been advanced for the purpose of

discharging an ancestral or a family debt, and the members of the family have parted with their ancestral or family property in satisfaction of such advance, such alienation is valid, if the alienee is able to show that he acted *bonâ fide*; that in truth and in fact, the money advanced was for the discharge of an ancestral or family debt; and that on independent inquiry he was satisfied it was an ancestral or family debt from which it was necessary to relieve them.

Whenever the alienation of any property is set aside, the alienee is entitled to get back his purchase-money from the person who received it, and where the person at whose instance the alienation was set aside has had some benefit from the purchase-money, he will be bound to refund the whole or lose his suit. *Awortchie* v. *Eshon*, March 7, 1871.

But where the alienee fails to prove facts which would justify a refund of the purchase-money, he loses his money.

If, however, part of the alienation is found to be justifiable and a part not, then the alienee will be entitled to the part upheld.

(i.) GIFT.

Gift consists in the relinquishment of one's own right and the creation of the right of another, in lands, goods, or chattels, which creation is only completed by the acceptance of the offer of the gift by that other.

It must be remembered, however, that gifts are oftener made of moveables such as goods and chattels, than of lands and other immoveables.*

To constitute a valid gift, an intention of giving or passing the property in the thing given to the donee by the donor, who has power so to do, is necessary.

The acceptance of such gift by the donee must be made in the lifetime of the donor.

The giving and acceptance must be proved and evidenced

* *Halm* v. *Hughes*, 1 F. L. R. 65; *Bimba* v. *Mansa*, 1 F. L. R. 137.

by such delivery or conveyance as the nature of the gift admits of.

What is given by a person in wrath or excess of joy, or through inadvertence, or during minority or madness, or under the influence of terror, or by one intoxicated, or extremely old, or afflicted with grief or excruciating pain, or what is given in sport, is void.

Where anything is given for a consideration unperformed, or to a bad man mistaken for a good one, or for any illegal act, the owner may take it back.

The acceptance of a gift may be made publicly or privately, having regard to the nature of the gift; but the acceptance of a gift, consisting of immoveable property, must be invariably made with as much publicity as possible. Acceptance is made—

(i.) By rendering thanks with a thank-offering or presents, alone or coupled with an utterance or expression of appropriating the gift ; or

(ii.) Corporeal acceptance, as by touching; or

(iii.) Using or enjoying the gift; or

(iv.) Exercising rights of ownership over the gift.

In this country gifts invariably clothe themselves with the semblance of a sale, and therefore, where formal acceptance is wanting, the owner can take back his gift.

Gifts, in the European sense of the term, as far as regards immoveables, seem to be unknown here.

If the donee is in possession, either alone or jointly with the donor before the gift, the continuance of his possession is sufficient without any new delivery, provided the donee expresses his acceptance in the manner set forth in (i) above.

Every gift when completed is irrevocable, except in gifts between parent and child, which can be recalled or exchanged at any time by the parent in his or her lifetime, or by his will or dying declarations.

A gift is not rendered invalid—

(a) By being made in contemplation of death and

subject to a conditional right of resumption in case of the donor's recovery; *

(b) By being made dependent on a contingency; or

(c) Because the donee is a minor, provided some one on his behalf makes the necessary acceptance; or

(d) Because it is voluntary.

Anything given in return for a gift, as a token of the acceptance, cannot be recalled so long as the original gift is in the possession of the original donee.

(ii.) MORTGAGE AND PLEDGE.

A pledge is the delivery of a thing or chattel to a creditor as a security for money advanced or due, on condition of his restoring it to the owner after payment of the debt, and subject to a conditional power of sale if the loan or debt be not paid at a certain specified time.

The creditor is not bound to defend the title of the owner of such security.

A moveable thing or chattel given as security for a debt is a pledge.

An immoveable property given or conveyed by way of security for a debt is a mortgage.

The person giving an immoveable property as security is called the mortgagor; and the person to whom such property is given is called the mortgagee.

When the mortgagor discharges the liabilities for which an immoveable property is mortgaged, he is said to redeem the property.

When the mortgagee enforces any right given to him by his contract of putting an end to the mortgagor's right to redeem, whether by selling the property, and out of the proceeds of the sale satisfying the debt on the property, or by transferring the property to another person, or by

* *Asandua* v. *Hayfron and others*, before Macleod, C.J., 1887, a case of *Donatio mortis causa.*

becoming absolute owner of the mortgaged property, he is said to foreclose.

Where a person is the security given for the payment of any sum of money, the person is called a pawn, and the transaction, pawning; but since the Gold Coast Ordinance, No. 1, 1874, this has been declared illegal.

A mortgagee has no power to foreclose without first giving reasonable notice to the mortgagor, and in his absence, to the immediate relatives of the mortgagor, of his intention so to do.

Where real property has been mortgaged, the mortgagee is absolutely entitled to enjoy, without any hindrance whatsoever, all profits accruing therefrom, nor is he accountable for the profits so enjoyed.*

Where continuing interest is charged for the principal, the mortgagee may reimburse himself for any trouble or expenses he may have put himself to, for and on behalf of the mortgaged property.

A mortgagor can redeem at any time he please, provided he repays all monies due on the property, whether such monies be the principal debt or interest, or expenses incurred on behalf of the property.

No mortgagor or mortgagee, or their respective successors, can transfer to another any rights which he may have under the mortgage without notice to the other party to the mortgage transaction. The mortgagor may assign or transfer his right of redemption to a third person.

To make such an assignment or transfer of mortgage rights valid, it is necessary that some of the witnesses of the original transaction be present, if available, or the mortgagor have notice of the person to whom such assignment or transfer is made.

The person to whom a chattel is pledged has the right to use it, nor is the pledgor discharged if the thing pledged is destroyed by use : e.g. Kudwo pledges his cloth to Kwow

---

* *Amonoo* v. *Abbakuma*, 1 F. L. R. 157 ; *Ashong* v. *Barng*, 1 F. L. R. 153.

for a dollar. Kwow has the right to use the cloth, and Kudwo is bound to repay the dollar so long as the pledgee can restore the cloth, even if in a torn and worn-out condition.

No person can sell a chattel pledged to him until the owner on being requested to redeem has failed so to do. Where the owner is dead or not to be found, his immediate successors or relatives must have notice of the intended sale of such pledged article before the pledgee can safely sell.

The pledgee cannot purchase from himself any article pledged to him unless the owner thereof, or some one claiming through him, has gone into accounts with the pledgee and consented to his taking the chattel, in full or part satisfaction of the debt.

Where a mortgagee or pledgee realizes his security and finds there is still a balance due, he cannot call on the mortgagor or pledgor to make up the difference. If his security has turned out insufficient, he has to thank himself for his simplicity. The debtor, however, is bound to make good the balance, if the creditor sold it by his instructions or with his approval. If, on the other hand, the security realizes more than the debt, the surplus must be paid over to the debtor or his personal representative. Once a pledge or mortgage, always a pledge or mortgage.*

(iii.) LOANS.

A loan is the lending of an article to another person called the borrower, for the use of such borrower, either gratuitously or for valuable consideration.

The property in an article borrowed remains in the owner, whether the borrower himself have it in his possession or not.

The borrower is bound to exercise the greatest diligence

* *Incruma* v. *Marmoon*, 1 F. L. R. 157.

and care for the safety of the article borrowed, for if the thing borrowed is injured through his carelessness, he is bound to make an equivalent restoration.

If the thing borrowed be injured or lost by act of God, he is not liable if his own negligence did not conduce to such loss or injury. If the thing be lost by any other cause whatsoever, the owner at his own option can claim the value or an article of like nature and quality.

Where the borrower fraudulently deals with property borrowed, or uses it for a purpose different from that for which he told the owner of the thing, he is liable, not only to return it, but also to account for any profits accruing therefrom.

E.g.: A lends his cutlass for a month to B, who said he wanted to cut some bamboo trees. B does not use it to cut bamboo trees, but to cut down odum wood. A can claim his cutlass back before the end of the month, and compel B to give compensation from the proceeds of the odum wood.

If B had not shown for what purpose he required the cutlass, A could not demand any compensation.

The most common kind of loan is that for money. Here the lender invariably asks for a surety or security, and in the absence of a special and distinct contract, the rate of interest is fifty per cent. on the sum advanced, the principal and interest being payable at an indefinite time not less than a year, and even then after notice. The said interest of fifty per cent. is added once for all; other lower rates are fixed, according to an agreement of the parties. Among the Wassaw people, for each extension of time not less than a month an extra interest is charged.

(iv.) Sale.

Dealing with the native law and custom relating to the sale of land, where the English language or a written instrument is not used, the careful student will doubtless not fail to observe that, of all things, land is about the last thing which became the subject of an out-and-out sale. Owners of land were as reluctant and unwilling to part with their land and inheritance as was Ephron, the Hittite, to sell a burying-place to Abraham, as recorded in the Holy Writ. Rather than sell his land, the Fanti landowner prefers to grant leave to another, a friend or alien, to cultivate or dwell upon it for an indefinite period of time, thus reserving unto himself the reversion and the right to resume possession whenever he please.

This is the reason why the first European settlers could not buy the freehold of the site of their forts and castles, but had to give pay-notes, securing to the owners of the land certain annual rents.

Before the prohibition of slavery and pawning on the Gold Coast, rather than part with the family inheritance, members of a family have cheerfully volunteered to be sold to raise money for the payment of a pressing family liability. But in process of time, and especially since the emancipation of slaves and the prohibition of slavery, the sale of lands has been of more frequent occurrence in the coast towns.

The inhabitants of the more inland districts are very conservative, but the native laws and custom relating to the sale of land have not changed at all, and the decisions of the Judicial Assessors thereon are as applicable to-day as then.

To constitute a valid sale of land on the Gold Coast there must be—

1. Competent contracting parties ;
2. Mutual assent of such parties ;
3. The marking out or inspection of the land and its boundaries, and, if necessary, the planting of boundary trees, and fixing of boundary marks ;
4. Valuable consideration, that is gold, money, or chattel, paid, given, or promised ;
5. The payment of *Trama* (earnest money) to the

vendor or his representative, in the presence of some of the members of his family and witnesses.

1. To find out who are the competent contracting parties, one must know whether the land about to be sold or purchased is—

(a) Land appurtenant to a stool; or

(b) Land held in common by the members of a village community or a company; or

(c) Ancestral property; or

(d) Family property; or

(e) Self-acquired property.

(a) To every stool (*Bogya Egwa*) to which annual sacrifices are made, are attached lands under cultivation, or forest, or habitable, and in such lands the family, including the servants and others, the immediate dependents of the stool community called domestics, have a life interest. The blood relatives of the original owner, the purchaser, with the occupant of the stool, however, possess a greater and superior interest in such stool property, but the occupant of the stool alone cannot sell or alienate any portion of such property. *Per* Sir David Chalmers, Judicial Assessor:—

" I apprehend that not even the regular occupant could alienate property without some concurrence by the people of the stool who have an interest in it, and are usually consulted on such a matter." *

If one of the people of a stool (*Bogya Egwa*) convey any stool land on his own authority, and in so doing no doubt intends the best interests of the stool, yet such transaction is not binding on the stool or the members thereunder so as to give a valid title to the land.

(b) The village community is a corporate body, of which the members are the resident families or family groups residing in the several households.

These village communities are scattered over the length and breadth of the whole of Guinea. The headman of the

* *Barnes* v. *Atta*, 1 F. L. R. 169.

village is in some places so by hereditary right, in other places he holds his position by election. In places where the right. is hereditary, the members of the village community, by and through the council of the village elders, have a right of veto to his election. Land owned by the village community can be sold, when, there being a public liability, the inhabitants of the village are unable to contribute money for the payment of such claim, and the village council decides to sell such land or a portion thereof. The headman of the village, acting together with the members of the village council, alone can sell the land; but where the plot is in the occupation of some one, that person is entitled to make the first offer for it. So, also, in cases, where land is owned by a company, the person who can act for the company is the president of the assembly of captains controlling and managing the affairs of the company. The captains in a body, with their president, may sell lands belonging to the company whenever any pressing or special need arises, causing the alienation of such property for purposes of the company, expedient or imperative.

(c) Ancestral property is any moveable or immoveable thing which has descended to a person from an ancestor however remote; all savings made out of such moveable or immoveable thing, and all purchases or profits made from the income, or from the proceeds of the sale thereof, follow the character of ancestral property, also every immoveable property acquired on partition of, or in exchange for, property which has so descended.

Per Chalmers: "I consider that the new tenements took all the incidents of the one for which it was substituted, and was therefore in Degraft's lifetime in the same position as if it had been land of inheritance to which he had actually succeeded." *

(d) Family property is any moveable or immoveable thing acquired—

* *Barnes* v. *Mayan*, 1 F. L. R. 180.

i. By the joint labour of the members of a family. One of the most common instances of this is the building of a house by the members of a family; or

ii. By the contributions from two or more members of one's family.

(e) Property is designated self-acquired or private, where it is acquired by a person by means of his own personal exertions, without any unremunerated help or assistance from any member of his family; or without any advance or contribution from the ancestral or family possessions of his family.

The owner of self-acquired property, whether such property consists in land or otherwise, can sell or deal with it as he thinks fit.

But where any land, lost by an ancestor or any of his successors, has been recovered by a member of the family out of his private resources, such land is considered to have been purchased for the family, and is not self-acquired property, unless the members of the family were made distinctly to understand at the time of purchase that it will not resume its former condition as the ancestral property.

It should be noted, while on this point, that, with the exception of the coast towns, where there is much contact with European ideas, self-acquired or private property in its strict sense does not exist over the whole country, because the family group is of the patriarchal type.

The occupant of a stool and the head of a family each occupies a position somewhat similar to that of a Roman paterfamilias.

But in this country the head of a family holds the family possessions in trust for himself and the members of the family.

All the family possessions are under his control, and all acquisitions made by the family are made for him, and fall into the common stock, and all the self-acquired property of a person which remains undisposed of at his death descends to his successors as ancestral property.

It is a universal custom that if an individual holds property in severalty, that is, as sole owner and possessor, it will in the next generation relapse into a state of joint tenancy.

If land be free to-day in the hands of its acquirer, it will to-morrow resume its fetters in the hands of his heirs. Absolute, unrestrained, and exclusive ownership, enabling one person to deal with his immoveable property, is the exception. For the father is restricted by his brother, the brother by his sister's sons and daughters, and the woman by her own issue. In the English law, individual property is the rule; the converse holds in the Gold Coast.

The head of a family has greater powers of alienation over moveable than he has over immoveable ancestral property and family property. He can alienate such moveable property in gifts to any of the members of the family, for their education, support, or getting a wife for any member of the family.

If the family, therefore, find the head of the family misappropriating the family possessions and squandering them, the only remedy is to remove him and appoint another instead; and although no junior member can claim on account from the head of the family, or call for an appropriation to himself of any special portion of the family estate, or income therefrom arising, yet the Customary Law says they who are born and they who are still in the womb require means of support, wherefore the family lands and possessions must not be wasted or squandered.

The head of a family cannot, without the consent of or notice to all the principal members of the family or the greater part thereof,* alienate any part of the family immoveable possessions, and if such consent is secured, the alienation must be for the benefit of the family, either to discharge a family obligation, or the proceeds of such alienation must be added to the family fund.

In answer to the Judicial Assessor, as to how such

* *Gaisiwa* v. *Akraba*, 2 F. L. R. 94.

consent should be signified, the Chiefs said * :—" It would be necessary for all the members of the family to meet and discuss, and if there were land to be sold, all the members would meet and get strangers to be witnesses, and the family would concur for payment of the debts. As many members as could be got should represent the family. When such meeting and discussion has once been had, the sale remains good. It would be proved by the strangers who were witnesses."

The right of one of the senior or elder members of the family to rescind or set aside sale of ancestral or family land, such person having opposed the sale, has been the subject of a decision of the Full Court, presided over by Chief Justice Marshall in *Bayaidee* v. *Mensah.* †

The Court said :—" Although it may be, and we believe it is the law, that the concurrence of the members of the family ought to be given in order to constitute an unimpeachable sale of family land, the sale is not in itself void, but is capable of being opened up at the instance of the family, provided they avail themselves of their right timeously, and under circumstances in which, upon the rescinding of the bargain, the purchaser can be fully restored to the position in which he stood before the sale. This, obviously, is not the case, whereas here the purchaser has possessed for a series of years (fourteen years) in undisturbed ownership, has cultivated and improved the land and established a home upon it. We are of opinion that whatever right of impeaching the sale the family possessed, is barred by their acquiescence and the plaintiff's continued cause of undisturbed possession."

The principle enunciated has been followed in two important decisions, *Asraidu* v. *Dadzie,*‡ and *Bokitsi Concession Inquiry.* §

2. The intending purchaser having discovered the proper persons from whom he could buy, and who could give him

---

* *Awortchie* v. *Eshon*, 1 F. L. R. 170. † 1 F. L. R. 171.
‡ 1 F. L. R. 174. § 2 F. L. R. 160.

a good title, now enters into negotiations with them, and in the course of these he makes known to them what he seeks to buy.

It has been already stated that in ancient days the sale of land was not of general or common occurrence, and to-day there are some parts of the Gold Coast whose inhabitants will not sell any of their lands.

But the sale of the produce on one's land is a very ancient custom. In the palm-oil producing districts there exists the custom of selling the palm crops of a specified field, for one or more seasons, and the purchaser is entitled to enter on the land with his servants to gather the nuts and make the oil on such land. While engaged in this work they may eat some of the plantains there growing, but must not remove any for sale.

On the same principle landowners sell growing timber for a lump sum of money, which the purchaser has the right to cut down on and remove within a reasonable time, from a piece of land, the name of which is given, or the boundaries thereof are mentioned or shown. When the trees are cut down the land reverts to the owner, although the felled timber can be removed afterwards. Unfortunately, it has been found in several instances, that landowners have been made to put their names and seals to documents in the English form, under the belief they were selling only the timber on such land, when, as a matter of fact, they were parting with the entire ownership of such lands. It is satisfactory to state, that many conveyances of this kind, having been detected by the Concessions Divisional Court at Axim, were abandoned by the claimants thereof.

The right to collect or manufacture rubber on payment of a lump sum is more in the nature of a licence for valuable consideration than of sale of the rubber.

Generally when any land is sold, and the ownership is parted with, the purchaser becomes the owner of everything, including the minerals in such land, for the common saying is, "If you find a treasure-trove on your land, you are entitled to it; it is your luck." But in such mining districts as Wassaw, Sefwhi, Apollonia, and Aowin, the purchase of lands does not include the minerals. The ownership of the minerals is vested in the king's stool. When the purchaser mines, he is bound to give to the stool-holder the usual Ebusã; if, however, he allows others to mine, he is entitled to claim from them one-third as his Ebusã, and of this the stool-holder gets a third.

3. When the owners of the land consent to sell, a day is fixed for inspecting the land. The owners of land adjacent to and abutting upon land under inspection are invited to be present, so that disputes as to boundary marks may be averted in the future. Where the land is a town plot, and the intending purchaser knows it, an inspection may be waived.

In the contract of sale, whether of immoveable or moveable property, one is ever reminded of the saying, *Obi nto nantwi anamon*, "Nobody buys the footprints of a bullock."

4. Having determined upon the identity of what is to be sold, and the interest which the buyer is acquiring, the price is fixed, and is payable in gold or silver. In former days purchases were made by barter. The Fanti word for trading is *Batta*. This word is used by Asanti and other traders, and is not a corruption of the word "barter." *

5. Then is paid the earnest-money (Trama). This binds the contract, for without the payment of Trama to the vendor no contract exists, and he is at liberty to sell the land to some one else for a larger price; the intending purchaser can withdraw his offer and repudiate the contract without being liable to any damages, although the Trama becomes forfeited; but if any part payment has been made, it is doubtful whether it can be recovered. In this connection is the expression, "If you have not eaten anything you do not pay for it." *Basel Mission Factory* v.

---

* *Cobbold* v. *Taweia*, 1 F. L. R. 179.

Bruce, 2 F. L. R. 99, will repay a careful study, and will be found very interesting, instructive, and useful. In that case the defendant purchased a piece or parcel of land from one Jacob Vanderpuye, on April 23, 1899, for one hundred and seventy-five pounds, of which he paid eighty pounds down; the balance, ninety-five pounds, was to be paid three months afterwards. The purchaser did not receive a deed or any document, but at the trial he called evidence to show, and the Court found, that the sale was a valid one by native law. The plaintiffs alleged they had bought from the same Jacob Vanderpuye a larger piece of land, of which this formed a portion, for three hundred and eighty pounds, and had received a deed of conveyance for the same on June 19, 1899, which had been duly registered as required by sect. 17 of the Registration Ordinance, 1895; and, further, as they were not natives, the Customary Law relating to sales should be disregarded. The Court decided that the land in question had been validly sold to the defendant prior to its sale to the plaintiffs, and gave judgment in favour of the defendant, and this was, on appeal, confirmed.

The Trama is sometimes distributed among the witnesses to the contract, as token of their presence when the bargain was struck; but it is more usual for the vendor on receiving the Trama to give to the witnesses a distinct amount of money.*

The drinking of palm-wine, rum, gin, or other spirits is not an essential part of the contract of sale.

In Appendix XII. will be found a form of document which has been extensively used by the author for many years. It was prepared for those who were anxious to hold or possess some documentary evidence of their title to property validly acquired in accordance with the requirements of the Customary Law. The form is now translated into the Fanti language for the use of persons who prefer to conduct their business in their own language.

---

* *Quay* v. *Aywoodsuah*, 1 F. L. R. 163.

In the absence of agreement reserving the crops on the land which are to be removed as soon as possible, or within a specified time by the owner, the purchaser of a piece of land is entitled to all that is thereon and within it.

He who offers anything for sale thereby implies he has a right or is authorized by the true owner or owners to sell and part with the ownership therein, and to give a good title to the purchaser. Where the title is found defective, the purchaser can demand his money back, and all expenses incurred must be repaid by the seller, whose personal representatives are not liable. If, therefore, a man buys from another, and after the death of the seller the purchaser discovers his title defective, he has no remedy, for if he wished to protect himself, he should have specially contracted with the seller for good title and included his successors or heirs. No earnest-money (Trama) is paid in simple purchases or in barter. In the sale of lands and slaves, and for a large quantity of goods at one sale or transaction, Trama must be paid.

In contracts for the sale of chattels and merchandise, as soon as Trama is paid, the purchaser is entitled to their possession on payment of the agreed price. If he fail to complete the purchase, he forfeits the Trama, but he does not seem to be liable to any damages for breach of contract. The vendor cannot compel the purchaser to perform his part of the contract; on the other hand, in the absence of the Trama, the purchaser cannot, by tendering the price agreed upon, compel the vendor to give him delivery. The respective positions of the parties, and their freedom from liability, are tersely stated in the well-known trade expression, current on the West Coast of Africa, " No buy, no pay."

(v.) TESTAMENTARY DISPOSITIONS.

The Customary Law knows nothing of wills in writing, and even in the matter of testamentary dispositions the members of the family exercise much influence.

Cruickshank describes the ceremony of will-making, as he calls it, which is still common among the people. "In view of death, the head of the family summons around his death-bed his relations. He instructs them about the state of his affairs, and how his property was acquired, and how to be disposed of. He is most particular to furnish them with proofs respecting the acquisition of his pawns and slaves, mentions the names of the witnesses to the transactions, the circumstances under which they took place, and the sums paid for them, in order that his successor may be enabled to defend his rights, in the event of their attempting to obtain their liberty or redemption at the death of their master. He also recounts the names of his debtors with the sums which they owe to him, as well as the debts which he owes to others. His death-bed declarations, made in the presence of responsible witnesses, are always received as evidence in the event of litigation afterwards." The curious inquirer may here be informed how suggestive are the death-bed scenes of the patriarch Jacob, as recorded in the sacred writ (Gen. xlix.), and that of King David.

Now, it has been affirmed as a general proposition by Sir Henry Maine, in his "Ancient Law," that in all indigenous societies a condition of jurisprudence, in which testamentary privileges are not allowed, or rather not contemplated, has preceded the latter stage of legal development in which the mere will of the proprietor is permitted, with more or less restrictions, to override the claims of his kindred in blood. And even among the Romans, a will was never regarded by them as a means of disinheriting a family or of effecting the unequal distribution of a patrimony, and the rules of Law preventing its being turned to such a purpose increase in number and stringency as the jurisprudence unfolds itself. *Samansiw* is, in fact, not a word that accurately conveys the conception of a will as understood by an English lawyer, for the idea of making a disposition of property to take effect after the death of the giver, as has been noticed by observant European travellers on the Gold Coast, is really opposed to the fundamental principles of the ties binding the members of the family.

Without doubt, the custom of making wills with respect to self-acquired property is of modern growth, but no one can tell when the practice first began. Death-bed dispositions, known as *Samansiw*, seem to be recognized, not so much because of any assumed right to make such a disposition, as because, from feelings of affection, respect, or even superstition, the last wishes of the deceased are considered to be entitled to weight, among the members of his family. And this idea runs through the Customary Law relating to testamentary disposition of property. In fact, the only disposition of property known to the early Customary Law was a transfer followed by immediate possession. Contact with British rule in the old settlements gave rise to the practice of reducing into writing such transactions, and writing has in some localities become common, not so much because it is essential for the validity of transfer, but because it is a permanent record of such occurrence.

A stool-holder, or chief, or head of a family, or the manager of family property, has no power by testamentary disposition to alienate any part or portion of the family estate, moveable or immoveable, from the family. He may suggest some one to be his successor, but on his decease the people of the stool or members of the family may or may not act upon his suggestion or recommendation (*Coffie Yammoah* v. *Abban Cooma*).

The owner of self-acquired property can in his lifetime deal with it as he pleases, and where he intends to give the whole or a portion of it to his child by a freeborn wife, Adihiwa, or to any person not a member of his family, he does so before his death. As soon as he dies, his successor is entitled to all the property he died possessed as heritable and ancestral estate, subject to the usual rules of inheritance; of course the successor may give heed to the expressed desires of the deceased, who may have been so taken ill suddenly as to have been unable to accomplish his intention respecting the disposal of his property.

Where the owner of self-acquired property gives testamentary directions as to its disposal among the members of his family, who thereby take such property as heritable or ancestral property, the person, who would otherwise have succeeded to the deceased, cannot ignore such dispositions, and the persons benefited have a right to enforce such bequest.

E.g. Kwesi, owner of Addum and Donpim lands, four bendas, a house, and twelve pieces of salagha cloth, makes testamentary disposition, bequeathing Addum land to his son Kudwo, Donpim land to his youngest niece Araba, two bendas to Aduku, his younger brother, two pieces salagha cloth to Baidu, his friend. The said Kwesi had a mother, elder brother, and three sisters him surviving. By the Customary Law, his son Kudwo cannot take Addum land unless his father placed him in possession before his death; Araba is entitled to Donpim land, and can enforce her right to possess the land, she being of the heritable blood; and it is only on the failure of her issue to succeed that the other members of her family come in. Aduku also is entitled to take the two bendas, but Baidu cannot compel delivery of the two pieces of salagha cloth, if the mother, eldest brother, or the sisters refuse to deliver them to him. The owner of self-acquired property, after solemnly making his testamentary dispositions, may subsequently revoke a part or the whole of them.

Where a woman, having issue or descendants, possesses self-acquired property, her testamentary declarations as to the disposal of her property among her children and grandchildren are binding. When she fails to make such disposition her mother is her successor, then her children by seniority, failing whom, her sisters and brothers by seniority. So long as her children and their issue are alive, the right of the brothers, sisters, and sisters' issue is subordinate to that of her own children.

The property of her son, which a mother succeeds to, is at her absolute disposal, and she can do whatever she pleases with it; but she has only a limited or at the most a life interest in property which comes to her from her deceased daughter leaving issue.

E.g. Amba has two daughters, Effua and Abba, both having issue, and sons Kwesi, Kobina, and Kwow. Effua, the possessor of four bendas, and Abba, the owner of a piece of land and some valuable beads, and Kobina, possessing a house, chattels, and some money, die, each leaving children, but without making any testamentary disposition: the mother takes the property of her son Kobina, and of this she has absolute control. She may appoint the youngest son Kwow to be Kobina's successor, or even give the estate of the deceased son to any of her grandchildren by her daughters Effua and Abba, and such person will hold the property as heritable or ancestral property. The said mother has only a limited interest, however, in the estate of her daughters, for the right of children to succeed to their mother is superior to that of their grandmother.

A stool-holder, who had kept his self-acquired property distinct from the stool property, to the knowledge of the senior and immediate members of the stool, can make a valid testamentary disposition of such self-acquired property to a member of the family. The Customary Law does not permit any person to bequeath to an outsider a greater portion of his property than is left for his family. Nor does the Customary Law permit any testamentary disposition, by a man weak in intellect, or imbecile, or insane, or under the influence of fraud or misrepresentation, to stand, or to be regarded at all.

It is not only on the death-bed that a man can make testamentary disposition. A person can make his testamentary disposition while enjoying perfect health; but at the time it is made, the witnesses must be distinctly told by him his words are his *Samansiw*, to take effect after his death. A subsequent *Samansiw* does not necessarily cancel or revoke a previous one, unless it is incompatible therewith.

Where a person, by testamentary declaration, releases

his debtor from payment of any claim he may have against
him, or directs that a person in possession of the testator's
chattel shall retain it as his own, it is binding on his successor and other members of the family, who cannot claim
from such debtor the amount of the debt, or from such
legatee his legacy; for, says the Customary Law, what is
given under such solemn conditions cannot be recalled; the
acts of gratitude should be cherished, and an act of restitution that calms a guilty conscience pricked with remorse
should be respected.

Persons coming under the Marriage Ordinance, 1884,
should clearly understand that, unless they leave a will
made in strict compliance to and in accordance with the
English Statute of Wills, they die intestate, for at present
no provision exists for the granting of probate on the
recognition of any other form of will. *Re Anaman
deceased,* 1 F. L. R. 221.

CHAPTER VII.

SUCCESSION.

THE first important rule which one has to learn and ever
bear in mind when dealing with matters of succession is
that the right of inheritance is only through the female,
and pedigree is traced through the female line and *that* only.*

There is no such thing as succession, in the proper
English meaning, in a family owning ancestral property.
The whole family, consisting of males and females, consti-
tutes a sort of corporation; some of the members being
coparceners, *i.e.* persons entitled to a portion of the property
on partition (cutting Ekar), and others who are dependents,
and are entitled to reside in the dwelling-house for life, such
as sons and daughters, subject to good conduct and not disputing right of the family. Partition being extremely rare,

* *Abbacan* v. *Bubuwooni,* 1 F. L. R. 213; *Parker* v. *Mensah,* 1 F. L. R.
204; *Holdbrook* v. *Atta,* 1 F. L. R. 211.

the idea of heirship scarcely presents itself to the mind of any member of the family. The members are entitled to reside in the ancestral house, and to enjoy that amount of affluence and consideration which springs from their belonging to a family possessed of greater or less wealth.

The head of a family holds his property either in severalty or in coparcenary, and this depends whether the property is self-acquired, family property, or ancestral property, and, if the last, whether it be attached to some political or public office.

The right of inheritance to ancestral property attached to a public or political office, varies as to whether such property is enjoyed with or without the immediate or remote control of any person. For example, in the case of a captaincy (Tufuhin) or other commanding position in a fighting force, without election no one can fill the post left vacant by his father or uncle or brother.

Where the property is under or subject to another stool or head of a family, either by commendation or subjection, or by any other means, the superior lord or head of the family has an ultimate and absolute right of veto, whenever the person selected or elected by the retinue or members of the family is considered unfit or unsuitable by him.

E.g. Kudwo, brother or nephew of X deceased, is chosen by his family to sit on the stool under Y, whose chief he was. If the blood relatives and domestics and bondmen of the family concur, the proposal must be confirmed by king Y, before Kudwo can be placed in the room of X deceased. And on the failure of the blood relatives, domestics, and bondmen to present a suitable person, the king may himself choose one of the blood relatives; and this person will succeed if accepted by the major part of the family or people of the subordinate stool, otherwise one of the domestics or bondmen is to be appointed as the manager or trustee for life or for a specified period of the family possessions.*

The owner of self-acquired real property dying intestate,

* *Amfoo* v. *Yardonua* 1 F. L. R. 198.

is not succeeded by his sons, they being outside the line of inheritance, but by his mother and her issue according to seniority.

Persons in the line of succession are :—

Mother.

Brothers, according to seniority.

Nephews, by seniority.

Sisters.

Sisters' daughters.

Failing these—

Mother's brothers, by seniority or election.

Mother's sisters.

Mother's sisters' children.

Failing these and their stock, the domestics in whose veins runs any of the heritable blood, take by seniority. Next, the head domestic; lastly, a member of the tribe. Provided always that a man is invariably preferred to a woman. Hence the saying, "Obaa odan bayin" (a man is the mainstay of a woman).

There are therefore four kinds of successors, viz. Real, Proper, Ordinary, and Extraordinary.

The Real successor of a person is his mother.

We call those persons *Proper* successors who are the uterine brothers and sisters of the deceased, and the issue of such sisters; but never can the pedigree be traced out in the line of the male.

Ordinary successors are such persons as are descended from the maternal grandmother :

E.g. : A person's uncle or aunts, and the issue of such aunts.

Extraordinary successors are :—

(i.) Issue by a house domestic with a male person of the heritable blood (Dihi).

(ii.) Domestic.

(iii.) Clan or tribal relative.

The rule of succession may be made plain perhaps by the following pedigree or table of descent :—

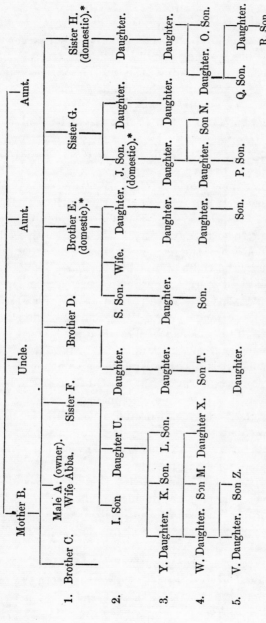

* Married to a slave or domestic in the house.

In the above pedigree A, a male, is the owner of self-acquired property. On his death, his wife Abba does not succeed to his property, but his Real successor is his mother B; she waiving her right, his brothers C, D, and E take by seniority. Failing the brothers C, D, and E, his successor is found among his nephews, that is, children of his sisters F, G, and H.

The nephews are I, son of his sister F; and J, son of his sister G. These take by seniority; if, therefore, J, the nephew by his younger sister G, is older than I, J has a better right to the succession.

If the nephew I or J be older than the brothers C, D, E, such nephew can be preferred over the brothers C, D, E, and the sisters F, G, H, to succeed A, and although the brothers are capable to succeed, yet any of them can waive his right in favour of one of the nephews. On the death, however, of the nephew, the right of the brother passed over or who waived his right revives. Failing the brothers and nephews, the next persons in the succession are K and L; next to them are M, N, and O, then P, Q, and R. The persons so named are those who can be placed on the stool, if any, and can become head of the family. If any of them cannot succeed when it is his turn, and there is no proper person available, then S, a son of E, by a domestic of the house, or a suitable domestic is appointed manager of the property. It seems that where a house-born son as S is appointed guardian trustee, or manager, he holds his post for life, although he can resign in favour of any of the proper successors becoming fit to inherit.

The sisters F, G, and H are the natural and proper guardians of the property during the incapacity or minority of the proper successors, but their management of such property and their control goes by seniority, the eldest, F, taking before G and H. Where the nephews are capable to look after the property, they take by turns: e.g. if the three sisters had three sons each, after the death or deposition for misconduct of the eldest son of the eldest sister, one of the sons of the second sister will be entitled to succeed to the uncle's property, and on his death the eldest son of the youngest sister will be next entitled, and one branch will not be exhausted before those of the other branch come in.

Suppose K, a son of U, the daughter of F, who is the sister of A, had died, leaving self-acquired property. After his mother he will be succeeded by L, then by M, his nephew, who will be in his turn succeeded by Z, his grandnephew, and not by O, the great grandson of H, who cannot succeed until the issue of Z's sister, V, becomes extinct. When that line becomes extinct, some say any son of Z by a domestic takes in preference to O, who is blood relative, and the ordinary successors of K, both persons tracing descent from a common ancestress B, and failing the descendants of B, the persons entitled must be found by finding the descendants of A's aunts.

When a person such as A dies, having his own acquired property, moveable and immoveable, he is not succeeded by his sons, free-born or domestic, whose only right is that of a life interest in the dwelling-house built by their father, the deceased, on a land not family property. For if the house be built on family land, the children have only right of occupation during good conduct. If any one living in the house of his father deny the right of the proper successor, or commit waste or injure the house, or encumber or sell it, he thereby forfeits his life interest. Such person must make the necessary repairs, and may quit if the successor requires it for himself as a residence.

Mr. Eminsang, giving his opinion on *Boham and another* v. *Marshall* (May 18, 1892), says : "By native law, Anna Boham had a right to the house, as she was the sister of John Boham. By native law, she was the only heiress at the time. She could by native law have power to give the house to the children for their natural lives. Of the part so given to the children, unless Marshall gave the children an equivalent, he could not turn them out of the house.

Marshall can pull down his portion of the house, if he did not interfere with the other portion.

" By the Court : By native law, the person succeeding to property could not dispose of it to beyond his lifetime, unless with the consent of the families. In this case, the plaintiffs being the children of John Boham, have the right to remain in their father's house during their lives, unless for good reasons. If the children do not live in their father's house, still if they can go and live there as they will, the heir could not break the house down and dispose of the materials. The heir is the one to repair the house, and if the children are in a position they contribute towards the expenses."

The latter part of this opinion is, we submit, erroneous. Children who leave their father's house for their own family or private house, cannot stop the father's successor breaking down the house, and if they alone reside therein, they must keep the house in repair. Where, however, the successor resides in the same house, he of course sees about the repairs.

In *Halmond* v. *Daniel*, August 22, 1871, Chief Koffie Chie and others laid down the law, in answer to the inquiry, If a man went from his family, cleared land, and on that land built another house, would not his children be entitled to live in it after his decease ? that "if a man had a father, either by country marriage or otherwise, and the father lived in the house with the wife and child, and he died, all the deceased's property, except the house, goes to his family. The father's gun and sword and house go to the son, and the saying is, 'the father dies and leaves his house to the son.'

" The family take the property, but do not turn away the child. The son lives in the house with the family of his father, supposing they had nowhere else to live, and the son does not turn them away. If it is a family house, the head occupies as head ; yet he does not turn away the son from the house, except the son, after he has grown up, finds himself competent to build and leaves for the purpose of doing so. But he would not under any circumstances be turned out by the head of the family.

"The family would not be turned out for the son's accommodation. If they had nowhere else to live, they would live in the house. Where there is room enough for all (son and family), the head of the family arranges the rooms to be allotted to each. My answer of the descent of house to the son applies in case it has been built by the father. The family would be allowed to live in it if they had nowhere else to go; if they had, they would leave the father's house to the son. The son could not sell the house except with consent of the family."

In the coast towns, one now and then comes across what at first sight seems to be an exception to the general rule of succession. There are some families where succession goes from father to son; but this has reference only to the dignity or title or office, with such property or insignia going with it, and which was in the first instance created with it. Such a position is quite distinct from that of head of family, although a person may hold the two offices at the same time : e.g. B is head of a wealthy family having and possessing a large retinue. The townspeople make him their king or chief, and give him by general contribution a sword, robes, drums, etc. If at any time the people depose him, the only property they can take from him will be what was handed him on his installation as king or chief, at which time he took the oath of office, swearing to be true and faithful to the interests of his subjects. And unless the members of his family remove him, he nevertheless continues head of his family, although another person be given the public honour and office.

Where the deceased is a slave or domestic, his master or mistress is entitled to take all the property, but if another slave or domestic is appointed as successor, the master or mistress takes from the personal effects whatever he or she pleases.

If a person whose ancestress was a slave die without issue, there being no descendants of the ancestress's master or mistress, his fellow domestic takes his property as successor : *e.g.* B is great-grandchild of C, a donkor of A ; D is descendant of A, and there are in the family (i.) several domestics, (ii.) but one domestic. On the death of B, D may keep B's effects or give some to such one of the domestics as he please. If there be no descendant or heir of D her surviving (i.), the head domestic succeeds ; (ii.) the one domestic takes, and no tribal or clan relative can take preference, for the donkors invariably acquire their owner's tribal name, and bondmen often join the master's tribe.

He who succeeds a person owning self-acquired property is liable for and bound to pay the private debts of the deceased, whether the assets are or are not sufficient. An heir, if he sees that his deceased relative is greatly indebted, can give the body to the company of the deceased, and on the body being buried at the expense of the company or the public, the heir and his family are not liable at all for any debt of the deceased. Any property left by the deceased is sold by the public to defray any burial expenses.

In the early part of 1891, Chief Justice Hutchinson sought information on certain points of the Customary Law from the late Edmund Bannerman, of Accra, that eminent solicitor and advocate whose knowledge of the Customary Law and long experience in the Law Courts were unsurpassed. The Chief Justice put these questions :—

1. As to property which the deceased himself acquired : I understand that it descends as follows—(*a*) to his eldest brother by the same mother ; (*b*) to his eldest sister by the same mother ; (*c*) to the eldest son of his eldest sister ; (*d*) to the eldest daughter of his eldest sister. Is this correct ? And who is the next heir ?

2. As to property *inherited :* I suppose the rule is the same, except that you have to go back (as far as possible) to the person who originally acquired the property, and trace the descent from him ?

3. Where does the *mother* come in, supposing her to be alive ?

4. Does a *woman's* property acquired by her descend in the same way, or do her children inherit it before her brothers and sisters?

5. Can a child ever (and if so, under what circumstances) be heir to its father's property?

6. Is there not a custom in some places for a stool or stool property to descend to the late chief's son?

7. Can a man appoint as heir to his property, inherited or acquired, a person who is not the next heir according to native law? If so, what formality is required?

8. The rights of the heir : Does he ever take the property as his own absolutely, or is he bound to allow some share (and if so, what) to the other members of the family?

9. The duties of the heir : Is he bound himself to pay all the expenses of the funeral and the funeral custom, and all the debts of the deceased?

10. Suppose a person not the heir, with the heir's consent, performs and pays for the custom, does he thereby acquire any right to the property of the deceased, or to be reimbursed?

11. Can the other members of the family supersede the heir; and if so, on what grounds; and can a mere majority do it?

12. If a man dies without any known heir, who takes his property, and who is bound to bury him?

13. Can a bastard inherit the property of his mother and of her other, legitimate or bastard, children?

Similar questions were sent to Mr. G. E. Eminsang at Elmina.

Mr. Bannerman's opinion relates specially to the Accra district, but it will be noticed that the Accra customary laws differ very little from what have been explained herein. Says Mr. Bannerman : "Before answering the first question, it will be as well to explain that there are two forms of marriages obtainable in the Accra country proper, namely, what is known as the *two-cloth,* or *sweetheart,* and the other is *six-cloth,* or legal marriage. With reference to the first, personal property only descends as follows: (a) to the uterine brothers of the deceased, the eldest taking first; (b) failing the brothers, the uterine sisters and their children take by seniority.

"The children by the *two-cloth* marriage do not come in at all.

"(c) With reference to the second, that is, *six-cloth* marriage, real property descends the same as personal property, with this exception, that it is inherited in conjunction with the children of the deceased of that marriage, and such real property cannot be disposed of without the children's consent. It must be borne in mind that in the Accra country males take precedence of females, and if minors, the eldest female takes charge until the eldest male be of age. I am well aware that opinions varying in part to mine have been given, but it is most absurd to think that there should exist two forms of marriages, one superior to another, and yet the claims of the children of one marriage to their father's property is the same as the claim of the children of the other.

"(d) Property acquired by the deceased, he can either in writing or verbally will away to whomsoever he pleases, but should he die intestate, it then descends according to (a), (b), and (c).

"Property inherited descends precisely in the same manner as property acquired, with the exception that the deceased has no power to will it away, as in the case of property acquired.

"The mother does not come in at all, but the inheritor of the property is bound to take care of her *durante vita,* and at her demise to bury her decently.

"A woman's property acquired by herself descends to her children and their children; failing them, then to brothers or sisters according to age.

"No child can inherit his father's property except under the circumstances related in (a), (b), and (c).

"There are instances where the son has inherited the

stool and property *strictly attached* to the stool; *e.g.* the case of King Frederick Dowoonah, of Christiansborg, Accra; but generally inheritance of stool jumps from one branch of the family to another and back again. Should the holder of the stool, however, acquire any property of his own *durante vita*, that property cannot go to the inheritor of the stool, but must descend as stated in (*a*), (*b*), and (*c*).

"No man can appoint an inheritor to property which he inherited, but the property acquired by himself. The inheritor appointed may be a person who is not the next heir, but such person must go through the formality of custom, making expenses of funeral and paying all the deceased's just debts.

"The right of the heir of personal property is absolute, but he is bound to assist any member who is in real distress.

"The heir is bound himself to pay all the just debts of the deceased's, and also the expenses of the funeral custom.

"Any person not being the heir, but who with the heir's consent performs and pays for the custom, does not acquire any right whatsoever to the property, but has simply to be reimbursed for what he has expended.

"The heir can be superseded by other members of the family on the ground of insanity, imbecility, extravagance, etc. There need not be a majority to supersede him. Two or three of the nearest members are quite sufficient for the purpose.

"Should a man die without any known heir (a thing utterly unknown as regards natives), his property would be taken charge of by the owner of the house in which he stayed when he came into the country, who will see all funeral expenses and debts paid; and should any heir ever turn up, he or she alone is responsible to him or her.

"Any child can inherit the property of his mother, bastardy being a thing hardly recognized in this country."

Bosman, writing on inheritance, says: "The children they have by their wives are indeed legitimate, but all along the Gold Coast (they) never inherit their parent's effects except at Accra only. The right of inheritance is very oddly adjusted, and as far as I could observe, the brothers' and sisters' children are the right and lawful heirs in the manner following: They do not jointly inherit, but the eldest son of his mother is heir to his mother's brother or her son, as the eldest daughter is heiress of her mother's sister or her daughter. Neither the father himself nor his relations as brothers' sisters have any claim to the goods of the defunct. In deficiency of the above-mentioned heirs, the brothers or sisters take their place; but if none of them are living, then the nearest relation of the mother of the defunct comes in.

" The eldest son, supposing the father a king or a captain of a town, succeeds him in his office only; but besides his father's shield and sabre he has nothing more to pretend to. So that 'tis here no manner of advantage to be descended from rich parents, unless (which seldom happens) paternal love obliges them to bestow somewhat on their children in their lifetime, which must be privately done, otherwise the relations after the father's death will oblige the children to return it to the utmost farthing." (Bosman, letter xii. pp. 203, 204.)

John Barbot, the agent-general of the French Royal Company of Africa and islands of America, who was a contemporary of Bosman, in connection with this custom, says: "The best reason the blacks give for such a constitution, is, that the dividing of estates or goods among so many persons as generally compose their families, so many wives and children, would occasion endless disputes and quarrels amongst them; or this, that children relying too much on their father's wealth, would live lazily, without any inclination to employ themselves in some business, to avoid lewdness, wantonness, and debauchery. Whereas being now sensible from their tender youth that they have nothing to expect from their father but a bare maintenance during his life, they are much the readier to betake themselves early to learn some profession by which they may maintain themselves handsomely when their father is no more ; and even to maintain their father's family after his death, as many do."

CHAPTER VIII.

SLANDER.

WORDS which cause or produce any injury to the reputation of another are called defamatory, and, if false, are actionable. False defamatory words, when spoken, constitute slander. Where a person has been found guilty for using slanderous words, he is bound to retract his words publicly, in addition to paying a small fine by way of compensation to the aggrieved party. Words imputing witchcraft, adultery, immoral conduct, crime, and all words which sound to the disreputation of a person of whom they are spoken, are actionable. The native custom is more in accordance with natural justice, equity, and good conscience than the English law, which has been denounced by many a learned judge. Says Lord Chancellor Campbell, in *Lynch* v. *Knight and Wife*, "I may lament the unsatisfactory state of our law, according to which the imputation by words, however gross, on an occasion however public, upon the chastity of a modest matron or a pure virgin is not actionable, without proof that it has actually produced special temporal damage to her." Instead of the word "unsatisfactory" I should substitute the word "barbarous," said Lord Brougham on the same occasion.

Meredith remarks: "The law against witchcraft is particularly severe, inasmuch as it generally extends to all under the same roof; as it is supposed they possessed some portion of the malign influence." What makes it a serious offence is that witchcraft is considered *hereditary*, and to call a person *Ayen*, wizard, witch, implies that every member of such person's family is possessed of an evil spirit capable of doing infinite mischief, and the less one has dealings with any of them the better.

So much annoyance, mischief, and injury is caused by the reckless imputation of witchcraft, that many a woman has been known to commit suicide, unable to bear the disgrace of a false imputation.

It would be well if other judges and magistrates follow what was done by Mr. Justice Richards in *Bedua* v. *Ochua*.

An effective way of punishing a person guilty of slander of serious consequences, is to make him walk through the town or village carrying a heavy stone in front of an officer of the Court, who, at convenient halting-places, beats a gong; the guilty slanderer is compelled to recant his base falsehoods, and to confess his disgraceful behaviour, amid the sneers and jeers of the multitude. The heavy stone so carried is called *oturbiba*.

CHAPTER IX.

MODES OF ENFORCING PAYMENT.

THERE are several modes of enforcing payment of liability more or less common. I. "Dharna," a practice well known in India, especially in the native states. The word "Dharna" is said to be an exact equivalent to the Roman *capio*. The person who adopts this means of enforcing payment of his claim goes early in the morning to the door or house of the person against whom it is directed, or to the place where the debtor usually follows his occupation. Here the creditor, covered over with white clay or in sackcloth and ashes, and having a supply of food sufficient for one meal, seats himself on a mat or on the bare ground. He informs the debtor that unless the debt is paid to the last farthing he will not go away, and if the debtor goes out this creditor follows him everywhere. Instances are known where the debt not having been paid the creditor has died of starvation. Sometimes, as the day draws to a close, the creditor swears to commit suicide if the debt be not paid before sunset. If in such a case the debt be not paid, and the creditor doth commit suicide, the debtor is bound to bear the funeral expenses in addition to paying the original debt and making substantial compensation to the family of the deceased creditor. But when the creditor swears that if by a certain time the debt be not paid he and the debtor must both forfeit their lives, the debtor cannot save his life by simply paying the debt and a compensation ; he too must take away his life.

It is worthy of notice that in the Brehon law, if a person has a legal claim against a man of a certain rank, and is desirous of compelling payment, the law authorizes him to "fast upon him." Notice, it says, precedes distress in the case of the inferior grades, except it be by persons of distinction or upon persons of distinction ; fasting precedes distress in their case. (Ancient Laws of Ireland.) This institution is said by Sir Henry Maine to be unquestionably identical with one widely diffused throughout the East, and known by the Hindoos as "Sitting Dharna," which consists in sitting at your debtor's door and starving yourself till he pays.

II. There are two kinds of Panyarring, namely, (a) persons, (b) chattels.

(a) Among the coast tribes and members of the same tribe, panyarring of persons was not customary. When a member of a different tribe was found in a distant place he was liable to be seized with all his goods, and detained in bondage for a debt due by a member of his tribe till such debt had been paid to the satisfaction of the person or creditor who had so detained him.

(b) A creditor whose claim remains unsatisfied after repeated demands, followed by unfulfilled promises of payment by the debtor, is entitled to seize his debtor's goods and chattels, usually of a higher value and retain them till his claim is satisfied in full. The creditor has no power or right to sell the goods so seized or to use them; but he is under no obligation to take any special care of them, or to account for their safe custody or keeping.

Panyarring (pronounced payaring) is rather a law than a custom, and although sometimes prostituted to bad purposes, is frequently the only way to recover a just debt. If exercised unlawfully, the amount of damages to be paid as satisfaction is so much as to cause the financial ruin of the wrong-doer.

III. Payment of debts is also enforced by the debtor being detained in custody, imprisoned in chief's prison or at the village lock-up till payment is made. The debtor meanwhile has to subsist himself or get his family or friends to do so, failing which he is forced to do hard labour by way of return for his board. So effective is this custom that, except in very rare cases, the debtor's family quickly make a contribution and pay the debt in full. During the administration of the African Association and Governor Maclean, judgment debtors were never subsisted by their creditors. On their friends failing to look after them, they were compelled to earn their food by being put to some remunerative occupation within the precincts of the prison.

PART II.

FANTI LAW REPORT OF DECIDED CASES.

———◆◇◆———

THE FAMILY.

ABBA QUASSUA *v.* THOS. WARD.

September 1, 1845.

Consawment Money—Husband and Wife—Accounts.

PLAINTIFF in this case complained that the defendant, her husband, according to the country custom, had been treating her ill, and not using her as she considered a wife should be.

Complaint examined and found that he had not been treating her well. It appeared likewise that he refused to allow her to go away back to her family, who lived at a distance, alleging that she was due him on account. This account, on examination, seemed to consist of some small items which she had gotten on different occasions to sell, and of no great amount. This was declared unclaimable, considering that the plaintiff or her family had not received any *consawment* money according to the country custom at the time he took her, and it is hereby accordingly declared unclaimable. The plaintiff was likewise to consider herself free from any claims which the defendant might have upon her, inasmuch as from his own conduct to her, he had not performed his duty to her as a husband is generally considered according to the custom of this country.

AGGRYBA *v.* ABAN.

September 1, 1845.

Marriage—False Charges—Dissolution.

The plaintiff in this case complained that during the time she had lived with the defendant as a wife he had used her ill, and endeavoured to get up a false debt against her and her family, by leaving in her hand some pieces of lead, iron, etc., going away and alleging afterwards that this was gold. This was disproved afterwards, and the defendant convicted thereupon by his own town chiefs. He did not, when brought up before me, even attempt to substantiate it. The plaintiff, in consequence of her own refusal to return and live with him, was declared free from any claim which he might have upon her.

ECCUAH AHINFUA *v.* QUASHIE GHAN.

Anamabu, October 7, 1845.

Father's Liability—Child's Maintenance.

Plaintiff claims for her daughter Adjuah Bakoom's lying-in and support charges from defendant, the father of a child, begotten with the said daughter.

Judgment for plaintiff, 9 ackies and costs.

YOW PENIN *v.* WILLIAM DUNCAN.

October 11, 1869.

Before D. P. CHALMERS, Judicial Assessor.

Assessors : Chief JOHN MAYAH and Chief KOFI AMOAH.

Marriage—Essential Ceremonies—Dowry—Consawment—Dissolution—
Ill-usage—Theft—Tanbiba.

John Mayah, sworn :—

What are the essential acts or ceremonies to constitute a valid marriage according to the custom of the country ?

When a man intends to have a certain woman for his wife, he applies to her family, asks her to be given in marriage, by taking to the family, according to his means, two flasks of rum ; or 2 ackies of gold dust (9s.), or 4 to 6 ackies, according to his means. Upon this, if the family approve, they agree to give the woman.

Next follows the matter of dowry.

That depends on the family. If they tell the man that they require dowry to be paid, they state the amount they wish, sometimes one ounce or nine ackies. If the woman's family did not wish for dowry, the application of the man with the rum would make a valid marriage.

Next custom to be performed by the man is preparing some clothing for the intended wife. Gold is given to the mother of the woman, called Tanbiba, signifying money for the mother, for cooking against the time of marriage.

Would the request and consent with the first present alone make a valid marriage ?

Ans. : It would. The preparation of the clothing and gold would not affect the marriage ; the man would give them afterwards.

Kofi Amoah :—All that the witness Mayah has stated is correct, according to the custom of our country.

If a wife steals from her husband, does that break the marriage ?

No. It is not customary for a husband to turn his wife away in such case. The case must be looked into to see if the marriage is to continue. If that is proved, the husband has the option of continuing or discontinuing the marriage.

If he elects to discontinue, what steps must be taken ?

If husband says he does not want his wife, the wife goes away with all the property she possessed at the time of marriage ; if the wife refused to remain, everything that had been given the wife must be refunded.

Is any ceremony necessary ?

The word of mouth of the husband is not sufficient. It

is necessary to chalk the woman. The husband chalks her on the shoulders, for unless chalked the woman would not be at liberty to marry again.

How is the chalking proved?

The woman goes about to the neighbours showing the marks and telling, "My husband has chalked me." If a woman should falsely represent such chalking, the family would have to make satisfaction to the husband, paying about two flasks of rum. Though there has been no theft, if the husband wishes to be quit of his wife, he may chalk her and let her go. He cannot do so without assigning cause. It is inquired into by the family, and they judge whether the cause is sufficient.

Is a husband beats or illuses his wife, is she at liberty to leave him?

Not without the case being gone into by the family of the man and woman. If not investigated, and the wife should marry again, the first husband would be entitled to have compensation from the second husband; the amount would vary according to the man's position—6 ackies up to 2 ozs.

When marriage is suspended and parties wish to renew, is any ceremony used?

When the woman has stolen from the husband, it is necessary, in the event of renewal, for the wife to give a sheep unto the husband by way of satisfaction.

On October 12, 1869, judgment was delivered :—Find that the plaintiff was married to his wife *Eccuah Chinwah* according to the custom of the country.

That a husband cannot validly put away his wife without going through certain ceremonies.

That the plaintiff has not performed these ceremonies.

Consequently that cohabitation with the said wife by another man was unlawful.

Find that alleged cohabitation by defendant proved. But not proved that defendant enticed or seduced *Chinwah* to leave her husband.

Find that plaintiff is entitled to compensation from the defendant; under the whole circumstance, restrict the amount to 1 ackie, *i.e.* 4s. 6d.

(Signed) D. P. CHALMERS.

In the hearing of this case the following evidence was given among other :—

September 20, 1869.—Plaintiff my husband brought rum and engaged, and afterwards brought cloths and married me. No money was sent, only cloths. He did not ask my family when he took me to wife, and paid the expenses charged by my first husband. I know the law in the country to which I belong, and the reason why none of my family was asked when I married plaintiff, (was that) plaintiff paid all the expenses charged by my former husband without dispute; plaintiff paid to my former husband about 4 ozs. 8 acks.

October 7, 1869.—*Per* Kofi Koomah. *Eccuah Chinwah* my niece has been married to plaintiff legally, according to country fashion. The ceremonies were not performed, but took her to be his wife. The presents should have been given to me. The marriage can be made good at any time by paying the dowry. No dowry has been paid to me. *Eccuah's* father and mother are both dead. *Eccuah* is not niece to me through her father or mother, only by tribe. I am not brother either to her father or mother. I am the chief man of the tribe. The presents are paid to the chief. If father or mother were alive, the presents would have been paid to them, but I must have been informed. Know defendant; have seen defendant at Dominassie. *Eccuah* lived with plaintiff about two years.

Cross-examined: I know country custom of marriage. Plaintiff asked *Eccuah* from me in marriage. A person who did not apply properly for a woman in marriage, but seduced her, would be fined. When a woman has been properly asked in marriage, though ceremonies not fully

performed, if any trifle had been given as earnest, if she
was seduced, the husband would be entitled to compensation.
When plaintiff asked for *Eccuah*, she had not been married.
Plaintiff brought me 2 flasks of gin, and 2 flasks of rum.
Eccuah's mother was living when plaintiff proposed
marriage. When it was time to fulfil the marriage, plaintiff
brought nothing to me. The marriage gifts were brought
direct before me. It is necessary for the man to buy some
clothing, beads for the women, and I saw you send these.
I could accept these things without monies also being given.
There was no money. It is customary to send gold dust;
plaintiff sent some; the mother returned it, because she did
not know if the marriage would be prosperous. I gave my
consent to this marriage. The gold sent was 8 takoos,
i.e. 6*s.* Plaintiff undertook to cook according to custom for
eight days. I invited friends. On the death of the mother-
in-law plaintiff contributed to the customs.

When a man detects his wife stealing from him, it
breaks the marriage. If they wish to renew, the one in
the wrong must give satisfaction—3 ackies, *i.e.* 13*s.* 6*d.*

LINTOTT BROTHERS *v.* SOLOMON.

April 18, 1888.

Before FRANCIS SMITH, Judge.

Family Property—Alienation—Consent of Senior Members essential—
Marriage—Domestics—Succession.

James H. Brew: As chief, I have been in the habit of
deciding cases referring to the law of descent, and I have
decided cases wherein the ceremonies connected with native
marriages are brought in. In certain respects the law of
native marriages is not so different from that of the law in
England. The party seeking the hand of the daughter of
another, would apply to the parents of the girl for her; and
on the parents expressing their willingness to give their
daughter to the man, he would give them headrum without

doing anything more. That would make the woman his
wife in the eyes of the native law. But if he were desirous
of going through the remaining ceremonies in addition to
the headrum, he would send the trousseau, give a party to
his friends, and in the evening the friends of the lady would
accompany her to her husband's residence with lanterns not
dimly burning, and leave the wife with her husband to
complete the ceremony. The headrum is given to the father,
and in case of a slave to the master or mistress, as the case
may be. In the absence of the father, to any person standing *in loco parentis.* The party receiving the headrum
distributes it amongst his family, and in some cases amongst
his friends.

The law as to descent is from uncle to nephew, the eldest
son of the eldest sister taking, that is, where the party
dying does not make a will according to native notions.
But where there is a brother of the deceased uncle, he steps
in before his nephew.

Where there are freeborn in the house and slaves, the
country law is that slaves cannot inherit as long as there
are any of the blood surviving. They may inherit by
will, or, where the blood is under age, one may be selected
from the slaves to succeed. There is a vast distinction
between legitimate and illegitimate children known to
native law. If a man has children by a woman for whom
he pays no headrum, the children are not legitimate
according to native law, though they may become so by
their parents marrying. Children cannot succeed unless
under the will of the parent, or by express declaration of
all the family, given during the lifetime of the deceased.
Ancestral property cannot be willed absolutely as if it were
acquired property, but the last surviving member of a family
can dispose of it as he thinks best. If emancipated slaves
take advantage of their emancipation by leaving the family
and severing their connection, they have no right to the
property of the family, and whatsoever they acquire becomes
their own property. Those of the blood would be those

coming out of the womb of the head. All who issue from her are all of the blood. The children begotten by those of the blood are termed household children. The emancipation is useless unless you take the benefit of it. The grandchild of an emancipated slave would still be a slave, if he does not sever the connection. If there are two cousins, A and B (males), and A is a (*sic*) family, and there are issues of A with a slave in the house, and there are issues of B with an outsider, the issues of A would take in preference ; but if A and B are females, the issues will take equally— that is, the senior branch would take first. If a mistress takes a slave, and through that branch one child remains, he will take in preference to the descendants of the brothers of the mistress.

If one buys a slave, and that slave has a child, and he wishes to marry that child, he will give headrum to the mother. The exact ceremonies will not necessarily be followed. Cases are known in which the headrum is not paid. This might prejudice the issue of the blood. If a master has a child by a slave, and the master's sister has a child by an outsider, the sister's child will take in preference. Illegitimacy is no bar to issue of the female side as to succession.

The head of the family cannot dispose of any of the family property without the consent of the family. No qualification, excepting that of birth, is needed to be the head of the family, and this head must be from the female side.

By birth, I mean it must come from the blood, the seniority taking precedence. The father might be disposed not to regard the children by a slave for whom he paid no headrum, and in that case they would be prejudiced. The household children stand next in succession to those of the blood.

If the father does recognize the issue of a slave of his, that issue's rights are not the same as issue of a lawful marriage. The issue of the lawful marriage would necessarily succeed first.

If there are three sisters, A, B, and C, and A has a son lawfully born, who has a grandchild from a slave in the house, and B has sons and daughters, and C has a daughter, who marries outside and has a child, the children of B, with regard to the family property, would take first. But if A, B, or C has acquired property of her own, the line of descent of each must be extinguished before the property of the one can go to the other line.

Judgment for plaintiffs with costs.

Mr. Renner for plaintiffs.

Mr. Sarbah for defendant.

DE GRAFT *v.* ABBA MANSAH.

September 9, 1871.

Before CHALMERS, Judicial Assessor.

Marriage—Accounting—Second Marriage—Wife.

To show cause why you, having refused to live with plaintiff as his country wife, and having left his home, should not be ordered by this Court to pay him the sum of £40 12s. 7½d., the same being amount incurred by plaintiff on your account according to the custom of the country.

Chiefs: It is the practice for elder wife to be consulted by husband on taking " second wife." If husband takes a second wife without doing so, it is not cause for discontinuance of the marriage, but it brings dispute, and husband must give elder wife satisfaction.

Defendant being interrogated, states that she does not wish to continue marriage with plaintiff. Plaintiff is willing to renew and do such things, and pay satisfaction as may be appointed by the Court.

Remitted to Chiefs Thomson, Martin, Robertson, and Mr. Morgue, to receive from *Abba Mansah* for *De Graft* such of the articles given by him to her as may be serviceable, the value of which shall go *pro tanto* towards satisfaction.

Judgment for plaintiff, £30 10s.

KOFI SACKIE *v.* ACCOSUA AGAWA.

July 28, 1873.

Before CHALMERS, Judicial Assessor.

Marriage—Recovery of Consawment*—Liability of Mother-in-law.*

Recovery of the headmoney from defendant, whose daughter declines marrying plaintiff.

Chiefs : 1. When a man takes a woman as his wife, is it customary for him to pay a sum of money to her mother as a dowry ? Yes.

2. Is this dowry given as a " gift " to the mother, or can it, under any circumstances, be recovered back by husband ? It is recoverable in a case of dispute between husband and wife, which has led to a discontinuation of marriage. The money given as dowry by the husband does not always go to the mother alone, but also to the father, as well as the nearest relations. On a discontinuation of marriage, accounts are gone into between the husband and wife as to their separate expenses, and a balance is struck, which becomes payable by the one on which it lies. .

3. Can the mother be made liable to pay the lump sum of dowry, if it had been divided among others ? The application is made to the head of the family, who consults and acts with others.

4. If a woman deserts her husband, is her family liable ? Yes.

5. If a woman deserts her husband, can the husband claim any money from the mother-in-law which he has expended in maintaining her ? The family of the wife will be liable for all the property which the wife possessed when she left her husband, if supplied by the husband.

Judgment for plaintiff, Chiefs Attah and Mayan to settle matters of account in dispute between the parties.

HANNAH JONAH *v.* ADDACOO.

October 9, 1873.

Claim of £12 8*s.*, expenses incurred by plaintiff and her family during the illness and subsequent death of one Effua Marnan, wife of defendant and daughter of plaintiff.

Chiefs: A woman is a man's sweetheart, and not his wife, until he provides her family with rum or money as a substitute, when she becomes his wife.

Plaintiff charged the following:—

	£	s.	d.
Native Doctor	4	10	0
Medical Comforts	1	16	0
Coffin	1	7	0
Burial Ground	1	7	0
Grave Diggers	0	5	0
Funeral Obsequies	1	5	0
Silk Pillow	0	4	6
Cloth for Coffin	0	13	6
Midwife	1	0	0
	£12	8	0

Defendant said I sent the plaintiff 8 ackies in gold (£1 16*s.*) and a ring (2 ackies), and a gallon of rum, because I loved the deceased. That is more than is usual in this country.

JUDGMENT.

On account of the iniquitous charges made, I had intended to relieve the defendant from all payment; but under all the circumstances, I decree that the offer of the defendant be accepted. £2.

ADJUAH CHIBA *v.* AGOOWAH OF MOREE.

October 21, 1873.

Custody of Children—The Right of the Mother.

JUDGMENT.

No person has a right to detain a child from her family, and the plaintiff has had a right to demand the girl Accosuah ever since she went into defendant's possession, and the defendant has had no right to refuse to give her up nor to demand any money for doing so. The defendant seems to have treated this girl kindly, and to have kept her well; but, it must be remembered, she has had the services of the girl in her house working for her. I wish it to be distinctly understood that I refuse any payment to be made to the defendant as though the girl belonged to her as a slave; it will only be as compensation for the expenses the defendant has incurred in clothing her. Her services I consider an equivalent for her food. I order the girl to be given up to her family at once, and award £2 to the defendant to be paid by the plaintiff as compensation for the girl's clothing and expenses, which are not covered by the services given by the girl.

PATRICK JONES AND HARRIET JONES *v.* J. F. MENDS.

April 22, 1872.

Before CHALMERS, Judicial Assessor.

Breach of Promise of Marriage.

JUDGMENT.

I find that the defendant asked the plaintiff in marriage, and that his proposal was accepted by her and by her parents on her behalf. That the understanding was that a country marriage should at once be entered into, which should be converted afterwards into a marriage in the face of the Church. Find that no time was fixed for the second marriage; that there is no proof of the defendant having refused to fulfil this part of the agreement, and that he has not incapacitated himself from so doing by the contraction of any other lawful marriage. In these circumstances the cause of action is not sustained, and judgment must be for defendant. The country marriage, upon defendant's own statement, still continues, and the plaintiff is entitled to the privileges which belong to that relation.

JOHN DANIEL NEIZER *v.* E. P. DONTOH.

March 5, 1874.

Before JAMES MARSHALL, Judicial Assessor.

Breach of Promise of Marriage and Seduction—Measure of Damages— Custody of Child.

Chiefs Chiboo of Assin, Thompson, and Robertson.

If a man promises to marry a woman and breaks the promise, has the woman any remedy against him?

In our country, if a man wishes to marry a woman, he sends his friends to her parents and asks their permission to marry the woman. If they consent to give him the woman, and afterwards he refused to be married to her, there would be no penalty; palaver set. But if he had already provided the necessary things, as gold from 4 to 8 ackies, and some cloths, and some rum or money as a substitute, then there would be a penalty if the man refused to marry the woman. The penalty is that the man forfeits what he has provided, and if there has been connection between him and the woman, he has to pay money to the parents.

If there is a child, the man would have to make provision for the child. In such a case, the parents would be the plaintiffs.

If the man provides for the child, it belongs to him when it grows up, *i.e.* when fit to part from the mother, about four or five years.

According to the law of the country, if a woman is made enceinte by a man, her family ought to give the man notice of it in about two months after she became aware of it. Loss of service is no ground for compensation.

It is the custom in our country, that if a man has a daughter, and a man has connection with the daughter, the father may claim one ounce, and then, if the man wishes to marry her, he begins to provide the necessary money and other things, and to ask her parents. But if the parents do not wish the marriage, they can claim nothing but the one ounce. If the woman prove pregnant, the man should provide for her during her pregnancy.

If the man denies her being pregnant by him, the parents support her until after delivery, when the matter is decided by the appearance of the child. This is decided by the midwives.

In this case, our opinion is that the defendant should pay one ounce and the Court expenses, and that the father should attend until she is delivered, and that if it be then found the child is the defendant's, the plaintiff should have further claims on himself. If it be found not to be his child, the father is to have no claim.

JUDGMENT.

Verdict for plaintiff—compensation £5, and each side to pay its own costs.

MARSHALL *v.* DAWSON.
September 15, 1885.
Before HECTOR MACLEOD, J.

Maintenance of Illegitimate Child—Proper Person to sue—
Satisfaction—Measure of Damages.

Chiefs Sackey and Kofii Yammie.

The plaintiff claims £30, being amount expended on Margaret Boham before and after her confinement of the illegitimate child of which defendant was the father, and £50 for the maintenance of the child during minority.

Plaintiff is a person in *loco parentis.*

Curia : I find that defendant is the father of Margaret Boham's child.

The following questions were put to the chiefs by the Court :—Is the defendant liable for the medical expenses and . . . connected with the birth of this child.? Yes? Is the defendant liable for the maintenance of the mother during the seven months she was laid aside from work ? Yes. Is there any other expenses for which the defendant is liable ? Yes ; these are the midwife and other expenses attending the birth; and as the defendant does not wish to keep the woman, he ought to pay compensation, but only half what is usual, because she was not a virgin. We think perhaps £10 would be suitable. *Marshall* is the proper person to sue.

Curia : This is a case to be decided altogether by native law. I find that defendant must pay the following sums :—

	£	s.	d.
For Maintenance of Margaret Boham, seven months, at 20s.	7	0	0
Medical expenses during pregnancy	3	9	3
Fooshiw Tam	2	0	0
Midwife expenses of birth	2	17	3
Illness after in-lying	1	13	6
Compensation	10	0	0
Total	£27	0	0

Costs, £1 18s. 9d. ; Execution stay, one month.

SEY *v.* ABADOO.

July 7, 1885.

Before HECTOR MACLEOD, J.

Infants—Native Law—English Law.

Claim : £6, being rent for occupation of premises belonging to plaintiff.

Appellant (the plaintiff) admitted that the defendant is under twenty-one years, and argued—

(1) That the lodgings in this case were a necessity ;
(2) That judgment was against the weight of evidence ;
(3) The case should be decided according to native law.

Respondent not called upon.

JUDGMENT.

This case must be decided according to English law. The father of this infant told it that he had already provided lodgings for it. It was therefore unnecessary for the infant to enter into a contract for other lodgings; and the fact that Mr. *Sey* did not know that the infant was already supplied, is not material. Appeal dismissed, with 21*s*. costs. Decision to be enforced by Court below.

ASHON *v.* ATTA PENIN.

July 25, 1888.

Before Commissioner RAYNER.

Betrothed Woman—Seduction—Damages—Difference between Dowry and Consawment.

Plaintiff sued defendant for £3 12*s*., alleged as paid for headrum.* Facts proved. Defendant, while engaged by another man, was seduced by plaintiff, who was bound to pay, and did pay, all the expenses paid by this man on

* *Consawment.*

behalf of the woman. Plaintiff and defendant then lived together.

Held, *per* Chief Sackey. Plaintiff cannot recover what he thus paid. It was not headrum, but satisfaction money, and if the man had liked he could have still continued the marriage. Hence, as no headrum was paid or has been paid, the relation of husband and wife does not exist. Headrum is paid to family, not to outsiders.

ELMINA ASSIZES.

BOHAM'S CASE.

June 15, 1892.

Before FRANCIS SMITH, J.

In re *Boham and Hayford—Native Marriage—Marriage Ordinance No. 14, 1884—Caveat.*

In the matter of an intended solemnization of marriage between *Joseph Alfred Boham* and *Helen Mary Hayford*.

A *caveat* in this matter was entered against the issue of the Registrar's certificate for the solemnization of the said marriage by *Ambah Kortaba*. Parties accordingly summoned to attend this Court to be examined concerning the premises.

Ambah Kortaba, sworn: I live at Atchinm, near Elmina. I know *Joseph Alfred Boham*. He is married to me according to native law. I heard that he was going to marry *Helen Mary Hayford*, and I entered a *caveat* against the marriage. I wrote a letter to the Judge, saying I wish to withdraw the *caveat*, but I had been coerced to do so by the plaintiff. Boham married me long before he knew *Mary Hayford*. Of my own free will I do not wish to withdraw the *caveat*.

By the Court: It appearing from the evidence of *Ambah Kortaba* that she is married by native law to

Joseph Alfred Boham, who intends now to marry *Helen Mary Hayford,* it is ordered that the Registrar shall not issue certificate.

DUNCAN *v.* ROBERTSON.

April 30, 1891.

Before W. E. CLEAVER, A.J.

Claim by Person in loco parentis—*S.C.O.* 1876, *sec.* 19—*Illegitimate Child—Expenses of Confinement.*

This is an appeal by the defendant against an order of the District Commissioner, bearing date the 17th day of September, 1891, in which the appellant was ordered to pay the sum of £12 15s., being money expended by the respondent, Hannah Duncan, on Amba, her ward, before and after her confinement of a child of which appellant is the father.

Mr. *Eiloart* appears for appellant.

Mr. *Sarbah* appears for respondent.

Mr. *Eiloart* addresses the Court, and argues that—

(1) Native law should not apply to this case. He cites sects. 14 and 19 of Supreme Court Ordinance, 1876, and relies upon argument that respondent did not show that " substantial injustice " would be done by strict adherence to English law, appellant being a European and respondent a native.

(2) That if native law applies, it is contrary to natural justice and equity if it has been rightly interpreted.

(3) Respondent *in loco parentis,* and, therefore, a joint *tort feasor* with appellant.

Mr. *Sarbah* replies—

(1) English law is not applicable.

(2) Bastardy Act never enforced.

(3) Appellant not European.

Mr. *Sarbah* cites *Marshall* v. *Dawson.*

Judgment of Chief Justice MACLEOD. Summons framed in accordance with that judgment. He further argues:—

Affiliation orders not in accordance with practice of this Court. Respondent does not claim damages for tort; the action is for money expended. Respondent did not encourage connection, therefore native law alone applicable, and *Marshall* v. *Dawson* applies.

Mr. *Eiloart* replies, and states that affiliation orders might issue, which would give *Amba* right to claim money expended for confinement, and respondent had her remedies against *Amba*. *Cur. ad vult.*

April 30, 1891. Judgment: I am of opinion that this is a cause which should be decided by native law. The appellant is not known to be, and there is no evidence as to his nationality; but admitting that he is a European, I think that where a man enters into concubinal relations with a native woman, his liabilities (and rights, if any) should be determined by the same rules, whether or not that man is a European or a native. The position of the one should be no worse nor better than that of the other.

The case of *Marshall* v. *Dawson* (Cape Coast, vol. vi. 420) appears to be almost identical with this case. The summons appears to have been drawn with reference to that case, and the decision of the District Commissioner appears to be strictly in accordance with the principles laid down in that case. I have not lost sight of a point, I think an important point, and raised by counsel for the appellant, namely, the respondent's connivance, or, at least, tacit consent to the immorality of her ward; but even in this particular, the case of *Marshall* v. *Dawson* appears to be similar, though there was very little on that point, and the Divisional Court did not appear to attach much importance to the point.

I am bound by the decision in *Marshall* v. *Dawson*, and therefore I must dismiss this appeal with costs, which I assess at £1.

QUAMIE ASHON *v.* JOHN SNYPER.

November 26 and December 17, 1869.

Wife not liable for Husband's Debt—Private Debt—Family Undertaking.

Where the relatives of a person undertake to pay his liabilities in his lifetime, they are bound to fulfil their undertaking even should he die in the mean time.

Chiefs: When a man is married country fashion and dies in debt, it is his own relations who have to pay his debt.

During his lifetime he applies to his relations for advice. Sometimes they undertake the debt for him. But without such previous voluntary understanding, the relations would not be held liable. The debtor himself would be liable.

There is no obligation on wife to pay any part of husband's debt.

Judgment of native Court at Mankessim affirmed.

INKRUMA *v.* KANKAN.

July 16, 1885.

Before HECTOR MACLEOD, J.

Head of Family—Claiming Debt.

Quamina Dansu [*per* the Court]: Did your stool belong to Kankan? *A.*—No, it was my own; he has his. *Q.*—Had Kankan any authority or control over your stool? *A.*—He had. *Q.*—What was the extent of that control? *A.*—Whenever he sent me anywhere I went.

July 18, 1885 [*per* MACLEOD, in judgment]. *Inkruma's* answers to my questions lead me irresistibly to the conclusion that when the Dompin palaver was before Judge Smith nearly five years ago, Dansu took out a summons to recover, not only his own property, but also that of *Inkruma,* and such action on the part of the head of a

family is of constant occurrence in the Courts of the colony,
though generally in cases affecting the rights in land, for
cases of this kind are rare.

ECCUAH BIMBA *v.* EFFUAH MANSAH.

November 25 and 26, 1891.

Before HAYES REDWAR, Acting Judge.

Gift—Family Property—Emancipation Ordinance, 1874.

Plaintiff for herself and the family of Aggrey, late King
of Cape Coast, seeks to establish her title to that piece or
parcel of land situate at Amissa Akyre in Cape Coast, the
freehold of which the defendant unlawfully claims.

JUDGMENT.

In a case like the present, where an entirely different
mode of tenure prevails from anything known to English
law, and where the alienation and devolution of property
proceed on principles the exact origin of which must ever
remain, to a great extent, obscure, owing to the absence of
any authentic records of native law, except of those points
which have been litigated and decided in this Court, it is
necessary to proceed with great caution, and, where customs
are not strictly proved in evidence, or have received judicial
recognition, to follow as far as practicable the analogy of
English law, disregarding any customs not so proved or
sanctioned by this Court. Native law, when not incorporated
by judicial decision in the law of this land under the provisions of sect. 19 of the Supreme Court Ordinance, 1876,
must stand therefore on the same footing as foreign law,
and must be proved by the evidence of expert witnesses.

Now, in this case expert evidence is not called, and
reliance is placed upon certain decided cases which, although

not conclusive on the points in dispute, throw the strongest light on them, enabling analogies to be drawn.

In the first place, the plaintiff, by a form of action unknown to English procedure, claims to establish her title to certain land, the freehold of which it is alleged the defendant unlawfully claims. That this action is in no way connected with or similar to a proceeding under the Imperial Declaration of Title Act, 25 & 26 Vict. c. 67, is perfectly clear, since the proceedings under that Act are not hostile proceedings, and the Act itself is expressly confined in its operation to England. But the form of action employed is one which has been in use in this Court for many years, and although it is difficult to see why proceedings should be taken in this form rather than in ejectment or for the recovery of possession, the Court is in this case relieved from the responsibility of scrutinizing its own practice in this respect by the consent of counsel at the bar; and, indeed, in view of the general aspect of the case as it appears to me, it is unnecessary to consider the point which was raised by defendant's counsel and subsequently dropped.

Looking at the plaintiff's case first. She contends that her ancestor King Aggrey merely gave a permission or licence to build on this land, the freehold of which remained in himself and descends to his heirs; and further, that the house erected by defendant's ancestor having fallen, further permission was necessary before it could be rebuilt, and this permission not having been obtained, the licence to build was annulled according to native law, since the house had been improperly rebuilt. No expert evidence, however, was called on this point, and reliance was placed upon the case of *Lyall* v. *Dougan* decided in this Court. But upon a comparison of the facts of that case with the facts in this, it is at once clear that the case for the defendant in this action is of an entirely different character, and that the question which the Court has to decide in this case depends entirely upon the credit of the witnesses called on both sides to establish the respective parties' positions. The claim of the plaintiff is based upon a pedigree showing her descent from Aggrey, but she admits that she is the descendant of a slave of Aggrey; and the question was then raised as to how the status of a slave to inherit is affected by the Emancipation Ordinance, No. 2 of 1874.* Defendant's counsel has argued that, as slaves cannot legally exist, the conditions of their inheriting property are swept away with the status of slavery. But upon referring to sect. 3 of that Ordinance, a proviso is found that nothing in that Ordinance shall diminish or derogate "from the rights and obligations of parents and of children, or from other rights and obligations not being repugnant to the law of England, arising out of the family and tribal relations." The true construction of that section is, in my opinion, that slavery, being repugnant to the law of England, is abolished by that enactment, but that any privileges or rights which the slave may have had before the passing of the Ordinance are saved, provided those privileges or rights are not in themselves repugnant to English law. Obviously there is nothing "repugnant" in the idea of a slave child inheriting its parent's property, and I hold therefore that a slave can inherit, under any native law permitting him to inherit under circumstances clearly defined and proved to exist. Now, in view of the decision to which I have come in this case, after a careful consideration of the evidence adduced on both sides, it is unnecessary to express any opinion as to the validity of the plaintiff's claim as a house-born slave to inherit King Aggrey's property, because unless I entirely disbelieve the evidence led by defendant,

---

* On December 17, 1874, a proclamation was issued by the Government forbidding slavery and dealing in slaves, and declaring that all children born after November 7, 1874, were free. This proclamation concluded thus: "But it is not intended by any of the aforesaid laws or otherwise to offer inducement to any persons to leave any master in whose service they may be desirous of remaining, or to forsake the *Kroom* where they have been accustomed to inhabit, and that it is intended to permit the family and tribal relations to continue in all respects according as used and wont, except only that of slavery, and such customs as arise therefrom, and are thereon necessarily dependent."

the question narrows itself to this: "Was this land given or
sold by King Aggrey to defendant's ancestors or not?" If
it was so given or sold, whatever may be the plaintiff's
claim to inherit, this land in dispute forms no portion of the
inheritance. Now, the plaintiff sets up an admission by
Bosumafi that the land was not hers but King Aggrey's,
and that the house only was her property. Upon what
evidence is this alleged admission based? I dismiss at once
the evidence of Prah as being of no value. I further dismiss
the evidence of plaintiff on this point, as she admitted in
cross-examination that she derived her information from
what she had heard from Tawiah, and that she was not
present when the admission was made. The admission, then,
must rest on the evidence of Ayensoo, and looking at his
evidence generally, and the mode in which he stood the
ordeal of cross-examination, I am forced to the conclusion,
from the general tenor of his testimony and its improbability,
that this witness's memory is at least defective, and his
knowledge of facts even more defective. He is unable to
answer any questions outside the alleged admission, and is
unable to give any clear account even on the very points
on which his evidence is of importance. So much for the
admission; I will now address myself to the evidence
adduced by defendant.

She states that her ancestor Bosumafi went to Aggrey
and asked for land to build on; that King Aggrey said she
was welcome to do so, as he had married into her family;
that subsequently he said he would make a present of the
land in dispute to his wife Insafuabbah and her son by
him; that because of this the three sisters—Kabbribah,
Insafuabbah, and Bosumafi—sent, as a thank-offering to the
King, the sum of twenty dollars in cash and other valuable
presents, which at first he refused, but that he subsequently
accepted, at least some of them. Now, most of the witnesses
of these transactions are stated to be dead, and the defendant
is herself an aged woman; but she tells her story in a
straightforward manner, and comes through the ordeal of

cross-examination with the main points of her testimony unshaken. Counsel for plaintiff has commented on the absence of witnesses to corroborate defendant's statements ; but these things occurred a long time ago, and it may well be that witnesses older than defendant have passed away. She says she was about twelve or fourteen years of age at the time, and she is now an aged woman. Amongst other things, she says that the three sisters contributed to the sum of twenty dollars, and that Kabbribah dying first, Insafuabbah and Bosumafi occupied the house that was built ; that neither could dispose of the land given by the King, or the house built, without the consent of the others ; and that it passed to the survivor Bosumafi, and thence to her (defendant) as her niece. Further, that the King gave the land to them to do what they pleased with it. It would seem, therefore, that the land was held after the fashion of a joint tenancy with benefit of survivorship. Now, plaintiff's counsel asserted that such a tenancy was unknown to native law ; but he called no expert evidence on the point, nor did he refer me to any case in which it has been held that such a tenancy is unknown or impossible according to native law.

The cases cited in the arguments do not convince me either that this transaction was merely a permission to build on the land without affecting the ownership of the freehold, or that a licence to build is revoked by the falling of the house built upon it. Indeed, the cases, if anything, guide me by analogy to the conclusion that this transaction was really a gift of the land to defendant's ancestors as members of Aggrey's wife's family, and that there was no intention to limit or control the subsequent disposition of the lands so given. I am doubtful, indeed, whether the transaction was anything more than a gift. I hardly think it was, in the strict sense, a purchase, although valuable gifts are alleged to have been made to the King. I pass over minor points in the evidence, and deal only with the broad facts before the Court.

A further point was raised by plaintiff's counsel that, according to native custom, a gift is revocable. He has produced no authority for this proposition, and the cases cited tend rather the other way. In the absence of any authority as to the native law on this point, I feel myself bound to be guided by the settled principles of English law on cases of this kind, and to hold that although it may be doubtful whether this was a purchase, even as a voluntary gift it is good as against the grantor himself, and those claiming under him.

Under the circumstances, the judgment is for the defendant and with costs. Let the costs of the defendant of this action be taxed, and let the plaintiff pay to the defendant the amount of her costs when so taxed.

GABRIE *v.* AFFRANQUAH AND Q. EBERI.

September 3, 1844.

Criminal Conversation of Plaintiff's Wife by Eberi, Slave of Affranquah.

Plaintiff, Chief of Mansue.

Defendant admitted offence. Ordered to pay to plaintiff as damages 2 ozs. gold, a sheep, and a case of rum, leaving it optional with his master, *Affranquah,* either to pay this sum or give up his claim to defendant *Eberi.*

AMPIMA *v.* DEAMUA.

Anamabu, September 5, 1844.

Family Debt—Contribution by Members—Domestics.

In this case plaintiff complains that the house or family, of which the defendant and himself formed a part, had fallen into debt. That the defendant, who is a slave of the house, wants to get off from it, and leave the house, contrary to a law that prevails among the natives of this country.

Defendant pleaded that he was no slave of the house, but free-born ; that he wished to go away from the house, and leave it to plaintiff and the rest of the family.

It appeared, during a lengthened investigation, that defendant is a slave of the house, was born therein, and had ever since lived there ; that he had at one time assumed the highest place in the house, during which he had sold off several members of the family as slaves, among whom was the plaintiff's brother and the plaintiff himself also ; and that he had since redeemed himself and returned to the family.

Decreed that defendant must either redeem himself from the family or still remain there, and pay his part of the debt that has fallen upon it. His redemption money was fixed at 2 ozs.

ISAAC GODWIN JONES *v.* PRECILLA WARD AND OTHERS.

December 23, 1895.

Before FRANCIS SMITH, J.

Family Land—Sale—Ruined House—Compensation—Contribution.

Claim £137 2*s.* with interest, being expenses incurred for the preservation and security of the late Richard Sam's house and land, etc.

Judgment was reserved in this case, and parties having been duly notified to attend and hear it, have accordingly done so. The opinion of the Referees upon the native law involved is made part of the case.

JUDGMENT.

The plaintiff seeks contribution from the defendants for expenses incurred by him on the repairs of the family house during the lifetime of his mother. This house fell into ruins, and the Government bought the ruins and site for public purposes, the proceeds of which sale were shared between the plaintiff and defendants. This right, which is claimed by plaintiff, cannot be determined by English law, the act being a voluntary one on his part, and not performed at the request of any of the defendants. Native law must decide the matter, and (a) accordingly, at the close of the case, the facts were submitted by me to three native experts, and the native law bearing on the facts was asked of them, and these Referees have submitted their opinion thereon. These Referees are not unanimous in their opinion, two holding one view (b), and the third a different view (c). The two hold that the plaintiff has no right to contribution from the defendants, whilst the third that he has. They do not disagree, as it appears to me, upon the general question of the right of a member of a family to have the expenses he has incurred in repairing a family house, by which the value of that house has been enhanced, shared amongst the family when such a house is sold; but the two have applied the law to the circumstances of this case, whereas the third has stated the general law. That law, as stated by the two, commends itself to me, and is consistent with equity and good conscience. The circumstances are, that the Government did not buy any house, but the ground on which were the ruins of a house. Had there been a house, the value of the property would have been increased, the Government would have had to pay more, and in fairness and equitably, the member by whose means this increased value has been obtained should receive his expenses. The money so expended on the house was practically lost when it fell into ruins, and the purchase-money was really given for the ground on which no money had been expended. By native law, therefore, and in this case the Court is bound by the opinion of the majority, the plaintiff cannot claim contribution from the defendants. I must nonsuit the plaintiff, but in view of the circumstances of the case the nonsuit will be without costs.

Court House, Cape Coast, December 4, 1895.

(a) DEAR KING,—A matter has come before me touching the right of a member of a family to be repaid his expenses of helping to repair the family house.

The facts are briefly these: During the lifetime of a person whom we shall call A, B her son now and again contributed money and materials to repair the family house where the mother and other members, except the son, were residing. After the death of the mother the house fell into ruins, and lately the Government have purchased the ruins and site for public purposes. The money paid by the Government was delivered to the son and eldest daughter on account of the family, and that money was accordingly shared by the whole family, the son and eldest daughter receiving the greater share, and the others in proportion. The son now has sued the members of the family amongst whom the money has been shared for contribution towards the expenses he has incurred, and as the determination of his right depends upon native law, I shall feel obliged if you will advise me on the following points :—

Is the son entitled to have his expenses shared amongst himself and the other members of the family ?

Does the fact that when he incurred the expenses he was doing so at the request of his mother, prevent him from claiming contribution from the other members ?

Would each member who has expended money on the house have the right to contribution from the other members?

When the money is unequally shared, would each be only entitled to contribute to the extent of his share, or must the expenses be equally divided amongst the members?

With kind regards,

I am, dear King, yours faithfully,

(Signed) FRANCIS SMITH,

Puisne Judge.

To King Amonoo IV. of Anamaboe and to Chief Andoh of Elmina.

Cape Coast, December 8, 1895.

(c) DEAR SIR,—I have the honour to acknowledge receipt of yours of the 4th instant, and note contents of same having reference to a case that has come before you, and your honour requesting my opinion or advice on native points stated therein. In reply I beg to say—

1st. B the son of A is entitled to have his expenses made towards the house shared amongst himself and the other members of the family, and B should have one-third, and two-thirds for the other members of the family.

2nd. The fact that he made the expenses towards the house at the request of his mother does not prevent him from such a claim, unless he had the means from other property of the family.

3rd. Each member who resided in the house with the mother cannot have right to such contribution for his expenses unless he was not residing then in the house.

4th. The expenses should not be equally shared, but in proportion to the amount of his share of the money, or his age in order.

I have the honour to be, dear Sir,

Yours faithfully,

(Signed) AMONOO IV.

—————

Elmina, December 13, 1895.

(b) SIR,—Your letter of the 10th inst. to hand, in the matter touching the right of a member of a family to be repaid his expenses of helping to repair the family house.

That during the lifetime of A, B her son now and again contributed money and materials to repair the family house, where the mother and other members, except the son, were residing. After the death of the mother, the house fell into ruins, and lately the Government have purchased the ruins and site for the public purposes.

The money was delivered to the son and eldest daughter on account of the family, and that money was accordingly shared by the whole family, the son and eldest daughter receiving the greater share, and the others in proportion. The son sued the members amongst whom the money has been shared for contribution towards the expenses he has incurred:

1. Is the son entitled to have his expenses shared amongst himself and other members of the family? Answer: No.

2. Does the fact that when he incurred the expenses he was doing so at the request of his mother, prevent him from claiming contribution from the other members? Answer: Yes.

3. Would each member who has expended money on the house have the right to contribution from the other members? Answer: No.

4. When the money is unequally shared, would each be only entitled to contribute to the extent of his share, or must the expenses be equally divided amongst the members? Answer: No. When the family shared the money unequally, by giving the son and eldest daughter the greater share, the members of the family must have had their reasons for doing so; the expenses are not to be divided amongst the members.

If the house in question was standing, and inhabited by any member of the family, or was under rent, and, as above stated, the son did not live in the house, but kept it in repair, and the house and site were purchased, the son or any members of the family who kept the house in repair, as by his or their keeping the house in repair makes the estate more valuable, therefore he or those members of the family who did so, would have a right to have their expenses first deducted out of the amount so paid, and share it amongst them, according to the extent of his or their expenses made in keeping the house in repair, and the balance of the money divided amongst all the members according to their connection (in blood), as the land and ruins belong to them all.

I am, Sir,

Your obedient servant,

(Signed) G. E. EMINSANG,

Head Chief.

Elmina, December 9, 1895.

SIR,—I have the honor most respectfully to acknowledge the receipt of your letter, No. 362/341, of the 4th instant, and beg to reply you according to paragraphs as follows:—

1st. According to the native laws, one person out of a united family may purchase house or build one, but such house will always be recognized as his own house, and it will only be considered a family house after the death of its rightful owner, but the next of kin to the party who owns the house will be recognized the rightful owner of the house; and will be the only person to have supervision over the house; the next of kin will be entitled to take entire charge of the house, and to dispose same.

2nd. The families can assist the next of kin to make the necessary repairs towards a house, if the next of kin is not in a position to do so; but their doing so will not justify any family to have supervision over a house other than the next of kin; their rendering such assistance is only a matter of form to keep the reputation of the first owner of the house.

3rd. Answer to paragraph 3.

The son is not entitled to share any expenses he may have incurred towards the repairs of any building with families, except the families choose to render him any assistance; and in rendering such assistance, the families will not be justified to have any claim after, or have any supervision over the house.

In reply to paragraph 4.

The son will not in any way be entitled to claim any contribution he has from time to time incurred towards the repairs of the house.

In reply to paragraph 5.

The family will be entitled to demand any contribution from any family or the next of kin towards the repairs of any building, although some of the families may contribute more or less than the others.

In reply to paragraph 6.

I beg to inform you that the next of kin is entitled to have the greatest portion of the proceeds realized from any property or building sold; although the property or the house may be in a ruinous condition, and the families may, however, render assistance, but such assistance will not refer to either young or great, since the next of kin is supposed to be the rightful owner.

I have the honor to be, Sir,

Your obedient servant,

Chief QUACOE ANDORH his × mark.

Witness to mark and writer :   (Signed) K. B. ANDORH.

PROPERTY.

BAINEE v. MENSAH.

February 14, 1853.

Mortgage—Foreclosure.

Plaintiff states he is accused of owing money to defendant's family.

Defendant states that a man named Konfu Quabina pawned a man Bondon to Ewea for 1 oz. 2 acks. These three persons are all dead, and Ewea's family have claimed from Yarquah, of Bondon's family, the amount paid for Bondon. Yarquah, having no money, gave a piece of ground to Ewea's family that they should use it. The ground has been in possession of Ewea's family since it was given to them by Yarquah. This was about twenty years since. Plaintiff only laid claim to the ground last year.

It was decreed that plaintiff should pay the amount of Bondon's price, 1 oz. 2 acks. In default, the land to remain in possession of Ewea's family, of which *Mensah* is a member.

QUAMINA ATTOPEE *v.* EFFUA NANCY.

February 21, 1853.

Building Tenure—Resumption of Land—Compensation.

Plaintiff states that the defendant gave him some ground, and now, after building a house on it, she wants it back. He now wishes her either to pay the expense of building the house or to receive payment for the ground.

The defendant adopts the former.

By the Judicial Assessor :—

Referred to Dawson and Mr. Clouston to say how much it will cost plaintiff to build as good a house as is now standing.

ROBERTS *v.* AWORTCHIE.

June 23, 1884.

Before HECTOR MACLEOD, J.

Company Land—Building Tenure—What Interest attachable—Judgment Creditor—Interpleader.

Isaac Robertson : This house could not be sold by *Quamina Awortchie*, because it is the public meeting-place of the company, and, if it chose, the company could turn *Awortchie* out without compensation. When *Awortchie* dies this house will belong to Awortchie's children.

The native law is that the creditors of a trader can sell the materials of which such a house as *Awortchie's* is built, and the company has no right to prevent the purchaser from removing the materials. In the circumstances of this particular case, the judgment creditor has quite a right to sell *Awortchie's* house, and the No. 2 company has no right to prevent the purchaser from removing the materials of which the house is built; but the judgment creditor has no right to sell the land itself, which belongs to the company. If part of the swish that *Awortchie* used was on the land before in the shape of a ruined house, then such part is the property of the company, and cannot be sold; but such part of the swish as defendant brought there himself, the judgment creditor can sell, and the judgment creditor can sell the woodwork belonging to *Awortchie*.

JUDGMENT.

MACLEOD, J.: I have heard the case for the claimants. I think that an order ought to issue, releasing the land from attachment.

Further, I think the claimants are entitled to half the swish composing the house; but according to their own case, native law allows the judgment creditor to sell for the purpose of removal such of the material forming the house, as was brought there by the judgment debtor.

Claimants: *Ayea* and *Antoney*, on behalf of No. 2 company.

QUAMIN DANSUE *v.* TCHIBU-DARCOON AND CANCAN.

December 18, 1880.

Before W. J. SMITH, J.

Stool Property—Occupant abdicating to restore Stool and Appurtenances.

Assessors: When a person is placed on a stool and he wishes to leave the stool, everything he received with it and everything he had made by use of the property passing with the stool were taken from him, and he must go alone.

* * * * *

Defendant, King *Tchibu-Darcoon,* King of Assin : Have chiefs and captains under me. The chief of Fessoo is the head chief. The captain of Dompin is under Yow Fencee. *Cancan* succeeded to Yow Fencee. The stool of Dompin belongs to the stool of Fessoo. All the property belongs to the stool. When a captain dies, another is placed there, and if he leaves, the property is taken and given to the new captain. This was the reason the property at Dompin was taken, namely, because it belonged to the stool, and I ordered them to be taken because he said he was going to leave entirely.

* * * * *

Amonoo, of Anamaboe : When a captain leaves the stool, he must not take the property away if the stool is subordinate to another.

JUDGMENT.

That the property taken at the village of Dompin belonged to the stool, and was legally seized by the defendants when plaintiff declared his intention of leaving the stool and going to Akim.

ATTA *v.* SAM AND OTHERS.

June 8, 1882.

Before N. LESINGHAM BAILEY, Acting Chief Justice.

Family Property—Succession—Slaves—Emancipation Ordinance.

In this case plaintiff claims certain lands by right of succession to one Otuah, whom he alleges to have been tenant in fee or absolute owner. The defendants claim to be joint owners of the lands by right of succession to one Odabin. After hearing the evidence on each side, I and the

assessors also have come to the conclusion that the plaintiff
has established his claim, and that Otuah was tenant in fee
of the lands in question, and that the defendants were his
slaves. On the death of Otuah, more than fifteen years
ago apparently, the right of succession devolved on the
plaintiff, who, however, permitted his younger brother
Tebiah to exercise rights of ownership over the lands in
question. Tebiah employed one Akon, as caretaker, and up
to that time the defendants were, and considered themselves
to be, the slaves of Tebiah. After Akon had been placed
in possession by Tebiah, one of the defendants, *Incomah*,
lived with him (Akon) as his wife or concubine; but,
between ten and fifteen years ago, Akon was ejected by her
from the lands over which he had been placed in charge by
Tebiah.   Tebiah I hold to have been simply the licensee
of the plaintiff, and consequently his possession was the
possession of the plaintiff.

The adverse possession of the defendants, therefore, commenced within the time limited by the Statute of Limitations (supposing such statute to be in force in the colony), a
point which I am not called upon to decide.

The point urged by Mr. *Eminsang* for the plaintiff, viz.
that as slaves freed by the Ordinance of 1874, the defendants
were not entitled to succeed to the ownership of his lands
on the death of their master, does not arise. The master
died before the passing of the Ordinance, and by native
custom, they, as well as his other property, devolved upon
his nearest blood relation in the female line. The fact that
Tebiah and Attah were the nearest blood relations of Otuah
was not put in issue, nor were the points in any way
relied upon by the defendants, neither were the plaintiff's
witnesses cross-examined on this head. Judgment will
therefore be for the plaintiff, with costs.

COBINA ASHON *v.* COBINA BARNG.

November 27, 1891.

Before HAYES REDWAR, Acting Judge.

Mortgagor's Rights—Palm-oil Districts—Palm-wine—General Rate of Interest.

Plaintiff claims £50 damages for trespass on plaintiff's land, called Ottookrooban, and cutting down thirty-four palm-trees.

Mr. *Roberts* for plaintiff; Mr. *Sarbah* for defendant.

Plea—Not Guilty.

Hearing resumed at 9 a.m., pursuant to adjournment.

Mr. *Sarbah* proceeds and calls the following expert evidence :—

Kofi Sackie, sworn : I am a Chief of Cape Coast. I have been accustomed to be consulted as to native law by this Court since the days of Chief Justice CHALMERS. In the case of a pledge of lands, the pledgee works on the land, and if there are palm-trees on the land, the pledgee has a right to cut them down. As to the neighbourhood of Cape Coast and Anamaboe, I know that at Anamaboe they make palm-wine, but whether some of them make oil I don't know. As to Cape Coast, they only make palm-wine there. In a palm-wine district the pledgee has the right to cut the palm-trees. In cutting the palm-trees the pledgee is not accountable to the pledgor. The pledgor's previous consent is not necessary to cut down the palm-trees. In the Fanti country the pledgee is not to account to the pledgor for the use of the land or of a man who is pledged. This is a universal custom in the Cape Coast district.

[By the Court.] It is the custom of the whole Fanti country. Before the pledging is made, the custom* must be explained to the pledgor.

* The word "custom" by interpreter objected to by defendants' counsel, who said that it should be interpreted as "matter."

[Examination continued.] Before the land is pledged, the pledgor tells the pledgee, "I am going to pledge my land to you." Then the pledgee says to the pledgor, "I am going to take your land on these conditions."

[By the Court.] The conditions must be agreed on. There are some lands that have no palm-trees, and on those lands it is agreed that the pledgee should work thereon till the loan is paid. On lands which have palm-trees producing wine, the agreement is that the pledgee has a right to cut the palm-trees for wine in lieu of interest. Being the law of the country, this is explained and agreed to before the pledging is completed. Whether this law is explained or not, the pledgee has a right to cut the palm-trees. I have never known a case in which pledgor has claimed an account from pledgee.

By the Court: If the pledgee takes from the land the amount of his loan and interest, is he entitled to continue cutting down the trees till he is paid ?

Witness replies " Yes."

[Examination continued.] I know one Inkrumah, and of a dispute between him and some one about land which had been pawned for years.

Dankin's land is situated in the Anamaboe district. The "conditions" I have mentioned before must be mentioned to both pledgor and pledgee. If the pledge be of land in a palm-oil district, there must be an arrangement that the pledgee shall take the palm-oil from the nuts. Where palm-oil is made, there is no cutting of trees for making wine for sale ; the trees are only cut for wine for the labourers. No permission is necessary to cut down palm-trees for him for labourers.

Not re-examined.

Cudjoe Imrah, sworn : I am Chief of Cape Coast, and I was once linguist at the King of Anamaboe's Court. I hold Court now and decide cases. Supposing a man wants to raise money and borrows on the security of his land, there is native law on the subject. When the pledgor pledges land to the pledgee, and when there are palm-trees on the land, it is arranged that he is to cut the palm-trees.

[By the Court.] The arrangement is on the basis of a native law. By the law it is so, but the pledgee is to be told of this. It is not necessary to tell the pledgee, inasmuch as he has taken your money, he has a right to take the crops and cut down the palm-trees.

[Examination resumed.] Interest is matter of arrangement. There is a legal rate on all the Fanti Coast; the rate is 50 per cent. Sometimes the lender is asked to take less than this rate, and sometimes he foregoes interest altogether. I have done that myself. At Anamaboe the pledgee has a right to cut palm-trees for wine. In a palm-oil district, you have to ask the pledgor for permission to make oil, because palm-oil is considered more valuable produce than palm-wine. In a palm-oil district, the pledgor's permission is not necessary to enable the pledgee to cut down palm-trees for wine for labourers. The native law of pledging is applicable to palm-oil districts as well as palm-wine districts; but, as I have stated, an arrangement also is made. The arrangement sometimes is that the pledgee charges no interest, in which case he is entitled to take the palm-oil; and sometimes it is arranged that the pledgee takes interest and goes shares with the pledgor in the proceeds of the sale of the produce of the land. In palm-wine districts, sometimes it is arranged that the pledgee is only to fell a certain number of trees for the wine, and that goes as a set-off against the debt. Where this arrangement is not made, the pledgee has a right to fell the trees to any amount until the debt is paid.

Cross-examined by Mr. *Sarbah*.

A pledgee advances £4, no arrangement is made as to interest, the boundaries are shown. In such a case the pledgee has a right to cut the trees to any amount.

[By the Court.] This Law is well known in the Anamaboe and Cape Coast districts.

By the Court: Upon a careful consideration of the

expert evidence, I find that by a preponderance of testimony the custom of cutting down the palm-trees by a pledgee until the debt is repaid is clearly and satisfactorily proved, and that therefore the plaintiff's claim for damages in trespass fails, as the defendant had a legal right to do what he had done, and which is the subject of this action.

The judgment must be for the defendant and with costs, to be taxed.

ABBAN v. SAGO.

January 24, 1883.

Before QUAYLE JONES, Acting Judge.

Emancipation Ordinance—Tenure-service.

Per QUAYLE JONES: I find that the land in question is the property of the plaintiff, and that defendant and his ancestors occupied as slaves in the first place, and since the abolition of slavery, on an implied contract of fulfilling the services and bearing the responsibilities which would have devolved on them as slaves. This being so, as long as defendant fulfilled these services and bore these responsibilities, the plaintiff would not have been entitled to recover the land in dispute. But the defendant having refused to continue to perform such services and bear such responsibilities, ceases to have any interest in the land, and plaintiff is entitled to recover the same.

Judgment for plaintiff.

ACCUFUL v. MARTEY.

December 22, 1882.

Tenant—Family Land—Failure of Rent—Adverse Possession.

JUDGMENT.

I think it is clearly proved that the lands in question were originally Etsien's, and by the native law land descends by the female line to the children of the owner's sister.

Donkum was Etsien's son, or rather one of his sons, and was permitted at his father's death to occupy the land together with the other children, paying a portion of the produce to Etsien by way of rent. This permission was continued to Abocue's children, among whom was *Martey* the defendant; but for thirty years no rent had been received from the defendant. I cannot, however, bring myself to hold that the defendant's possession was adverse possession. I feel quite clear that the defendant was well aware of the tenure under which he held, and that he was in fact permitted by native custom to receive and cultivate the land, but had no right of ownership in it.

KOFI AMONOO *v.* ADJUA ABAKUMA.*

June 7, 1871.

Before CHALMERS, Judicial Assessor.

Mortgage—Redemption—Intermediate Profits—Accounts closed.

To render payment to plaintiff of the value of the palm-wine, yams, and other produce of a certain land, known as Soldofoo, which proceeds you have unlawfully retained and converted to your own use for the last six years, and which plaintiff estimates at £97, or thereabouts.

JUDGMENT.

In this case the plaintiff claims £97, being the value at which he estimates the use and profit had by the defendant from the lands at Soldofoo, which, by proceedings in 1865, before the Mayor's Court, and again recently in this Court,

---

* *Incroma v. Murmoon*, April 13, 1882, before Lesingham Bailey, C.J., the Assessors, Chiefs Robertson and Botchi laid down the Customary Law thus : " No right of possession by a mortgagee could vest the ownership of mortgaged lands in such mortgagee. No length of even adverse possession would entitle a mortgagee to oust the claim of the mortgagor, the mortgage-debt having been satisfied.

it has appeared, were held by the plaintiff and his ancestors in pawn for a loan made to the ancestors of the defendant. It appears that by the custom of the country a creditor who holds land in pawn is entitled to the use and produce of the land as well as the interest of the money borrowed. I must remark on this arrangement, that it gives a very large advantage to the lender over the borrower, where the land, as in the present case, is of considerable value; and this consideration makes me, I confess, the less favourable to such a claim as is now made—to the effect, at least, of inducing me to inquire somewhat strictly that the circumstances which are necessary to sustain the claim should have been thoroughly fulfilled.

It appears from the evidence that during the six years which constitute the period to which this claim relates there has been a joint use of the land by the people of the King of Anamaboe and the defendant's people. This shows that what the defendant was doing was perfectly well known, yet no steps were taken on the King's part to exclude her or her people. All that was done was that on some occasions the person who says he was in charge for the King of Anamaboe, asked persons who were working on the land to account to him for what they took. The names of such persons were not taken, nor is there in strictness any distinct proof that they were sent by the defendant, though she has not disputed this. It is true that for a year Kuow Saman, while occupant of the stool, took possession of the land, driving away, it seems, defendant's people. After this he was deposed and left the land, and the present King succeeded, and soon after his succession, the defendant made payment of the sum found due by the Mayor's Court. Unfortunately the payment miscarried and she obtained no valid discharge, but it was made in complete good faith on her part; and after so doing, she was, in the absence of notification to the contrary, well entitled to "*think*" she had a good right to the use of the land. It does not seem that any such notification was given to her; on the contrary, the joint use of the land by the plaintiff's and her people, appears to have continued without the plaintiff making any exclusive claim; neither did the plaintiff apply to her for payment for the 8 ozs. found due by the Mayor's Court, which, though paid by the defendant, he had not received. I must further state that the actual value received by the defendant from the land is left a good deal conjectural, the witnesses for the plaintiff, who lived on the land and who speak to produce removed by people supposed to belong to the defendant, giving nothing but very indefinite statements on this subject. Taking all these considerations into account, and taking into account also that a very considerably increased amount of redemption money for the land has been assessed by the Court without any mention being made by the plaintiff of this claim, which redemption money has been paid; and taking into account also the clear opinion stated by the chiefs, that after a land has been redeemed, nothing should be said about intermediate profits, which I think is a right and just opinion, I must advise the King of Anamaboe that this claim should not be sustained.

Judgment therefore for defendant.

***

ECCOBANG v. HAGAN.

May 29, 1885.

Before BRANDFORD GRIFFITH, A.J.

Trespass—Long Possession without Rent of any Kind—Notice.

Referees: Mr. Sarbah and Chiefs Essell and Sacky.

Q.—By the Court: The owner of land gives permission to a person to cultivate a portion of the land; this person and his heirs continue cultivating the land for upwards of forty years, paying no rent and giving no produce to the owner; by native law, does this prolonged possession destroy the title of the original owner? Referee: I say and affirm that such prolonged possession does not destroy the title of the original owner.

It makes no difference if the permissive occupier inter-marry with the niece of the original owner.

The original owner can re-enter upon the land at any time. The original owner could not enter on the land and take the produce at any time without consent of the occupier.

The original owner cannot enter on the land at any time and "clear away bush"* without giving prior notice to the occupier that he required the land.

The owner of the land might cut down palm-trees on this land at any time, as they either ought not to have been planted by the occupier without the previous consent of the owner, or they were there at the time the land was lent.

JUDGMENT.

The Court finds that the portion of the land called Oduassie, claimed by the plaintiff, is held by the plaintiff at the will of the defendant, and that the defendant before entering on the land gave notice thereof to the plaintiff, and that the defendant by entering on the land after such notice and clearing the land and cutting palm-trees thereon did not commit a trespass.

GRANT *v.* AMISSAH.

November 20, 1883.

Before N. LESINGHAM BAILEY, Esq., Chief Justice, and Mr. Justice MACLEOD, Puisne Judge.

Family Land-building Tenure—Adverse Claim—Ejectment.

This was an appeal against a judgment of Mr. Justice MACLEOD for the defendants on November 3, 1883, in an action brought by the plaintiffs to recover possession of a

----

* ["Clear away bush" means to till or cultivate the land.—ED.]

piece of land alleged by them to have been granted to one of the plaintiff's predecessors in title, one *Charlotte De Graft*, and subsequently conveyed to the plaintiffs.

Mr. *Maxwell* was for the appellants, and Mr. *Williams* for the respondents.

Mr. Justice MACLEOD delivered a written judgment as follows:—

Upon the 15th of November, 1883, I gave judgment in the Court below for the defendants, and it is therefore not easy for me to view the case from the standpoint which ought to be taken by a Judge of Appeal. I have, however, listened with care and attention to the arguments addressed to the Court by the counsel for the appellants, and I still remain personally satisfied with my judgment of November 3, 1883; but I desire to add a word or two regarding the interpretation which I have thought it right to put upon the certificate of the measure of land granted to *Charlotte De Graft*, as that certificate appears upon page 16 of Vol. I. of the Register of Town Lots, for according to my views of the case upon that interpretation depends the issue.

The certificate begins by saying that an actual measurement has been made of a lot of land upon the Saltpond Road on the one side, but it does not say that the lot upon or on the other at the back. It simply narrates that this second road is at the back of the lot. That, therefore, does not necessarily mean that the lot extends from road to road. From the description so far, it may so extend or may not. Next follows a statement of the actual measurement made of the lot; and it is declared to be (in the direction with which we are concerned) 120 feet. Then, for the first time, we get something clear and distinct; 120 feet never change. I allowed this clear and distinct measurement to control and regulate the previous general description, and in doing so I think I adhere to the ordinary canons of interpretation. In a word, I held that in that direction *Charlotte De Graft* had only a right of 120 feet, and through her father she transferred her rights, which, through Mr. *Grant*, senior, and *Enchey*, came into the ownership of the present plaintiffs. There is nothing to show that Mr. *Grant* got from Mr. *De Graft* anything more than his daughter possessed. If I am right, so far, the plaintiffs have only established a right to 120 feet from the Saltpond Road. Now, does the Saltpond Road end at the ditch or at a wall? That is an important question, for if it ends at the wall, part of *Mary Amissah's* house stands upon the 120 feet, whereas if it ends at the ditch, the house is clear of the 120 feet.

Under these circumstances, the first occupants (of whom we know anything) of the land in dispute are the defendants, and I think they ought to remain there till some one with a better title makes his appearance.

The Chief Justice said that it was with considerable regret and great hesitation that he felt compelled to differ from the judgment just delivered, and from that of the Court below. Still, while recognizing the great pains and care which had been bestowed by the Court below upon this case, he could not bring himself to interpret the certificate No. 15 (upon the construction of which the whole case was admitted to turn) in the way that Court had interpreted it. . He then read the certificate, and said that although the description of the land granted was not such as would have been employed by a lawyer, it appeared to him sufficiently clear.

He could not but interpret the words as meaning that the plot of land lying between the Saltpond Road on the south and the Napoleon Road on the north was granted by the then Lieutenant-Governor on December 31, 1850, to the plaintiff's predecessor in title, *Charlotte De Graft*.

It is true that the certificate goes on to say that the land had been measured from north to south, and was certified to be 120 feet; but that appeared to him to be merely a matter of description, which could not affect the operative portion of the grant which, if his construction was correct, gave the land between the two roads above mentioned to the grantee.

He observed that the Court below had suggested that the roads may have been altered since the date of the grant, but there was not a tittle of evidence that he could see in support of such a suggestion. The Court below had also viewed the land, and found that by measuring, not from the Saltpond Road, but from a point some 27 feet to the north of it, 120 feet was left between that point and the Napoleon Road, and that the land claimed in this action would thus be excluded.

But why measure from that point ? Why not take a point 27 feet to the south of the Napoleon Road, which would still leave only 120 feet of land, but would include the land in question ? He considered that the probabilities were also in favour of this view. The defendants had, on first squatting on the land in question, asked permission to do so from the plaintiffs or their predecessors in title. Then, too, why should the original grantee have asked for 120 feet from any given point off the road instead of from the road itself ?

On the whole, and looking at the terms of the certificate No. 15, he felt bound to dissent from the judgment of the Court below.

Ordered : That the judgment of the Court below be reversed, and that the plaintiffs do recover possession of the land in dispute. Costs to be appellants'.

CUDJOE QUAY v. AYWOODSUAH.

July 28, 1871.

Before CHALMERS, Judicial Assessor.

Sale—Trimma or Earnest-money—Ceremonies—Burthen of Proof.

Per Chief Kofi Yammie : If a mother was purchased by her husband and she had children, except they belong entirely to their father's house, they would be entitled to succeed to his property. They are his slaves. He could

not sell his own children except the son were unruly. If
uncle pays money for niece, he pays as one of same house,
and the child on whose account the money is paid lives in
the house. When I say on account of the child, I contem-
plate that the father's necessities would have (if he had not
got the advance from the uncle) compelled him to pawn the
child to a stranger. The child would be a pawn, so that it
might be redeemed whenever money could be raised; or
if not, then would continue living in the house. If the
brother who advanced the money should predecease the
borrower, the child comes back into its father's hands,
through his succession to his brother. Re-interrogated,
states that the child in his uncle's hands would be a slave.
Re-interrogated—white man's palaver is very difficult,—
states that the child would be pawn to his uncle. A man
cannot owe a debt to himself. When a mother belonged to
another family, and you received the mother for money,
the son has nowhere to go to, is your property entirely.
Brothers, if of different mothers, would be of different
family; if of same mother, of same family. Brothers who
were of different family, would not succeed to each other.

JUDGMENT.

The claim of the plaintiff to hold Adjuah Aywoodsuah
and her relatives as slaves depends for its validity on the
absolute sale of Aywoodsuah to Quamin Ahin; it lies on
the plaintiff to prove this, and without it he has no case.
His proof is dependent on the statement made by the
mother of the witness Kofi Ahin (who is now dead). That
witness certainly alleges that the information of his mother
was that an absolute sale had taken place; but no accompanying circumstances are stated, such as the *payment of
earnest*, or of the *ceremonies denoting sale*. Moreover, an
absolute sale is improbable; if the advance had been received
from a stranger, it is much more likely that the father
would have pawned the child than sold it absolutely, especially for the comparatively small sum of 1 oz. 2 ackies; and

from the evidence of Chief Yammie, before whom the case formerly came, it does not seem that the fact of the sale was at that time stated to him. His decision seems to have been based on the fact (that) merely that money was paid by Quamin Ahin on account of the child, coupled with an assumption that on being transferred to him it passed into a different family from its father's. But this last was obviously a mistaken supposition, as appears from Quacoe Ahin (as is stated by both parties) having succeeded to the property of Quamin Ahin on his death. I consider, on the whole, that the burden of proof has not been satisfied, and I must dismiss the claim to hold the defendant as a slave.

Judgment is therefore for defendant.

JOHN HALM v. REBECCA HUGHES.*

November 15, 17, and 19, 1869.

Before CHALMERS, Judicial Assessor.

Interpleader—Family Property—Gift.

To show cause why you shall not be ordered by the said Court to give up possession of the house known as Bosoo's house, seized and taken possession of by the Bailiff Minew, by virtue of a writ of *fi. fa.*, issued from the said Court in *Re Hughes* v. *Halm* at your instance, the said house being the property of the said plaintiff and his said brothers and sisters, to wit, Lucy Halm, John Holdbrook, Thomas Hughes, Josiah Martin, Elizabeth Hughes, William De Graft, and the children of *John* and *Lucy Halm.*

---

* From the evidence it appears that Mr. *Hughes* bought from Thompson Bosoo's house, which was then in possession of his nephew, Mr. Thompson, by right of inheritance. *Hughes* did not take possession, but gave it to his married sister, Mrs. *Halm*, who took possession with her children, and made such repairs as were necessary.

Mr. *Hughes*, the donor, spoke to the donee, his sister, about her quarrels with his wife and children; told her, " I do not like it—there is that house for you," pointing towards Bosoo's house. Donor did not mention the children.

Chiefs : 1. A family house is when a person had an ancestor and that ancestor died, he inherited the property and the ancestor's house, such house is called family house.

2. A house would also be called a family house if it was built from the proceeds of inherited property.

3. A family house descends to the heirs in succession ; the succession is by the mother's side.

4. Owner is not at liberty to sell family house.

5. The next succeeding members of the family would oppose him, and if he persevered, would turn him off the possession, saying, " you are likely to ruin this house."

6. A person who has not inherited, however rich he may be, cannot constitute his house a family house.

7. If a family house should be sold to a stranger it would cease to have the qualities.

8. Under some circumstances a brother might be bound to provide a married sister with a house, *i.e.* if she and her husband were poor and he had means, and also to keep it in repair.

9. Such ·a house would be considered a family house. The sister would leave children who must inherit the house. The sister could not sell the house.

10. This form would be used in making over such a house. The donor must say : "I dash this, or give it to you."

11. When a house is presented to a sister, it belongs also to the children and descendants. (This in answer to question, if it is necessary in the gift to make express mention of the children.)

12. If the sister is not poor, and the brother, nevertheless, gives her a house, that also would be a family house.

13. Could the house be seized for the sister's debts ?

When a brother made a present of a house to his sister, knowing that she had children, but when there was debt incurred by the family or debt incurred by the sister, it would not follow that the debt should be paid, and she must consult with the children : "there is this debt which I have incurred, let us consult how we can contribute towards its payment." If the family could contribute, well and good. If they did not, and the mother proposes to sell the house, the house would be sold.

14. But if the children did not consent ? Then the mother could sell the house.

15. If children did not consent to their mother's making away with the house, they must pay the debt, or work for it.

16. If neither mother nor children were willing to sell the house, what would the creditor do ?

The mother and children must pay the debt.*

17. If house is not occupied, could the creditor take possession for his debt without consent of the mother and children ?

The creditor could not.

JUDGMENT.

November 19, 1869.

Find that the house claimed and known as Bosoo's house, was constituted a " family house " to Mrs. *Lucy Halm* and her family.

That such a house is not liable to execution for debt. Therefore find for the plaintiff in this summons.

Order the execution to be withdrawn.

* Creditor could originally in such a case put the debtor and her children in logs, panyarr any of them or their family till debt is paid, or sit dharna.—ED.

SAMUEL TOKOO *v.* KWOW ASIMA.

January 26, 1870.

Before CHALMERS, Judicial Assessor.

Interpleader—Family House—Debt.

Per Samuel Christian : The house being a family house, it would not be seized for debt. Whole family must concur in sale. The present members of the family may agree to put away the house.

When a man gives his whole property for his debt, I understand it to mean his own—not family property.

January 28, 1870.

Chiefs : It is always the case, when a member of a family has a debt and the debt is known to the whole family, and they all consent and speak on behalf of the debtor and give security for the debt, it would become necessary for the family to part with present. The family are not responsible, having made no agreement to be so.

The defendant should have ascertained clearly from plaintiff what the property consisted of, whether a part of it was family property. If he understood plaintiff to mean that the house was part of the property given in security, he would not attach it without intimation to the family and their consent.

Failing to do this, it is not to be understood that the family house was included.

The land or the house in question is known as a family house. There is no division; it is all one. It could not pass for the debt of one member.

MARY BARNES *v.* CHIEF QUASIE ATTA.

July 17, 1871.

Before D. P. CHALMERS, Judicial Assessor.

Property attached to Egua (stool)—Debt of Deceased Chief—Liability of his Family—Alienation.

The claim of the plaintiff is that the land claimed by her was conveyed to her late husband by Kofi Koomah, in satisfaction of a debt due first by Quacoe Atta, afterwards by Quacoe Ennoah, who had both been occupants of the stool now held by Chief *Atta*.

The facts stated on behalf of the plaintiff are that Quacoe Atta, whilst King of Cape Coast, owed a debt to Mr. and Mrs. *Barnes;* that Quacoe Ennoah succeeded him, undertook his debt, and also contracted some further debt of his own; that on the death of Ennoah, Kofi Koomah, who was his uncle, was applied to for payment, and having no money at command to meet the claim, gave this land, which was accepted by Mr. and Mrs. *Barnes* as equivalent. There is a discrepancy in the statements of plaintiff and defendant in regard to the acquisition of the land; plaintiff says it was purchased by Quacoe Atta and descended to Ennoah; defendant, that it was purchased by Ennoah; and this view is best borne out by the evidence, although not of material bearing on the case at issue.

In order to the validity of the transfer, it is necessary that Kofi Koomah should have been in a position in which he had power to put away the property belonging to the stool. He was not regularly in occupation of it, and there is some dispute whether he was fully, or to what extent, in charge of its affairs at the time; but assuming that he was, *I apprehend that not even the regular occupant could alienate property without some concurrence by the people of the stool who have an interest in it, and are usually consulted on such a matter.* Here there was not only no concurrence, but there is evidence of dissent. The presents which inferred indebtedness were not accepted, but expressly refused by the people, on which Kofi Koomah took upon himself to hand over the land on his own authority, in so doing, no doubt intending the best interests of the stool. Yet, I apprehend it was not an act binding on the stool, so as to give a valid title to the land that is now in the defendant as occupant of the stool. He will, however, be responsible for the debt of his predecessor on its amount being proved.

Judgment for the defendant.

QUAMINA AWORTCHIE *v.* CUDJOE ESHON.

March 7, 1872.

Before CHALMERS, Judicial Assessor.

Trespass on Land—Sale of Family Property—Rescission of Sale.

Chiefs: When a man is head of the family and he has to sell land in case of debt having arisen in the family, is it necessary that he inform the members of the family and get their concurrence before the land could be sold ?

If the purchaser know that the land he had to purchase was a family land and the man from whom he was purchasing it was the head of that family, he would not make the purchase from the head without requesting him to get the concurrence of his family. And if he paid his money to the head of the family without this, his money was considered lost, in respect he was fully aware that the land was family land.

If he did not know it, it would be that he was a stranger, and he would get back his money from the head of the family.

Interrogated: Whether any limit of time within which family must interpose if they desire to set aside a sale ?

There is no limitation of time—even after lapse of time.

Interrogated: How consent should be signified ?

It would be necessary for all the members of the family to meet and discuss, and if there were land to be sold, all the members would meet and get strangers to be witnesses, and family would concur for payment of the debt: as many members as could be got should represent the family. When such meeting and discussion has once been had, it remains good; it would be proved by the strangers who were witnesses.

JUDGMENT.

Sale set aside, and Quamin Tawiah, who sold the land, ordered to restore to *Quamina Awortchie* 5 ozs., the amount he had received.

FULL COURT REPORT.

QUASIE BAYAIDEE *v.* QUAMINA MENSAH.

March 27, 1878.

Sale of Family Land—Impeachable Title—Possession—Improvements.

The plaintiff here seeks to recover from the defendant a piece of land called " Odoomassie," the possession of which, he says, the defendant has unlawfully deprived him. The judgment of the Court below was, that the plaintiff should recover the land, against which judgment the present appeal is brought.

It appears from the evidence that *Bayaidee* purchased the land from Kofi Aigin for the price of 1½ preguans; that Kofi Aigin was the owner of the land; that his purchase took place fourteen years ago, as plaintiff states, and in any case, a very considerable number of years ago ; that upon purchase *Bayaidee* entered into possession of the land and cultivated it, and that his possession was not disturbed until seven months before he brought the suit in September last.

The ground on which the appeal was maintained was that

the land was family land ; that Kofi Aigin, although the occupant of the stool, could not make a valid sale of the land alone, and that one of the members of the family, Eccua Assabill, protested against the sale at the time it was being effected. Now, although it may be, and we believe it is the law, that the concurrence of the members of the family ought to be given in order to constitute an unimpeachable sale of family land, the sale is not in itself void, but is capable of being opened up at the instance of the family, provided they avail themselves of their right timeously and under circumstances in which, upon the rescinding of the bargain, the purchaser can be fully restored to the position in which he stood before the sale.

This is obviously not the case, whereas here the purchaser has possessed for a series of years an undisputed ownership—has cultivated and improved the land, and has established a home upon it.

We are of opinion that whatever right of impeaching the sale the family possessed is barred by their acquiescence and the plaintiff's continued course of undisturbed possession.

And we order that the judgment of the Court that he should recover his land be affirmed, with costs of this appeal.

ABROBAH v. CHIBOO.

January 26, 1883.

Before QUAYLE JONES, Acting Judge.

Land—Sale by Slave—Master's Consent necessary.

Per Robertson : A slave has no power to sell his master's land without his master's permission. A slave does not inherit land from his ancestors. If a man sold land to bury his mother, that would show he was a freeman, because, if he were not, the master would have to defray the funeral expenses.

The leave a slave must have to sell such land is not a mere consent, but a formal consent given in the presence of and with the approval of his master's family.

Judgment for defendant.

DADDIE *v.* QUEATEABAH.

February 22, 1884.

Before HECTOR MACLEOD, J.

Family Property—Unauthorized Alienation—Mortgage—Forfeiture of Interest.

A member of a family who, without the knowledge and consent of the other members, encumbers the family property, forfeits thereby any right or interest which he or she may have had in it.

Calling on defendant to show cause why she should not be ordered by the Court to deliver to plaintiffs their family houses which she had, unknown to the plaintiffs, mortgaged to one J. W. Sey, and which were advertised to be sold.

Defendant admitted that, unknown to plaintiffs, she mortgaged the three houses to Mr. Sey; she also admitted they were family property, that she had no right thus to mortgage the houses, and that she was not one of the elderly members of the family.

Daddie, plaintiff, said as follows: I knew nothing of the debt which defendant incurred to Sey. I am not aware that any member of our family knew of the debt. The first intimation which I had of this debt or mortgage was the notice of sale posted in the houses. When I asked *Queateabah* about it, she told me she had incurred a debt to Sey, who married her daughter, and that she hoped to be dealt easily with. She said she had gone to Sey with her sister Fosuah and her daughter, Sey's wife. There was no family debt; it was *Queateabah's* private debt, contracted without our knowledge. *Queateabah* is a member of our family, and if there had been any family debt, we would all have contributed to its payment. She told us she had incurred this debt about four years ago. We have had no interview with Mr. Sey about this, because it was not our palaver. Ambah Amissah, who is sick, is the present head of our family, and she was appointed our head. Defendant is not the head of our family, neither is she second in the family. Ganbah is next to Amissah. Our family knew nothing about the mortgage. We knew nothing about her doing so until we saw the notices for sale. I represent the family in this action. Fosuah is defendant's younger sister.

Chiefs Essel and Kuow Kuta, on oath, said: In consequence of the action of defendant in mortgaging to Sey those three houses without the knowledge of the heads * of the family, which she had no right to do, that she had forfeited thereby any right in the house which, as a member of the family, she may formerly have had.

MACLEOD, J.: I adopt the opinion of the Chiefs, and declare that, in consequence of the conduct of defendant, she has forfeited any right in the three houses, which as a member of the family she may formerly have had. In making the declaration, I think I am substantially satisfying the ends of justice, and though my judgment in this action cannot directly affect the rights of Sey under his mortgage; still, it may enable him to judge whether, in view of this judgment, he is likely to find a purchaser of the rights of the defendant in those three houses.

ASSRAIDU v. DADZIE.

Cape Coast Records, vol. xii. p. 729.

July 23, 1890.

Before HUTCHINSON, C.J.

Family Property—Gift—Mortgage—Sale—Sec. 19 *of S.C.O.* 1876—*Loss of Right to sue or recover Possession—Adverse Possession.*

This case must be decided according to native law, that is, I ought to give the same judgment that a native Court,

* Elders.

judging honestly and in accordance with native law and custom (such law and custom as is referred to in section 19, of the Supreme Court Ordinance, 1876) ought to give.

The land in question was family land. About ten years ago, Kobina Kwenu, late chief of the family, was dead; Ochrimpi was the person entitled to be established as his successor, but he had not been installed (being a sick man), and there was no one on the stool ; Ochrimpi, however, was in charge of the stool and of the family property. He gave Ochua a piece of the family land ; she says that he gave it to her absolutely to do what she liked with it ; and she says that there were then only five of the elders of the family living, and that all these were present when he gave it to her. On the 9th of July, 1881, she having built a house on the land, mortgaged the land and house to Abadoo for her own private debt; on the 29th of April, 1882, Abadoo, under the power of sale in his mortgage, sold the property to Eddu, and shortly afterwards Eddu sold it to the defendant *Dadzie*. The first sale was by auction, the bell was rung through the town, and the sale was as public as possible. *Dadzie* took possession, fenced the property round, put up other buildings on it, spent a considerable sum in improving it, and has been in possession ever since his purchase. At the time of the sale to him Affedi was on the stool. He was, I think, not the person entitled to be installed on Ochrimpi's death, for the plaintiff, who was then and had been for many years in Salagha, had a better right. Still, the plaintiff being absent, Affedi was the person in charge of the stool property. He died about two years ago, and on his death the plaintiff was placed on the stool.

The first question is whether it was possible by native law for Ochrimpi, with the concurrence of those heads of the family who were then in the country, to make an absolute gift of part of the family land to Ochua. I think that the chief and all the heads of the family concurring can make an absolute gift of the family land; but the only

evidence that has been given on the point is to the effect
that, if any of the heads are absent and do not concur in
the gift, those absentees are not bound by it. And the
reason why they are not bound is, not that the land belongs
to them (for even the chief on the stool is not the owner
of it, but only the trustee or manager for the family), but
that it belongs to the family, and the consent of all the
members of the family then living must be obtained before
it is given away. But in this case it is not merely claiming back the land from the donee, but claiming it after it
has been sold eight years, all the members of the family
who were then in the country knowing that it had been
sold, and after the purchaser, without any objection from
any member of the family, has spent large sums of money
in building on and improving the land.

What would a native Court do in such a case? It
must be noticed that the right to set aside the gift made
by Ochrimpi is not a personal right of the plaintiff's. Family
land does not belong to the chief : he is merely the trustee
of it for all the family. The right to set aside the gift and
the subsequent sales was the right of the family ; and the
question is whether or not the family, through its chief for
the time being, can enforce that right after any lapse of
time, however great, and after full knowledge of and
acquiescence in the dealings with the land during all that
time by all the members of the family except the two who
were absent from the country.

There is apparently no positive rule in native law limiting the time within which an action for recovery of land
must be brought. Chief Sackey, however, gave some illus-
trations of cases in which the right to recover would, in his
opinion, be held by a native Court to have been lost.
Doubtless, there is no positive rule of native law as to the
circumstances which would deprive an individual or a
family of the right to recover land. But judging from the
opinion expressed by Chief Sackey, and from what I have
heard of the procedure of native Courts, I think that

where the chief and all the family who are in the country have seen the land sold and have said nothing for eight years, and have allowed the purchaser to suppose that the land belonged to him, and to build and spend money on it, the right of the family to claim the land again would, according to native and custom, be held to be lost. I have little doubt that a native Court, applying the general principles of native law and custom, and deciding according to what they thought fair and equitable, and in accordance with those principles, would so decide. That is the way, therefore, in which I think that I ought to decide.

I dismiss the action with costs.

The plaintiff having applied for a rehearing, the Court, on November 5, 1890, gave the following judgment :—

This case has been reheard and evidence taken on the point raised in the affidavits filed by the plaintiff in this application for a rehearing, viz. that Chief Sackey's view of the native law applicable to the case was wrong.

I have always found it hard to discover what is the native law upon any point whatsoever. And the reason is because there does not exist any native law, which is the same throughout the colony or over any considerable area. It would be strange if it were otherwise, considering the few opportunities that were until recent times of friendly communications between distant tribes, the absence of Supreme Court of Appeal to lay down the law for inferior Courts or to enact new law.

The present question is as to the circumstances under which "family land" can be absolutely sold or otherwise alienated. Cases raising this question have probably not often come before the native Court ; for until lately there was (so I have often heard) no market for land, and it was rarely sold or given away absolutely.

This is not surprising, therefore, that answers of the chiefs who gave evidence in this case were contradictory and disclosed no principle. They were, in fact, so inconsistent, that I cannot place any reliance on them.

There is a definition of family land given by assessors in the case of *Halm* v. *Hughes* on November 19, 1869 ("Civil and Criminal Record Magistrates' Court," p. 461), and that case and *Awortchie* v. *Eshon*, on March 6, 1872 (C. Magistrate's Book 1, p. 50), and *Beyaidee* v. *Mensah*, on March 27, 1878 (vol. 1, p. 535), contain some information as to the circumstances under which family land can be alienated. The conclusion that I come to is, that it can be alienated by way either of sale or of gift by the heads of the family; and that, if all the heads concur, the other members of the family, including children and unborn persons, are bound by the alienation. I asked one of the chiefs who gave evidence in this case, whether one of the headmen who was temporarily insane would be bound; he replied "Yes;" and I think the answer, only a guess, was right.

Then, is a member who is absent from the country, bound? I can see no principle upon which infants and lunatics can be bound, and yet persons living abroad are not bound; upon which a man who, without fault of his own, is temporarily incapacitated from concurring can be bound, and not a man who voluntarily disables himself by going and living abroad.

The case of *Beyaidee* v. *Mensah*, decided by the Court of Appeal in 1878, is important, and I think concludes this case. There, the head of the family sold family land without the concurrence of the other members of the family and in spite of the protests of one of them to the seller and the buyer. After fourteen years' possession by the buyer, the family tried to eject him; but the Court decided in his favour on the following grounds: "Now, although it may be, and we believe it is the law, that the concurrence of the members of the family ought to be given in order to constitute an unimpeachable sale of family land, the sale is not in itself void, but is capable of being opened up at the instance of the family, provided they avail themselves of their right timeously and under circumstances in which, upon the rescinding of the bargain, the purchaser can be fully restored to the position in which he stood before the sale. This is obviously not the case, whereas here the purchaser has possessed for a series of years an undisputed ownership, has cultivated and improved the land, and has established a house upon it."

In the present case, the land is given absolutely by Ochrimpi, the head of the family, to Otua; and it was afterwards sold with the knowledge of all the members of the family then living in the country.

Now one member, who has been living in Salaga for many years, seeks to set the gift and the sale aside. Even supposing that he could have succeeded if he had brought his action within a reasonable time, I am of opinion that he cannot do so now.

COBBOLD *v.* QUACOE TAWEIA.

March 18, 1846.

Payment—Barter.

The defendant in this case having brought the amount of his debt, six ackies, in goods, to pay the plaintiff—a mode of payment often adopted by parties in this country, and in some cases (and under certain circumstances) sanctioned by the authorities—they were sent over to the plaintiff for the purpose of knowing whether he would accept them. They were shortly brought back with a message to the effect that he would see before he would accept them, whereupon the goods were ordered to be lodged in the fort and the defendant immediately released.

INHERITANCE.

JOHN AMAMOO AND OTHERS v. JOHN CLEMENT.

April 24, 1871.

Before CHALMERS, Judicial Assessor.

Right of Children to a Father's House.

Chief Mayan states that children of persons not married have no right of succession to property (moveable), but that if there was a family house and the child had been a good (dutiful) child to his father, he would have a joint right with other members of the family to inherit the house.

Curia: There is no proof of the marriage of the mother of plaintiffs to William Gordon Amamoo. Here the essential condition of their having a right of succession is wanting. It does not even appear that they have any joint right along with the family, this not being of the nature of a family house; at least, there is no evidence that it is such a house.

Judgment for defendant.   .

MARY BARNES v. CHIEF J. MAYAN.

June 24, 1871.

Before CHALMERS, Judicial Assessor.

Family House—Children's Right to Residence—Powers of Head of Family.

JUDGMENT.

This is an action to try the right to a piece of land with buildings thereon, part of a larger tenement, in De Graft Street, Cape Coast.

The land was formerly owned by Mr. De Graft, the father of Mrs. *Barnes*, who, for some time and at the time of his death, was head of his family (Twidan). Chief

Mayan, the defendant, is his nephew and successor as head of the family.

The ground on which Mrs. *Barnes* bases her right is that the subject in question was given by Mr. De Graft to her mother, who was one of his wives, and was occupied by her as a dwelling-place. It appears that Mr. De Graft's family house stood formerly near the Castle; that it was removed as well as other houses by order of the Government, at a time when that part of the town was opened up, and that the tenement now in dispute was assigned to Mr. De Graft, in lieu of the one from which he had been dispossessed. He received also a money compensation for the building, which it may be presumed he laid out in the construction of his new house. These things being so, I consider that the new tenement took all the incidents of the one for which it was substituted, and was therefore, in Mr. De Graft's lifetime, in the same position as if it had been land of inheritance to which he had actually succeeded. Keeping this in view, it is clear that it is not in Mr. De Graft's power (in accordance with Fanti laws), by any act of gift to his wife, to confer either on her or on her children an exclusive right of ownership. But, further, there nowhere appears in the evidence the slightest indication that it was his intention to do so. What he did was to give his wife a right to use and occupy for the purposes of a dwelling-house, and I consider that this right, but no larger or more exclusive ones, inheres in Mrs. *Barnes* as her child whilst she chooses to exercise it as one of the family. The judgment of the Court, therefore, is that Mrs. *Barnes* is entitled to the use of the premises occupied by her mother in such mode and for such purposes as may be consistent with that condition as forming part of a family house, such use to be had and exercised under the sanction and approval of Chief *Mayan,* the head of the family, and not otherwise. With regard to the hall raised above the room occupied by Mrs. *Barnes's* mother, which was erected by some other member of the family subsequently, Mrs.

Barnes is entitled to the use of that also, under the same restrictions and sanction as the lower story, but further with the condition of making adequate compensation to the persons who erected the same.

HALMOND *v.* DANIEL.

August 22, 1871.

Before CHALMERS, Judicial Assessor.

Children—Right of Residence—Father's House—Family Land—Head of Family—Duty to allot Rooms.

Per Chief Kofi Chee: If a man went from his family house, cleared land, and on that land built another house, would not his children be entitled to live in it after his decease?

The custom is that if a man had a father either by country marriage or otherwise, and the father lived in the house with wife and child, and he died, all the *deceased's property,* except the *house,* goes to his family. The father's gun and sword and house go to the son, and the saying is, "The father dies and leaves his house to the son." The family take the property, but do not turn away the child. The son lives in the house with the family of his father, supposing they had nowhere to live, and the son does not turn them away. If it is a family house, the head occupies as head, yet he does not turn away the son from the house, except the son, after he has grown up, finds himself competent to build and leaves for the purpose of doing so. But he would not under any circumstances be turned out by the head of the family. The family would not be turned out for the son's accommodation; if they had nowhere else to live, they would live in the house. Where there is room enough for all (son and family), *the head of the family arranges the rooms to be allotted to each.* My answer of the descent of house to the son applies in case it has been built by the father; the family would be allowed to live in it if they had nowhere else to go. If they had, they would leave the father's house to the son. Son could not sell the house except with consent of the family.

JUDGMENT.

There are two subjects of dispute: First, a garden which is in the possession of *Isaiah Halmond;* but the right to which the *Daniels* contend is not in him, but in *Henry Daniel*, as the present head of the family. Second, the house built by John Halmond at Amanful, which the *Daniels* contend is to be held and dealt with as a family house, but which *Isaiah Halmond* says belongs to him solely, claiming to inherit as the lawful son of John Halmond. Although claiming this absolute right in terms, he does not, in fact, set up more than a qualified right—a right to occupy, but without power of alienation. *Halmond* contends that the land pawned by old John Halmond in Amanful was not land of inheritance, but was acquired by himself through his having occupied and cleared it by his own labour. The evidence is decisively negative of this supposition. The statements of the old member of the family, Effua Circuah, as reported by Mr. Martin, and those of old Halmond himself, in the actions referred to by both parties, which statements were sustained in the resulting decisions, are enough to settle this matter; besides which, there is the utmost improbability that at a place peopled as Amanful is, land should have been lying ownerless at the time assumed. This being so, the bequest by old Halmond, which is assented to by *Isaiah Halmond*, would fail of the validity attributed to it, as he would not, in accordance with Fanti law, be entitled to dispose absolutely of family property, even to his son.

In regard to Halmond's right to the house of his father, he also fails. The house was built on family land and in substitution for an old family house, the remains of which are still existing on this land. The presumption is that the new house was intended also to be a family house. All feeling of respect for the ancestors, and desire to perpetuate their names, lead to this conclusion, and though Halmond had joined the Wesleyan Church, there is not the slightest reason to suppose that in so doing he threw aside those ideas which belong to no creed but to humanity itself, and are found habitually in association with the deepest religious feeling. There is nothing to rebut this presumption. The alleged bequest of land to his son and nephews by Halmond does not apply to the house. The Martins' evidence states that old Halmond expressly appointed his nephew, *Henry Daniel* (his successor by law), to occupy and attend to this house in the mode which is customary. Mrs. Halmond's statement of old Halmond having once desired her to remain in the house after his death, as otherwise he feared his children would leave it, whatever it shows as to the discussions he anticipated between his son and nephews, noways shows that he intended his son to have an unqualified right in the house, but distinctly the contrary.

I therefore think that both the garden and the house must be considered as family property ; nevertheless, it is just that *Isaiah Halmond*, as the son of his father, should occupy a portion undisturbed. He will, therefore, continue to occupy the garden he now possesses, but without right to sell or alien it. And he will occupy such part of the house as may be allowed to him and agreed on between him and the other members of the family.

To report the allotment.

FULL COURT REPÔRT.

WELBECK AND OTHERS, APPELLANTS *v.* BROWN AND ANOTHER, RESPONDENTS.

Before H. LESINGHAM BAILEY, C.J., SMALMAN SMITH and HECTOR MACLEOD, JJ.

Native Law and Custom—S.C.O. 1876, *Sec. 9—Cutting " Ekal "— Disinheriting—Compensation.*

James Welbeck appeared for appellants.

Mr. *Richards* for respondents.

The following judgment of the Court below as read over to appellant *Welbeck :*—" The plaintiffs seek in this action to recover from the defendants the estate of the late Peter Benjamin Johnson, and in making that claim they have appealed to native law and custom, but they have failed to satisfy me that native law and custom support their claim. On the contrary, I think that the opinion of Chief Robertson lays down good law according to native ideas. It is possible that some of the plaintiffs may have a claim against the estate for the assistance given to the deceased in the building of this house. That question does not arise here. I decide this case purely upon the principles of native law and custom, and according to that criterion the plaintiffs have failed to establish any right to any of the property belonging to the deceased, and that property must remain with the defendants. As all the parties live in Cape Coast, there will be no costs."

JUDGMENT.

BAILEY, C.J. :—Peter B. Johnson, the owner of the property in dispute in this case, was the uncle of the plaintiffs and the father of the defendants.

The property consists of a house and personalty of the alleged value of £300. It is admitted, on behalf of the defendants, that the site of the house was in part purchased by the deceased with money supplied by the plaintiffs, or some of them, and that they assisted him, either with money or labour, or both, in building it.

At the hearing, it was admitted that, by native custom, when members of a man's family assist him in building a house in the manner described, the members so assisting him have, at his death, the right to succeed him in such house as joint tenants, or rather as tenants in common. It was also admitted that, during his life, the owner of the house so built may disinherit any or all the members of his family ; and if he do so disinherit all of them, may dispose of his property in any way that he pleases.

Now, the plaintiffs contend that no valid act of disinheritance was ever done by the deceased ; the defendants on the other hand alleging that the plaintiffs were duly disinherited. The plaintiffs allege, and by the evidence of one Quansah have endeavoured to prove, that disinheritance can only be effected by the cutting of an "ekal"—one-half of which the head of the family keeps, and the other he gives to the disinherited member. That solemnity, the plaintiffs allege, and the defendants admit, was not observed in this case.

The defendants, however, allege, and by the evidence of their witnesses, I think, abundantly prove, that this custom has been, of late years, superseded by another; and one of the witnesses who, though called by the plaintiffs, gave evidence in favour of the defendants (Chief Robertson), states that the old custom of cutting the "ekal" was abolished in Cape Coast in Governor McLean's time, some forty or fifty years ago. He says that now it is sufficient that the owner of the house drive away from that house any nephew or niece whom he desires to disinherit, and that thereupon the act of disinheritance is completed, and the disinherited nephew, though he may have helped to build the house, ceases from that time to have any interest therein.

John Sarbah, a witness called for the defendants, gives somewhat similar evidence, though he appears in one part of his evidence to lay it down that the act of disinheritance is not complete till the value of the contribution of the disinherited to the building of the house has been paid.

To my mind the discrepancy, if such there be, between the evidence of Sarbah and Robertson is unimportant, and for this reason : they are speaking of a custom, if custom it can be called, which not only does not date from "a time to which the memory of man runneth not to the contrary," but actually dates from a time which is in the memory of men now living. How can this be called a custom? I know we are to give effect to native law and custom as it existed at the date of the passing of the Supreme Court Ordinance, viz. 1876. But the man who drafted that Ordinance was a lawyer, and I have no reason to suppose that when he spoke of "customs" he meant anything more or less than that word imparts to legal ears.

If my opinion be correct that this is no custom now— because we know the date of the beginning of it—it was no custom when the Ordinance was drafted some eight years ago.

It may be that the old custom spoken to by Quansah has fallen into disuse, and that so there remains no means by which a native can disinherit his nephews. I am not concerned with that ; but one thing does concern me, and that is, that the Courts should do all that is in their power to fix these fugitive will-o'-the-wisps called native customs, and transfer them to the records of the Court, rejecting all those which are alleged to be custom, but which do not bear the test to which I have subjected this one.

Mr. *Richards* has put it on me that I am upholding one custom, that of the devolution of property to nephews, while I am refusing to uphold another. True, but I am not inconsistent; one is alleged to be a custom, and neither side has offered any evidence that it is not a valid custom— valid, that is to say, as a legal custom ; while with regard to the other, if I am right, Mr. *Richards* himself has shown it to be invalid—in short, no custom at all.

I am of opinion that this appeal should be allowed, and that it be ordered—

1. That the decision of the Court below be reversed.

2. That the plaintiffs be permitted to enjoy the house in question together with the defendants as tenants in common, according to native law and custom, in every respect as though they had not been disinherited by the deceased P. B. Johnson.

3. That the plaintiffs be declared entitled to the personalty of the deceased P. B. Johnson.

MACLEOD, J. :—I do not find it necessary to give any opinion as to the meaning of the words " native custom," and I must not be understood as coinciding on that point with the Chief Justice.

Whether or not the plaintiffs were legally disowned by the deceased is to my mind a question for the Assessors, who are called in to assist the Court because they are supposed to be skilled in matters of native law.

They have given their opinion, and I see no reason why I should interfere with it.

SMALMAN SMITH, J. :—I concur in the conclusion at which the Chief Justice has arrived, but for somewhat different reasons.

We must of course conclude that the native customs to which the Supreme Court Ordinance of 1876 requires us to give effect in the administration of the law of this colony, must be such as in the contemplation and according to the principles of English jurisprudence would be regarded as customs, that is to say, such as have existed in the colony from time immemorial, or "to which the memory of man runneth not to the contrary." It cannot, therefore, be contended that an observance or course of conduct which may have sprung up within the last fifty or sixty years, and which native chiefs choose to designate a custom, should have the effect of law in this colony, or should be, so to speak, crystallized into law by the action of the Courts of this colony.

The intention of the Legislature was, in my judgment, to give the force of law to such customs of general and long-continued usage and observance as can be proved to have been in existence at the date of the Ordinance, and to have had at that date the essentials as well as the force of customs as by law established.

Now, the right of a man to disinherit in his lifetime those who would otherwise be entitled to share in his property after death, is proved to exist as a custom to my satisfaction.

The cutting of the "ekal" was a symbolic act which accompanied the act of disinheriting. I do not think, however, that the cutting of the "ekal" was essential to the existence of the custom, which is based on the *right* of a man to disinherit in his lifetime those who would otherwise be entitled to succeed him. When therefore the cutting of the "ekal" ceased to form a part of the ceremony, the right which by custom then existed did not cease to have the force of a custom, because the formalities which accompanied the act were varied in an important, though not an essential particular. Granted, therefore, that the right of a man to disinherit in his lifetime, still exists as a custom of the country, I have now to consider what formalities are necessary to render the act complete and operative. In ordinary circumstances, the solemn act of turning the persons whom it is intended to disinherit, out-of-doors, and in the presence of friends and relatives refusing to readmit them, amounts to a complete act of disinheritance. But where such persons have contributed to the building of the house from which they are shut out, they have, according to native custom and natural equity, a vested interest in that house. Where such are the facts, the act of disinheriting is not complete until compensation has been paid or offered to the persons ejected for their share or interest in the family house. Such were the facts in the present case. The payment of such compensation I regard as an essential element to the complete act of disinheritance.

The Chief Sarbah is the only witness, it is true, who speaks to this; but it does not appear from the notes that the actual facts of the case under notice were submitted to the then witnesses for their judgment. I do not find, therefore, that the evidence of the chiefs is incapable of being reconciled with the evidence of Sarbah.

The plaintiffs had a vested interest in the family house; they were entitled to compensation for that interest. This compensation was neither paid nor offered at the time of the alleged disinheritance, nor has it been since paid.

The alleged act of disinheriting merely consisted in turning the plaintiffs away from the house and refusing their readmission. The act was therefore incomplete and of no effect.

Under these circumstances the plaintiffs are entitled to share with the defendants in the family house, and are further entitled to the personalty of the deceased P. B. Johnson.

Chief Justice of opinion that the judgment of the lower Court should be reversed. Mr. Justice MACLEOD dissented from the opinion of the Chief Justice, and supports the findings of the Court below. Mr. Justice SMALMAN SMITH of the same opinion with the Chief Justice.

(Signed) H. LESINGHAM BAILEY, C.J.
     ,,   SMALMAN SMITH, J.
     ,,   HECTOR W. MACLEOD, J.

Upon hearing *James Welbeck* for the appellants, and Mr. *Richards* for the respondents, it is ordered that the appellants be permitted to possess and enjoy, in conjunction with the respondents, the house and premises—the subject-matter of this action—in accordance with native law and custom, and that the respondents do pay the costs of the action in the Court below, and of this appeal. It is further ordered that the respondents do deliver over to the appellants the personal property of the deceased P. B. Johnson.

SWAPIM *v.* ACKUWA.

September 22, 1888.

Before SMITH, J.

Family Land—Right of Children to live in Father's Resid.nce—
Ouster of Widow.

A review was allowed in this cause and the matter now comes on for argument.

Mr. *Eminsang* appears for the plaintiffs, Mr. *Sarbah* for the defendants.

Mr. *Eminsang* says that the house occupied by the defendants is part of the family house, and it was not a distinct house which was built on the land ; that by native law, if a husband built on family land with the assistance of his wife, the family of the husband can take possession of the house and turn the wife out. Even if the husband builds on his own land with the assistance of his wife, it is the same ; so also, if the wife built the house on the family land with the consent of the family, she can be turned out of the land by the family and quits, cites *Grant* v. *Amissah.*

After hearing *Sarbah,* case adjourned to obtain evidence on the Customary Law.

December 11, 1888.

This case was last before the Court on the 3rd of October last, when the opinion of certain chiefs on native law was ascertained, and it was thought expedient, in view of the difference of opinion, to consult other chiefs. Whereupon the opinion of the Kings of Anamaboe, (*a*) Mankessim, and (*b*) Abura, was obtained by letter, setting forth the questions which had been put to the other chiefs, and their replies have been received, and are now made part of the case.

Parties were duly notified that judgment would be given in this case to-day, and they accordingly attended.

JUDGMENT.

In view of the native law on the point, I must alter my judgment in so far as it gives to the defendants the right to remain in the house, and I declare that the plaintiff *Swapim* is entitled to the possession of the house. I give the defendants (*sic*) days to remove from the house. Each party will pay its own costs.

(*a*) By King Amonoo IV.: 1. The wife of the deceased husband, who was invited by a member of the family, has no interest in the house which both the husband and she built on the family land, except that of a mere occupant.

2. The family of the deceased husband would be entitled to the house.

3. Yes. The family would have the right to turn the wife out of the house, if they wish it. And she should only remain therein by the permission of the family, the wife having her own family, to whom she must go.

4. The family of the husband would be entitled to the house.

5. Yes. Her family would have the right to turn the children out of the house. The children could remain or continue in the occupation thereof by the permission of the family, the children also having their own family on their mother's side to go to. But this right of the family is seldom exercised but where occasion is given.

6. Yes. The person who succeeds to this land has a right to turn the wife out of the house, if he succeeds to the land as family property.

7. The person to whom the land descends has the right, after the death of the son, to turn the children out of the house, but this is seldom enforced. It is exercised when the children gave occasion. As the person to whom the land descends has right to the house, he could ask the children to go out on any occasion for any reasonable grounds, and where the interest of the family is at stake, or their right

is disputed, or even merely to secure and promote the interests of the family.

(b) By King Amfoo Otoo: 1. The interest of the wife who has built a house with the husband exists only in the lifetime of the husband.

2. [On the death of the husband] one from the family of the deceased husband is entitled to the house.

3. The woman would still remain in the house, if she will be married to the successor of her late husband; if not, she has no claim to the house.

4. The house or property of a deceased husband or father, according to native law, belongs to the family and not to the children.

5. The family have the right to turn the children out of the house, on this ground, if they are not on good terms with the father's family or successor, and are never entitled to father's house or property.

6. I give same opinion, that sons and wives have no right to claim a house or land belonging to sister's deceased brother, that is to say, it belongs to the sister.

BOHAM AND ANOTHER v. MARSHALL.

Elmina, May 18, 1892.

Before SMITH, J.

Family House—Tenancy of Children—Their Rights and Liabilities.

Eminsang: By native law, *Anna Boham* had a right to the house, as she was the sister of John Boham. By native law, she was the only heiress at the time. She could by native law have power to give the house to the children for their natural lives. Of the part so given to the children, unless *Marshall* gave the children an equivalent, he could not turn them out of the house. *Marshall* can pull down his portion of the house, if he did not interfere with the other portion.

Per Court: By native law, the person succeeding to property could not dispose of it to beyond his lifetime, unless with the consent of the families. In this case, the plaintiffs being the children of John Boham, have the right to remain in their father's house during their lives, unless for good reasons. If the children do not live in their father's house, still if they can go and live there as they will, the heir could not break the house down and dispose of the materials. The heir is the one to repair the house, and if the children are in a position they contribute towards the expenses.

EFFUA EDOOAH *v.* COFFIE AWOOAH.

July 23, 1869.

Before F. C. GRANT, Chief Magistrate and Judicial Assessor.

Senior Stool-holder—His Rights and Duties—Guardian—Subordinate Stool.

To return plaintiff's brother's property, which you wrongfully seized immediately after his decease.

Facts: Plaintiff says, my brother died at war between Fantees and Elminas. After the custom, defendant took all my brother's property, slaves, and pawns, and gave me only one woman and one girl to serve me, and told me he would train up my own son, and when he came of age place him on my brother's stool. I refused, and told him I belong to Acquannah family, Defendant to Abbrodie family, and not related to me.

Myself and defendant were of same father; different mothers. My father belongs to Acquannah family, and my mother belongs to Acquannah family at Assin, and belongs to Assin. My husband Essuman married me according to country law, and succeeded my father to the stool and property. My husband Essuman belongs to Abbrodie family. The son defendant wanted to put on my brother's stool was mine by Essuman. I am a free woman, and am not a daughter of any of defendant's slaves, nor was my brother.

Witness: Plaintiff sent me to tell defendant if a man buy slaves and one becomes wealthy and dies, the master places one of the fellow-slaves on the stool of deceased slave; but this man who is dead, and you want to take his property, I plaintiff am rightful brother (?) of deceased, and call upon you to give me his property.

Defendant said I must place his son on the stool of his uncle, my brother.

Defendant states plaintiff is not a slave; they are all brothers and sisters, and that my deceased brother told me so, and told us all to bury him when he died.

Opokoo is our grandfather; he bought Enquie, and ᒐnquie bought plaintiff's and her deceased brother's mother, and married her. I defendant am the nephew of Opokoo. My mother was Opokoo's sister. My mother is called Attah, and she was sister of Opokoo. He gave my mother, his sister, in marriage to Enquie. Opokoo died, and was succeeded by his slave Enquie. When Enquie grew old and was about to die, he made a verbal will. Plaintiff's mother died before Enquie. After her death, Enquie gave plaintiff and her deceased brother in charge to defendant's mother. Enquie died also. After his death plaintiff's deceased brother was asked to take his stool. He refused, stating he was a younger brother, but defendant being older ought to succeed before him. Defendant did not succeed, but Essuman was asked to succeed, being defendant and plaintiff's uncle. According to country law, during his occupation of the stool, plaintiff was handed over to him as his wife. At the time Essuman took the stool, I was allowed the use of palm-field, a very large one, too large for me to work. I divided it into two, and gave half to the deceased to work on it. Akoo succeeded Essuman, and I succeeded him. On the death of plaintiff's brother, as head of the family I made the necessary custom. After this I gave three persons to plaintiff to

serve her and work for her. I also took her son, by our
uncle Essuman, to serve me, to carry my gun behind me.
I would, when he came of age, place him on my deceased
brother's stool. I gave the son three boys to serve him;
the palm-field I gave to my late brother that also I gave to
plaintiff's son, and directed the three boys to work in the
palm-field and get money out of it for the future successor.
In this country, if you buy a slave and he had children,
they are to be considered as free in the house; they are no
more slaves. Plaintiff's deceased brother is my younger
brother; we are of different mothers, but one father.

When the deceased has no brother to succeed him, then,
and only then, the sister succeeds.

JUDGMENT.

The Judicial Assessor having convened a meeting of
the chiefs of Cape Coast to consider this case, finds that
defendant has acted in strict accordance to the country
laws. That defendant is the head of the house, and that
the same consists of two stools, a great stool and a small
one. That defendant sits on the great stool, and has control over the small stool. That defendant has acted wisely
in protecting the small stool, and acts as guardian to the
plaintiff's son, and will place plaintiff's son on the stool
provided he behaves himself. That, according to country
law, if plaintiff is a free woman, she is not entitled to any
property at all in the house, but being a slave entitles her
to claim through her son, which is not disputed by
defendant.

This Court therefore gives judgment in favour of
defendant, and orders him to take the supervision of the
property as he has hitherto done, and advises him to deal
leniently, kindly, and patiently with plaintiff and her son's
future interest of the stool of which he is the head and
guardian. The debts of the estates defendant will collect,
and when he is satisfied plaintiff's son will manage the
stool carefully and wisely, he will place him thereon as

under him; and to restore all property she has taken away
to Assin, and to live peaceably with her brother and
family in order to enjoy all the benefits accruing from the
stool.

COFFIE YAMMOAH *v.* ABBAM COOMAH.

November 3, 1869.

Before CHALMERS, Judicial Assessor.

Rule of Descent—Heir—Right of Selection by Members of Family.

For a trespass committed by you and your servants on
plaintiff's land called Impu-assam, and situate in the district of Gomuah, between Benyansang Ohimkookoodoo;
damage of plaintiff, £9.

November 5, 1869.

Opinion of Chiefs:

If Essa had property and Essa had a nephew, a son
of his sister, or a grandson, the nephew or the grandson
would be entitled to the property. It is custom to trace
the descent from a very old ancestor. Persons entitled
to succeed are:

First, brother; second, nephew; third, grandson; fourth,
great-grandson.

If he had more of these, but had sisters who had children, and children's children, who are considered, upon
consultations, part of the family, these would succeed after
each other. If deceased had a brother and sisters, if all
descended from one mother (if not all living at the same
place), the eldest sister would be nearest to the property,
and her children succeed. Then come in other children,
according to the ages of their mothers, unless deceased
himself names a child or states reasons. Sometimes if no
blood relation is entitled, a slave woman after purchase by
a member of the family. Her child would be entitled to
take; makes no difference in the succession of blood
relatives, whether they be in same place.

When a man has an heir, to whom he has objections stated to family, family has no right to consult on the reasons during testator's lifetime. But they do so after his death. Sometimes the testator's reasons are overruled. Sometimes they consent during testator's lifetime, and though agreeing to the testator's exculpations of the obnoxious person, do not afterwards adhere.

Rules of inheritance are not set aside at mere pleasure of owner, unless his reasons are judged sufficient.

Judgment for defendant.

QUASIE AMFOO *v.* AMBAH YARDONUAH.

May 17, 1871.

Before D. P. CHALMERS, Judicial Assessor.

Stool Property—Succession—Right to pass over—Election Veto.

Chiefs interrogated, say : The case has reference to the two persons who appear and have stated matters respecting the stool which is in contention between them. It has been stated that there was a man, Quamin Effor, who had four sons and one daughter; that the man bequeathed his property and stool to his children; that he died; that the stool was succeeded by Quasie Anka; he by Kwow Atta. Kwow Atta having died, the plaintiff wanted to take it. We find that one of the children has died. We have also heard it stated by the defendant, that after the custom of Kwow Atta had been finished, the relatives connected with the stool and the people who were not blood relatives, as well as the people of the place, agreed among themselves and placed defendant's son on the stool; that defendant did not agree to this, but the people did prevail and placed the son on the stool. It has also been stated to us that there was a will, in which it was laid down that the children of the deceased testator should take the stool. The question put before us by your Honour, to consider, was as to whether the relatives and slaves and people of the place were justified in placing defendant's son on the stool, contrary to what was stated by the will. In considering these matters, we find that the defendant in this case is the eldest child of the man Effor (testator) ; yet, as a woman, and because she is a woman, she did not succeed to the stool, but Quasie Anka, who was next to her, took the stool, and after him, Kwow Atta, and the next person would have been the plaintiff. We are chiefs, we have inherited to stools in like manner as the relatives of defendant have done ; we have slaves, people, and property connected with the stool, and we find, on the conclusion, that the succession to the stool in question and right of it lies with the plaintiff in this case, who was the next person to Kwow Atta, who should take the stool, and not the defendant's son, who was the nephew ; because the plaintiff has not succeeded to it nor died, so that defendant's son should succeed ; and we think that it is contrary to rule that people and relatives connected with the stool should join with the people of the place to consult and place defendant's son on it in place of the plaintiff. The people of the place could have no power to join people connected with the stool to put off the rightful person.

We find that the plaintiff is the rightful person for the stool.

JUDGMENT.

It was adjudged that the plaintiff be the rightful occupant of the stool, and ordered accordingly that he be placed thereon.

On the 24th May, 1871, this case was reopened by the learned Judicial Assessor, and at his request Amfoo Ottoo, King of Abrah, related what had passed before him and his councillors when they investigated this matter.

By King Amfoo Ottoo: Kwow Atta was a principal man, he was Master-of-Arms of the whole district of Abrah, and was chief over them. I was on a visit to Abonu at the

time of his death. On my return to Abakrampa the
plaintiff *Amfoo* came to me and informed me of what had
taken place, namely, that his nephew had been put on the
stool of Kwow Atta instead of himself. I replied that I
was anxious to attend at Donassi to make custom, and that
when I had done so I would inquire into matters. . . .
Accordingly, when I had stated this, I went to Donassi and
made custom.

After that we had palaver. First was that the defendant has summoned his sister, the present defendant.
Decision was in her favour; it was clear that he had
summoned her for nothing. As for the people of Donassi
who are people of the stool, the councillors still thought
that when Kwow Atta had died and plaintiff *Amfoo* was
his brother, they should have waited for the King's return
from the camp; and then for a case to be heard as between
them and *Amfoo* as to the reason and cause of their not
placing him on the stool, or of their objections they had
to him, so that these things might be talked over before
any one was placed on the stool. That, as concerned this,
Amfoo was right to complain.

The people of Donassi replied that they were dissatisfied
with the decision (viz. that the plaintiff should not be
passed over), and they said further that if the animal
found nothing and had no reason to give, that animal did
not make a hole in the ground to hide its young ones;
that *Amfoo* had done several wrongs, and they appointed
two persons who came before me to state these wrongs.
The wrongs of Osam (*sic*) in charcoal, red clay, and pepper,
etc., knowing that this person was my servant. The
persons who represented the people went on to state everything connected with *Amfoo*. I and the whole people of
Abrah were satisfied that they had made a case against
Amfoo, and that all was correct. They said further to me,
a person who would attend well on it, he is the person who
would be entitled to succeed to it, and not a person who
would not. Further, that I should compare the thing with

myself—how I was elected to the stool; and I thought of that because I was elected by the people to the stool, although I had an uncle who was a man of means, having about twenty slaves whom he had purchased, and has at present about fifty persons who could hold guns with him, and I have a brother who was next to me; that when the stool which I now occupy was vacant, and they wanted the rightful man to be placed on it; and though my uncle was alive, and the proper person to be elected, the people of the stool objected to him. They did not choose me either. They chose my younger brother, and after his death, took me. And if they had chosen Gaisi, Amfoo was his uncle, and was to *sit behind* him. Osam's case was brought to Cape Coast, and large expense was incurred. · The people of Abrah found that as for the reasons stated they placed Gaisi on the stool, they did right; they also found the decision given against him before was incorrect. I spent great attention on the case. I found they were correct. I, as a Judge, was on the side of *Amfoo*. The people said that at that rate, as they had stated, they had placed Gaisi already on the stool, I should state what ought to be done for *Amfoo* (the plaintiff), and I called on him to state what he claimed. He said that if they gave him 4 ozs., he would be satisfied, then Gaisi must inherit the stool. Then I said he himself will not have to sweep his house—give him two persons to sweep his house and carry his stool, also one woman to be with him. These to be given him in addition to the 4 ozs., so that he may, as it were, *sit behind* his nephew, and look after him on the stool. The 4 ozs. was given to *Amfoo* as a kind of compensation, in respect, that, being in the line to be placed on the stool, he had been passed over, and another person put in his place.

March 24, 1871.

JUDGMENT.

This cause is in substance an application by *Quasie Amfoo*, the plaintiff, to be placed on the stool of Quamin

Effor of Donassi, deceased; this is opposed by the people belonging to the stool. The Judicial Assessor has heard the statement fully on both sides. *Quasie Amfoo* is the person in the direct line to the stool, and would have succeeded thereto if his election had been supported by the people who have the right of choice. These persons, however, have passed over the plaintiff, and elected, in preference, his nephew Gaisi. This election has been confirmed by the King and principal persons of the district. The Judicial Assessor does not, under the whole circumstances which have been put before him, see cause for setting aside the appointment which has been made, which is hereby confirmed accordingly.

J. H. MOULD *v.* AGOLI AND ESSAN.

June 6, 1871.

Before CHALMERS, Judicial Assessor.

Head of Family—His Duties—Removal—Accounts.

JUDGMENT.

The question raised by the plaintiff is that of his right to receive from defendants and other persons of Abrobonku, the produce of the palm-trees belonging to that place. He claims on the ground of being headman, and he says that he is entitled as such to apply and appropriate a fourth share at his discretion without being accountable to the people. He has, it appears, been receiving this share until within a short time ago, when, on certain accounts being made of his past receipts, the defendants, not being satisfied about the manner of his disposal thereof, have refused to continue to make payments to him. The plaintiff has based his claim on his alleged inheritance from Adjuah Beraful, who, it is acknowledged, was at one time the owner of the land at Abrobonku. I do not think his descent is very satisfactorily established in evidence; but as the right he claims is not a patrimonial one so much as to be considered head of the family, and as such to occupy the stool of which the lands at Abrobonku are an appendage, it is the less necessary to give a decision on this question.

It is the fact that the plaintiff has been acknowledged as headman by the family for a considerable number of years, and has acted in this capacity; but the right of the family to displace him from that position on sufficient cause is in accordance with the laws and customs of the country.

The particular fault which the family, as represented by defendants, allege against Mould is that he had not applied certain moneys, amounting, as they state, to 7 or 9 ackies, for their benefit in such way as they consider proper. On the other hand, the plaintiff says he has applied this sum for the family in defraying the charges necessarily falling upon him in his character of headman, and also in the expenses of certain law proceedings which were taken with the purpose of recovering money from one Faidee, who, for a time, was in charge of these palm-trees, and received the proceeds for the family. The proof of the plaintiff having received these sums, is the statements of the defendants, which, however, the plaintiff does not contradict. As to the disposal of them, it is certain that the plaintiff must, from time to time, have been at some expense for the family; but the amount is conjectural, being uninstructed by any accounts. The plaintiff says he has expended more than he received. Upon the whole of this matter, the defendants have not proved misappropriation of the moneys by the plaintiff; but, on the other hand, he has not clearly established his averment that it has been all expended for the family.

It appears that there is not any member of the family, other than Mould, pointed out by age or position as suitable to take the stool in his place; and no one is proposed at present to occupy it. That is the state of things not likely to advance the interests of the persons concerned; and, in the whole circumstances, I think it best to remit to certain chiefs to arbitrate between plaintiff and the defendants, with full power to these arbitrators to arrange either for the continuance of the plaintiff on the stool on such terms as may be thought suitable, or for placing some other person upon it, should it appear to them that there is sufficient reason for removing him.

Remit was made accordingly to Chiefs Attah, Mayan and Attopee, who were present in Court, and accepted of the reference.

SARAH PARKER AND OTHERS *v.* MENSAH AND OTHERS.

June 6, 1871.

Before CHALMERS, Judicial Assessor.

Family Property—Liability of a Member of a Family.

JUDGMENT.

The question which the Court has primarily to consider in this case is whether the sale of the land at Quaduagah to *Quassie Mensah* under a writ of execution obtained by *Agoah Koomah* against *Joseph Adams* was valid. *The land belonged by purchase to Amoonoah, the mother of Adams;* and the family of Amoonoah, as represented by *Sarah Parker* and the others who concur with her in this action, now claim that the sale should be set aside and the land returned to them on the grounds :—

First : That the inheritor of Amoonoah's property was *Sarah Parker,* her eldest child, and not *Joseph Adams,* who, her eldest son, was not the eldest in the family, and therefore according to country law not the inheritor of Amoonoah.

Second : That the land having descended to Miss *Parker,* has become in her hands family land, which, by the custom of the country, is not attachable either for the debt of the head or of any member of the family ; and

Third: That the liability of *Adams* to *Agoah Koomah* was in no way shared either by Amoonoah or the family.

The first of these positions is true, Miss *Sarah Parker* and not *Adams* being the eldest child and inheritor of Amoonoah; and if the statement of the case which I have just referred to were comprehensive of all its incidents, the customary law of the country would render at once obvious the decision which should be given, and that would be that the land should be restored to Miss *Sarah Parker* as representing Amoonoah's family, and that the purchaser recover from the creditor of *Adams,* at whose instance and risk the sale was made, the price he has paid as well as collateral expenses.

But there are circumstances which render it necessary to inquire whether Amoonoah should be held to have been at least jointly responsible with *Adams* for the debt which at the first view seemed solely his own; for if she was thus responsible, I apprehend that I am in consonance with the country law in holding that her family could not recover back this land unless on the condition of satisfying the debt. Accordingly, I have found it necessary to look back closely into the circumstances out of which the liability of *Adams* arose.

The facts, according to the evidence, are these: A number of years ago (how many does not clearly appear, but at least sixteen years) *Agoah Koomah* obtained a loan of 7 ozs. from Amoonoah. This was to be repaid with interest of 50 per cent. *Agoah Koomah's* own statement is that the first payment she made was 5 ozs. 8 ackies; then, that she paid 1 oz.; then there was a payment of 5 ozs., which was made in cowries.

It is impossible to hold that *Adams* interposed in these transactions otherwise than as agent of Amoonoah. It is said she gave him the debt to collect and apply for his own use. It is quite possible that she did not exact from him a strict account of what he received, but here we have her name appearing as the judgment and incarcerating creditor, and receiving one of the final payments in person; whatever arrangement she had with *Adams,* she obviously, as regarded the debtor, sustained the character of creditor, *Adams* being her agent merely, through the payments made partly to him in that capacity and partly to herself in person, she had at this stage received full payment of her debt.

On this her duty to her debtor was plain. She was to grant a valid receipt, to take the original document of debt out of her agent's hands, and see that no further proceedings were taken by him against the debtor. It was stated by *Agoah Koomah* that on receiving the last payment Amoonoah gave no receipt, stating that it should stand over till *Adams* returned, who was· then absent from Anamaboe. The debtor was not bound to pay except on receiving a valid receipt, and if Amoonoah did as was stated, she made herself responsible that *Adams's* subsequent proceedings should be such only as she herself might lawfully have taken. It rather seems that this demur in giving a receipt must have referred to some of the previous payments. Nothing further seems to have taken place till 1861, when *Adams* took out a summons against *Agoah Koomah* at Anamaboe for £18. There has not been a suggestion that *Agoah Koomah* ever borrowed from *Adams,* or was indebted to him personally for this £18. Now, the extract from the book of the Anamaboe Court, which is in evidence, is remarkable. It contains the plea of the defendant denying the debt. Then the magistrate has noted : "The plaintiff produced a paper showing the defendant owed him £18." This to a moral certainty was the original undertaking of *Agoah Koomah* and her sureties, with the endorsement of a balance of 5 ozs. due, which I have noticed. Judgment was given for *Adams,* and upon that seems to have commenced a series of extortionate seizures, which were the ground of the recent judgment against *Adams.* And this action does not conclude the series. *Adams* afterwards, in 1863, has the

effrontery to raise an action against the sureties in the
original undertaking, and by means which could have been
nothing else than fraud upon the Court, obtained judgment, on which he proceeded to sell and seize the property
of the sureties. It is not a little significant that when he
was called to account on these proceedings in this Court he
obstinately refused to do so, and finally allowed judgment
to go against him by default, being aware that he could
make no defence. Now, it may be asked, what had
Amoonoah to do with all these acts of misconduct, or how
was she responsible ? It would be painful to suppose she
was aware of what *Adams* was doing, yet it is very
difficult to think that these seizures and sales taking place
at Anamaboe could pass unknown to her. But whether
this were so or no, she had put the means of perpetrating
those malpractices in the hands of *Adams*. She had
suffered him to have the documents after her own debt
had been fully paid. She had not recalled the agency
committed to *Adams*. Even assuming her to be free
of all connivance with the tortious proceedings of
Adams, and equally innocent of those who suffered by
them, a responsibility arises, on the plain principle that
where some one must be a loser through the fraudu-
lent acts of an agent, it is more reasonable that the person
who had employed and confided in the wrong-doer should
be the loser than a third party.

If *Agoah Koomah* and her sureties had claimed redress
from Amoonoah during her lifetime, it is difficult to say
how she could have refused it. Not only was *Adams* one
of her family, her eldest son, but it had been in consequence
of her own employ of him that he had been enabled to
make these extortions, and if the aggrieved persons had
constituted their claim by formal proceedings and had sold
this land, I do not see how such sale could have been
questioned. Now the land has been seized after it has
become land of inheritance, and according to general rule
not attachable. But I think this alienable quality of

family property must be reasonably construed. If there was an obligation subsisting in Amoonoah's lifetime, for which the land, whilst hers, might have been taken, it descended to her successor under the condition that she was bound to discharge such obligation by paying its amount to the persons entitled to claim. It is further to be observed that *Adams*, as a member of Amoonoah's family, has by his acts constituted a family debt which, it seems, in case of a subordinate member, the family are not in strictness bound to discharge, but would be in honour bound *unless they wished to cast the debtor out of the family*. Something like an undertaking to pay the debt is spoken by *Agoah Koomah*, viz. that Mr. Blankson, junior, interposed to prevent *Adams* being imprisoned, saying the family would see to the debt: whether for this reason or for any other, it is certain that *Adams* has not been imprisoned on the judgment obtained against him.

This sale has taken place without notice of any preferable claim, for it appears that the message sent by Mr. Blankson reached Quaduagah after the sale had taken place, and whatever was its purport, it seems to have been waived on the part of Amoonoah's family by their remissness in following it up, they having allowed a claim to the land which proceeded on a quite different ground adverse to their own to be fully litigated before setting up their right.

Having under review the whole circumstances that this sale should not be set aside—certainly not on any other conditions than of Amoonoah's family making full compensation to the purchaser for the price he has paid and all expenses, and also compensating *Agoah Koomah* for her expenses incurred in previous action—the expenses of this action will be payable by the plaintiffs.

[*Per George Blankson,* junior : I as one of the members of the family of Amoonoah claim to have a superior right

to any that can be shown by the defendants, inasmuch as I
have a right to cultivate and occupy landed property
which was owned by my grandmother during her lifetime,
and which was not bequeathed by writing to any particular
member of the family. But the title which I assert to the
occupancy is not confined to myself, but extends to all
members of the family. I state that Amoonoah did not
leave this land to *Joseph Adams*, nor on the eve of her
death did she leave a will either verbal or written making
her property attachable for *Joseph Adams's* debt. I also
state that Amoonoah never mentioned that this land was
attachable for *Joseph Adams*. To the best of my belief,
Agoah Koomah, one of the defendants, the judgment-
creditor of *Joseph Adams*, never in Amoonoah's lifetime
took any steps to inform Amoonoah as to the judgment
debt which existed against *Joseph Adams*. I claim on the
principle of the country law, that no real estate is salable
or attachable for debt unless by the sanction of the whole
family—neither for the debt of the head of the family nor
of any member. I maintain that the writ of execution was
directed only against the goods and chattels of *Joseph
Adams*, or against such real estate as *Joseph Adams* held
in individual right. Where an owner of land dies without
leaving will, and leaves a family who have to undergo
collectively the funeral expenses which may be made, and
supposing the family make such expenses, then whatever
the deceased may leave as real property would have to be
distributed among the members who made the custom.
The head of the family, no matter who he or she may be,
is supposed during life to look after the interests of every
member who may spring from him. If any member owes
debt during his lifetime, in default of payment the head
must pay it. Again, if the head contracts debt the whole
family must contribute. They are not to allow the head
to be imprisoned, even though the debt were contracted
without their knowledge. Therefore when Amoonoah
died without leaving a will, and the family made the

custom for her, it gave them right to inherit any property which she might have left. I as one of the members made custom.

When a woman leaves real estate, the eldest daughter, not the eldest son, is the inheritor—not for herself, but for the family. As a matter of fact, Amoonoah possessed the land. She left a family of sons and daughters. It is a feature of the country law that although my late mother was married according to Protestant religious rites, yet she could hold property in her own right independently of her husband. The head of the family who now claims is *Sarah Parker* of Anamaboe, who is eldest daughter of Amoonoah; she is my aunt; she took principal part in paying the debts of Amoonoah after her death, especially funeral expenses.]

ISAAC OCRAN *v.* QUAH BANDAFOO.

October 13, 1873.

Before CHALMERS, Judicial Assessor.

Ejectment—Land Aboo-Akoo, near Woontoo-Aga.

The property is at Quessie Ansah, between Abrah and Aga districts; bounded by Aban's, Amissah's land, and by the village Quessie Ansah.

Chiefs: Wills are made by word of mouth, and if not, it is easily discoverable who the rightful heir is.

If the grandmother was a slave, all her descendants remain slaves until redeemed.

Court: Has every slave a right to redeem herself?

A slave belonging to the country can be redeemed by her own family; but it is very difficult, as the expense would be great, and all her personal property whatever there, if she too have slaves, would have to be paid for.

In the case of a man dying and leaving property, and his blood relations appear to be too young to manage it, the property descends to an elderly slave as trustee, till the real successor comes to age. In the case of a slave becoming such a trustee, it would be his business to redeem all the blood relations of his master out of the proceeds of the property, and bring them to the house, and they would all succeed to the property in succession, and when all were dead, the property would go to the slaves.

The general rule of descent of property is that the nephew succeeds.

ARTHUR HUTTON v. KUOW KUTA.

December 6, 1878.

Letters of Administration—Family Property.

To show cause why the letters of administration, granted you to administer the estate of John Mayan, of Cape Coast, deceased, shall not be set aside and revoked in so far as they affect the family property held by the deceased, the same being the lawful property of plaintiff and others by the laws and customs of this country.

Colour is no bar to the right of succession in native law.

Judgment for plaintiff.

DINAH HOLDBROOK AND OTHERS v. ATTA.

December 22, 1882.

Before LESINGHAM BAILEY, Chief Justice.

Order of Succession—Family Property.

Chief J. Robertson stated, with concurrence of Chief Kuow Kuta, that in the event of land being held in common by three brothers and a sister, the children of the sister would, at the death of all (brothers and sister), inherit in preference to the children of the brothers, unless such brothers had married a woman of the same blood and family, and that this would be so, even though the sister had not been married according to native law, and if, in point of fact, her children were the issue of an illicit connection with a married man.

JUDGMENT.

The plaintiffs claim to be entitled to the possession of the land in question, as the children of Abbraba Kerantsua, who, with her three brothers, Chissie, Taweia, and Appia, held it in common, it having descended to them from the aunt or uncle, which is not shown in the evidence. Abbraba survived the three brothers, one of whom, Taweia, married, and had a son, Koffie Aboo. At the death of the brothers, the sister, niece of the purchaser (a person last seised), took possession of the land, and at her death her children, the present plaintiffs, took possession. Koffie Aboo, however, sold the land to the defendants, who have occupied it under a grant from him for a period of four or five years. The native law is very clear on the subject of inheritance, and there is no question that the land of a deceased uncle may be, and indeed of right is occupied by all the children of his sister, whether male or female, and descends at the death to the children of the female only; and therefore, although Chissie, Taweia, and Appia, were entitled to possession, together with their sister, during their lives, it descended to her children alone, to the exclusion of the children of either of her brothers.

These children are the plaintiffs, and as the defendants claim through a son of Taweia, I am of opinion that the plaintiffs are entitled to judgment for recovery of possession of the land.

SAM *v.* WILLIAMS.

February 24, 1883.

Before QUAYLE JONES, A.J.

Rule of Succession.

Per J. M. Abadoo: *Q.* A buys property and dies, leaving no brothers or sisters living born of the same mother, but one of such sisters left issue, who now survive. All the others died without issue. In such a case as this, can any one other than the issue of A's sister succeed to the property purchased by A ?

No one not being such issue of A's sister can succeed. They are the sole heirs.

MANSAH AND OTHERS *v.* DOLPHYNE.

May 11, 1883.

Before HENRY STUBBINS, J.

Succession by Domestics.

Per Chief Andor: The children of a man's slaves, begotten by him, take property in preference to household slaves.

Nonsuit, with liberty to sue again if evidence can be given that these were no children of Neizer.

ABBACAN *v.* BUBUWOONI.

May 25, 1883.

Before H. STUBBINS, J.

Rule of Succession.

Having called in Chiefs Robertson and Kuow Kuta, and they, finding that plaintiff claimed through the father's side and defendant claimed through the mother's side, and the law of the country being that the claimant through the mother's side takes the property,

Judgment for the defendant.

BURA AND AMONOO *v.* AMPIMA.

September 28, 1891.

Before HAYES REDWAR, Acting Judge.

Suzerainty—Subordinate Stools—Rule of Succession—Practice—Hearsay Evidence—Common Reputation—Town Stool Linguist—His Duties— Lachesse.

In this case the plaintiff's original claim was to recover from the defendant for himself and the Abonu people the five Darkem stools belonging to the Abonu people. To this the defendant pleaded "*res judicata*," but afterwards withdrew this special plea and substituted a plea of "entitled to possession."

Subsequently an application was made under Order III., rule 5, for the joinder of King Amonoo IV. of Anamaboe, as plaintiff, on the ground that his suzerainty over the stools of Abonu was in dispute in this cause. Leave was granted for the joinder, and the plaintiff's writ was amended, and stands thus: "The plaintiffs for themselves and the Abonu people claim to establish their title to the five Darkem stools for the town of Abonu." *

Plea, entitled to possession. This plea puts in issue the plaintiffs' claim, and obliges the defendant to prove lawful possession in herself. The plaintiffs' claim must, however, only recover on the strength of their own title, and not on any weakness in that of defendant.

The evidence in this case, although lengthy, is, when analyzed, much simpler than it appears to be at first sight. The plaintiff *Bura's* evidence as to pedigree consists of his own statement and those of the co-plaintiff *Amonoo* and Kofi Akubin, linguist of the town of Abonu, and he deduces a title by succession from Apotuduarkem, the first Chief of Abonu. Apotuduarkem came to Anamaboe, they say, to seek the protection of the then King of Anamaboe from the Asantis. This protection was afforded to him, and he was .

---

* Abonu town is in the neighbourhood of Cape Coast Castle.

granted the land now known as Abonu, by the King of Anamaboe. Apotuduarkem was succeeded by Kurankie-penin, his son, who was placed on the stool of Abonu, which was created under the protection of the King of Anamaboe, because Apotuduarkem's sister Drowa had no son. Kurankie-penin was succeeded by Inkrabia, who was succeeded by Okra, whose mother was, Brainua, the daughter of Drowa, who was the sister of Apotuduarkem. He was succeeded by Kofi Acquah, whose successor was Tchibu, the uncle of the plaintiff *Bura*, whose right has been recognized by King Amonoo IV. of Anamaboe. The woman Brainua was a niece of Apotuduarkem, and had two children, Okra (before mentioned) and a daughter, Yah Fuliwa, who had two children, Kofi Acquah (before mentioned) and a daughter, Orguetey. Orguetey had four children, Tchibu (before mentioned), Teney, a son, Breesee (eldest daughter), and Tenagaiwa (a daughter). Breesee had a son, who is the plaintiff *Bura*, and, therefore, a nephew of Tchibu, who was deposed.

The defendant's evidence as to pedigree is her own state-ment and that of Eccua Finiba, and she also deduces a title by succession from Apotuduarkem. She denies the story of her ancestor seeking the protection of the King of Anamaboe, and represents him as settling at Abonu independently of the King, and the town being subsequently a sort of dependency, or at the least, in alliance with the stool of Cape Coast. The King of Cape Coast, Cudjoe Imbra, however, gives evidence for the plaintiffs and does not support this view, although he cannot say under the protection of what stool the town of Abonu is. He appears to be a disinterested witness, and dis-claims any control over or alliance with the Abonus as a de-pendency of his stool. To return to the defendant's pedigree: Apotuduarkem, according to her case, was succeeded by Bruwa, a brother of Apotuduarkem, who brought one Pimpon as a slave from Asanti, where he, Bruwa, had been to trade. The stool of Apotuduarkem, according to her case, was brought to Abonu by her ancestors, and upon this stool

Bruwa was his successor. He was succeeded by Pimpon, who was a slave; and was placed in charge of the stool by Bruwa's direction. Pimpon was succeeded by Kurankie-penin, whose successor was Kaffu, who in his turn was followed by Orkra. Orkra was succeeded by Kofi Acquah, whose successor was King Amissa, who married King Acquah's daughter. King Amissa is stated by defendant to have been a nephew of Acquah and brother of defendant by the same mother, named Adjua Kuma, who was a sister of Kofi Acquah. The witness Finiba, however, contradicts this, and says that Amissa's mother was one Korkua, so that defendant's evidence is uncorroborated on this point, which is a most material point as affecting her claim to succession through the female line from King Amissa, under whom she claims.

Then arises a difficulty as to the admissibility of some of the evidence as to pedigree. The settled rule of English law of evidence on this point is to admit the oral or written declarations of deceased members of the family to prove a pedigree, and this exception to the rule, excluding hearsay, is founded on the difficulty of otherwise tracing descent and genealogy. Now much of the evidence adduced on both sides in this case does not satisfy the conditions of this rule, and counsel for plaintiffs has argued that, inasmuch as in this country there are no written memorials or history of families, and every matter of that sort depends on oral traditions, the evidence should be admitted. He argued that this had been done constantly, and that the rule, excluding hearsay, was of necessity relaxed by the Courts in cases of this kind. He said also that at the annual native festivals, a custom prevails of the linguist and other headmen and elders of the town giving a sort of recitation of the deeds of the ancestors of their family in which the stool of the place descends, and genealogies were often given, from which the history of the family could be gathered. Further, that hardly any other source of information existed. Now, in this case, the evidence of the witness Kofi Akubin is that of a linguist

and a linguist of the town of Abonu, and it has been shown
that it is the duty of a linguist to know the history of the
family in which the stool descends. A circumstance not to
be overlooked in this case is, that if the English rule be
rigidly applied, evidence on both sides of this case would be
rejected; and this, coupled with the circumstance that the
defendant's counsel has not objected to the admission of the
plaintiffs' evidence on this ground, weighs with the Court. I
hold, therefore, that, as a rigid adherence to the English law
in this respect would work injustice, the evidence in the
nature of *hearsay* adduced in this case is admissible. Apart
from this, even according to English law, evidence of common
reputation is admitted to prove rights affecting a large number
of persons, and therefore in the nature of public rights; also
of customs of manors and boroughs. Now, the right of
succession to the stools of Abonu is one which must
necessarily affect the people of Abonu, and on this ground
also it seems to me that hearsay evidence is admissible.

Dealing generally with the evidence in this case, there
is a discrepancy in the statement of the plaintiff *Bura*, as
compared with that of the co-plaintiff *Amonoo*, relative to
the length of the interregnum after the deposal of Tchibu
from the stool of Abonu; but his evidence on other points
has been corroborated; and looking to the fact that he is
illiterate, I am not disposed to allow a misstatement on one
point of secondary importance to outweigh the fact that his
evidence and that of the other witnesses as to the plaintiffs'
pedigree coincides on every material point.

Looking at the evidence for the defence, I find graver
discrepancies. It was stated that Chief Kudjoe Essel had
been in charge of the Abonu stools; but when called as a
witness for the defence, he appeared surprised at this suggestion and denied the fact. Notwithstanding defendant's
statement that she was born at Abonu, her witness Accundo
stated that she was born at Cape Coast, and when questioned
as to her pedigree, stated that King Amissa placed his
uncle Acquah on the stool of Abonu. Thereby not only

contradicting the defendant's evidence as to pedigree, but betraying an ignorance of the facts of the case. I cannot forget also, as a judge of fact, that when the written record of a Native Court was disallowed in evidence in this case, and the defendant's witness Ashun was questioned as to a record, he stated that no record was kept in the Native Court, and the linguist called to prove judgment and its purport, contradicted the evidence for the defence on this point. The evidence as to a letter from Elmina Prison, from prisoners confined there, fails to support the view advanced by the defence, and the letter, to my mind, is of the ordinary character of a threatening letter, and carries no weight with me as opposed to the evidence of the plaintiff's pedigree.

1. Upon the whole case for the defence, then, I find that there is nothing to show that Kofi Amissa ever occupied the stools of Abonu as rightful successor to Apotuduarkem, although he may have had *charge* of the stools as a sort of caretaker.

2. I find further, that even if he did occupy the stools as rightful successor to Apotuduarkem, the defendant has not succeeded in showing her descent from Amissa, through the female line, there being a conflict between her evidence and that of Eccuah Finiba on this point.

3. Upon the other hand, I find that plaintiff *Bura* establishes his right to the five stools of Abonu, as a descendant of Apotuduarkem according to the native law of succession; but having regard to the admission of his counsel, made in the hearing of this cause, subject, as regards the stool of Pimpon, to the right of any third party whose title can be made out to the right of taking charge of that stool, as to which the Court can express no opinion on the evidence before it.

4. With regard to the suzerainty of the co-plaintiff *Amonoo*, there has been a conflict of evidence, but the evidence for the defence amounts merely to a bare denial of this right, while the evidence for the plaintiff contains more probability in its general tenor, and some of the witnesses

for the defence even have admitted the existence of this right, while the co-plaintiff's case is supported to a certain extent by the testimony of such unbiassed persons as Kudjoe Mbra, King of Cape Coast, and Mr. Jacob Sey. I find, therefore, by a preponderance of testimony, that such a right exists, and that the co-plaintiff is entitled to place a chief on the stools of Abonu and to a general suzerainty over these stools.

5. The only other point raised by the defence requiring notice, is whether the plantiffs, by letter or otherwise showing a knowledge that defendant had litigated her claim and obtained judgment for the recovery of these stools against Akuban and Feakie in this Court, and not taking any steps to assert their respective titles, have been guilty of such delay or acquiescence as to amount to " *lachesse* " within the doctrine that " Delay defeats Equities." I am of opinion on this point, having regard to this delay being only for a short time, viz. two years at the most (the action being before the Court only in last July), and having regard to the dilatory habits of natives in this country, and to all the circumstances of the case, that this equitable doctrine does not apply, and that the plaintiffs are entitled to come to this Court.

Declare that the plaintiffs and every other person or persons claiming or to claim under them, are entitled to the possession of the five stools of Abonu, but subject, as regards the stool of Pimpon, to the right of any third party who shall make a title to the custody or charge of the said stool of Pimpon.

Decree that the plaintiffs be quieted in the possession of the said five stools of Abonu, which shall be delivered to the said plaintiffs forthwith. Let the costs, etc., etc.

Mr. *Sarbah* for the plaintiffs.

Mr. *Macmum* for the defendant.

AMEKOO *v.* AMEVOR.

Accra, September 29, 1892.

Before HUTCHINSON, J.T., C.J.

Administration Suit—Family Property—Native Law.

JUDGMENT.

The decision given on June 13, 1889, upon the application for letters of administration to the estate of Ametefi, was that property ought to devolve according to native law or custom, and administration was accordingly granted to *Amevor.* There was an appeal from that decision, but the appeal was abandoned.

According to native law, as proved in the application for administration, *Amevor* is entitled to manage the property, and he is entitled to the largest share of it, but he " ought" to give something—how much is not fixed by native law—to the other brothers and sisters and the children of Ametefi. Whether he can be by native law compelled to give these persons anything, or whether the duty to do so is only a moral duty, is uncertain. But unless he is legally bound to do so, the decree for administration by the Court ought never to have been made, and I think, therefore, that the Court in distributing the property, especially as the defendant is at variance with some of his brothers and sisters, ought not to give the whole to the defendant.

The only property that the Court can deal with at present is this £562 8*s.* 8*d.* and interest thereon, which is in the hands of the Basel Mission. *Amevor* in his accounts, sworn on August 10 last, shows that he has received £4867 9*s.* 9*d.*, and of that he only accounts for £700 8*s.* 8*d.* ; most of the rest, he says, has been taken by Ter Holma and the lawyers. And he also says that he and Ter Holma are in possession of deceased's land and houses. Ter Holma admits having received over £1000. I shall not, therefore, give either of them any part of this £562 8s. 8d. The third brother, Dsidso, admitted, in action of *Ter Holma* v. *Dsidso*, that he had received some goods of Ametefi's, but did not say how much; and therefore, as he has made no claim now, I shall give him nothing. It has not been shown that either of the sisters of Ametefi, or his widow, or his children, have received anything. I shall therefore divide the balance of the fund (after payment of the costs) amongst them equally.

Mr. *Bannerman* for plaintiff; defendant in person.

In re ISAAC ANAMAN, Deceased.

March 13, 1894.

Before FRANCIS SMITH, J.

Administration—Marriage Ordinance—Dying Declarations— Intestacy—S.C.O., 1876, *sect.* 19.

JUDGMENT.

This is an application by *Grace Amelia Anaman*, widow of the late *Isaac Anaman*, for a grant of letters of administration of the estate of her deceased husband. A notice to prohibit the grant was filed by *Jacob Anaman*, who was in due course warned by a warning in writing.

When the case came on for hearing, the contention by the counsel for *Jacob Anaman* was, not that the grant should not be made to the widow, though in the affidavit filed by Mr. *Jacob Anaman* on April 18, 1893, he claims to be the executor of the deceased, according to the tenor of his dying declaration, but that such a grant should be made with a verbal will reduced into writing subsequently annexed, which verbal will is said to have been made by the deceased, so that his intention as to the disposition of his property should be carried out by the administratrix.

The facts of the case are these. In the month of

October, 1887, the deceased was married to *Amelia Grace Anaman* at Anamaboe, according to the rites or usages observed by the Wesleyan denomination. On January 31, 1893, the deceased then being ill, made a declaration as to the disposition of his property, and died the next day.

There is, however, some conflict as to what were the exact terms of this verbal disposition, the widow stating that he made three declarations—one before· herself and Mr. *Anaman,* another before herself and Mr. Parker, and the third before herself and Amelia Ferguson; whereas Mr. *Anaman* gives evidence of one declaration. Assuming, however, that the deceased disposed of his property in the manner contended by Mr. *Anaman,* the question for determination is, Did the deceased die intestate ?

Mr. *Roberts* contends that as the late *Isaac Anaman* was married according to the provisions of the Marriage Ordinance, 1884, to prevent his personal property from being distributed in accordance with the provisions of the law of England relating to the distribution of the personal estates of intestates, he must have made a will according to English law, the word "intestate" in the Marriage Ordinance referring to a person dying without having made such a will.

On the other hand, Mr. *Sarbah* cleverly argues that the deceased and the widow being natives of the colony, native law and custom must, in terms of sect. 19 of Ordinance No. 4 of 1876, bind them, the Legislature having provided that such law and custom shall be deemed applicable in causes relating to testamentary dispositions; that, as by native law testamentary dispositions mean verbal dispositions, writing not being necessary by native law, a native who makes such verbal disposition cannot be said to die intestate.

That the word "intestate" in the Marriage Ordinance means a person dying without making a will, either in accordance with native law—that is, verbally—or in accordance with English law; that the rules 21 and 22 of Order

51, 2nd Schedule, Supreme Court Ordinance, 1876, are merely rules of procedure, and cannot override the substantive law, and quotes *Abd-ul-Messih* v. *Farra and another, Law Times Report,* vol. 69, p. 106.

That case established that similar rules in the Order in Council of December 12, 1870, conferring probate jurisdiction on the Supreme Consular Court at Constantinople were mere rules of procedure, and that the domicil of the testator must govern in all questions arising as to his testacy or intestacy, or as to the right of persons who claim his succession *ab intestato.*

In that case the domicil of the testator was Cairo, which is not British possession nor governed by English law, and the testator being domiciled in the Ottoman Empire, the law of Turkey became the measure of his personal capacity, upon which his majority or minority, his succession and testacy or intestacy depended.

The case, however, is distinguishable from the present, in that *Isaac Anaman* was domiciled in the Gold Coast Colony, which is a British possession and governed by English law. Unless, therefore, the provisions of sect. 19 of Ordinance No. 4 of 1876 override sect. 16, rules 21, 22 and 23 of Order 51, 2nd Schedule, Ordinance 1876, and the provisions of the Marriage Ordinance 1884, or the provisions of sect. 19, can be consistently carried out side by side with the above enactments and not in conflict thereto, English law must govern the present case.

Section 16 enacts that the jurisdiction of the Court in probate causes may, subject to the Ordinance and rules of Court, be exercised by the Court in conformity with the law and practice for the time being in force in England.

Section 19 provides for the application of native law when not incompatible either directly or by necessary implication with any enactment of the Legislature existing at the commencement of the Ordinance, or which may afterwards come into operation.

Now, the Legislature clearly had in view, in the framing

of sect. 16 and the said rules, the English Statute of Wills,
and has made no provision for the granting of probate of a
will executed in any other form than in the English form.
There is no power conferred on this Court to grant probate
with the will annexed, or probate of a will made according
to native law.

All that the Legislature says is, the Court shall, under
certain circumstances, observe native law in causes relating
to testamentary dispositions ; in other words, shall give
effect to them when practicable. Further, the application of
native law can only be made under the conditions specified
by the Legislature.

It requires no argument to show that the status of
persons who are married under the Ordinance is entirely
different from that of those married according to native law.
Rights are conferred by the former which not only are not
enjoyed by those married according to native law, but are
also inconsistent with the provisions of native law. Disabilities are created which are not known to native law.
But it is contended that it is only in case of intestacy that
these rights can be enforced, that is, where a person died
without making a will either according to English or native
law. Against this contention there is this argument : The
word "intestate" occurs in an Ordinance dealing with
marriage on the same footing as the law of England, and is
used in connection with the devolution of personal property
according to English law. The Ordinance does not regulate
the relationship between a man and a woman married
according to native law. Not, therefore, regulating native
marriages, except by imposing certain restrictions on
persons already married according to native law wishing to
be married according to English law, the meaning of the
word "intestate" must be found from its connection with
the subject of the legislation. And as it is used in connection with English law, its English legal signification
must be ascribed to it and not its native legal import. And
this view is further strengthened by the consideration of

the duty imposed on the registrar to explain to the parties the prohibited degrees of kindred and affinity, and the effect as to the succession of the property of either dying intestate.

I find, therefore—

1. That the application of native law under these circumstances. is incompatible with the enactment of the Legislature; and

2. That the person who is married under the Marriage Ordinance, dies intestate when he or she has not made a will according to the English Statute of Wills.

On these findings I declare that Mr. *Isaac Anaman* died intestate ; the widow is entitled to the administration of his estate, to be distributed in accordance with English law. Under the circumstances I allow no costs.

Mr. *I. J. Roberts* for *Grace Anaman*, the widow, applying for letters of administration.

Mr. *J. M. Sarbah* for *Jacob Anaman*, the caveator.

Where any person who is subject to native law or custom contracts a marriage in accordance with the provisions of this or of any other Ordinance relating to marriage, or has contracted a marriage prior to the passing of this Ordinance, which marriage is validated hereby and such person dies intestate, subsequently to the commencement of this Ordinance, leaving a widow or husband or any issue of such marriage,

And also where any person who is issue of any such marriage as aforesaid dies intestate subsequently to the commencement of this Ordinance,

The personal property of such intestate and also any real property of which the said Intestate might have disposed by Will shall be distributed in accordance with the provisions of the law of England relating to the distribution of the personal estates of Intestates, any native law or custom to the contrary notwithstanding.

Provided always, that where by the law of England, any portion of the estate of such Intestate would become a portion of the casual hereditary Revenues of the Crown, such portion shall be distributed in accordance with the provisions of native law and custom, and shall not become a portion of the said casual hereditary Revenues.

Provided also that real property, the succession to which cannot by native law or custom be affected by testamentary disposition, shall descend in accordance with the provisions of such native law or custom, anything herein to the contrary notwithstanding.

Before the Registrar of Marriages issues his certificate in the case of an intended marriage, either party to which is a person subject to native law or custom, he shall explain to both parties the effect of these provisions as to the succession to property as affected by marriage (Marriage Ordinance, No. 14, 1884, sect. 41).

Nothing in this ordinance shall deprive the Supreme Court of the right to observe and enforce the observance, or shall deprive any person of the benefit, of any law or custom existing in the said Colony and Territories subject to its jurisdiction, such law or custom not being repugnant to natural justice, equity, and good conscience, nor incompatible either directly or by necessary implication with any enactment of the Colonial Legislature existing at the commencement of this ordinance, or which may afterwards come into operation. Such laws and customs shall be deemed applicable in causes and matters where the parties thereto are natives of the said Colony or Territories, and particularly, but without derogating from their application in other cases, in causes and matters relating to marriage and to the tenure and transfer of real and personal property, and to inheritance and testamentary dispositions, and also in causes and matters between natives and Europeans where it may appear to the Court that substantial injustice would be done to either party by a strict adherence to the rules of English law. No party shall be entitled to claim the benefit of any local law or custom, if it shall appear either from express contract or from the nature of the transactions out of which any suit or question may have arisen, that such party

agreed that his obligations in connection with such transactions
should be regulated exclusively by English law ; and in cases
where no express rule is applicable to any matter in controversy
the Court shall be governed by the principles of justice, equity,
and good conscience. .(Section 19, Supreme Court Ordinance
1876.)

ADJUA AMISSA *v.* SUSANNAH KIMFULL AND WILLIAM FYNN.

November 26, 1894.

Before FRANCIS SMITH, J.

Family Property—Marriage Ordinance Will—Intestacy.

JUDGMENT.

This action was for trespass, but as the plaintiff's title
to the house and land has been raised by the defendants,
the question to be first determined is the ownership of the
house and land.   The facts are not in dispute.   The land,
originally, was Eccua Akroma's, *alias* Elizabeth Williams,
who got it from her husband.   Elizabeth Williams had two
brothers, William Fynn and Edward Jonah Fynn, their
mother being Eccua Kraba.   Eccua Kraba was bought by
one Sarah, so that William, Edward Jonah, and Elizabeth,
were domestics of the house of Sarah.   William Fynn
married Margaret, *alias* Araba Dodua, and the defendants
are two of the issue of the marriage.   The mother of
Margaret was Eccua Brobraba, and she was bought by the
said Sarah, so that the defendants are also domestics of the
house of Sarah.   On the death of Elizabeth Williams, who
had built a house on the land, William Fynn succeeded to
the property and built another house on the land, and on
his death, his brother Edward Jonah succeeded, and he also
built a house on the land, which is the subject of the present
action.   As the last of the blood relatives of Elizabeth,
Edward Jonah, who had married but had no issue, devised

this house absolutely to his wife, who survived him, making other devises affecting the other houses and portion of land, and the plaintiff is now claiming the property as her niece. It is further admitted that before building, Edward Jonah sent to inform the women of the House that he was not going to take the house anywhere, but that he was going to build it in the house. This case depends entirely upon native law, and must be decided accordingly.

Mr. *Sarbah,* for the plaintiff, contends that as Elizabeth Williams obtained the land from her husband and not from Sarah, and as Edward Jonah Fynn built the house without the help of any of the members of the family, he being the last survivor from the same womb as Elizabeth, he became absolutely entitled to the property and could dispose of it as he liked. And having by his will left it to his widow, the plaintiff, who is her heiress, is now the owner of the property.

On the other hand, it is contended that though Elizabeth received the land from her husband, yet she being a domestic of the house of Sarah, who could have dealt with the land as if it were her own, the land became family property, so that notwithstanding that Edward Jonah Fynn was the last survivor from the same womb as Elizabeth, he was still a domestic of the house of Sarah, and succeeded to the family property as such domestic. Hence he could have no more than a life interest in the land. Also as to the house, his interest therein was the same, and on his death the house and land passed to the other domestics in. turn. It was therefore not his property to dispose of it absolutely.

The facts of the case, with the variation of names, were submitted by me, with certain questions thereon, to the King of Elmina, the King of Anamaboe, and Chief Hama, and they have given me the native law thereon. There has, however, been a difference of opinion, two holding the same view, that is, the King of Elmina and Chief Hama, and one, the King of Anamaboe, the opposite view.

The opinion of the King of Elmina is that Edward Jonah

Fynn did not and could by no means become absolutely entitled to his sister's property, viz. the land with the houses built by his sister and brother William, by virtue of his being the last from the same womb. He being a domestic as his sister and brother of the house of Sarah, he had only a life interest in the property, the property passing, at his death, and in the absence of the blood relatives of Sarah, to the fellow-domestics of the same house in turn, including the children of William and Dodua.

Edward Jonah Fynn had no greater than a life interest in even the house he himself built on the land, whether his fellow-domestics assisted him in the building or not; whatever Edward Jonah Fynn had in life, whether by means of personal labour or by inheritance, were regarded as family property, and were, therefore, descendible after death to the surviving domestics.

"Edward Jonah Fynn not having more than a life interest in the house he built, it would be against native law to dispose of it as he has done."

If Edward Jonah Fynn did not even care to inform the fellow-domestics that he was not going to take the house anywhere, but that he was going to build it in the house, he would still have no more than a life interest only in the house. The fact of his being a domestic limits his interest to a life interest, and prevents him from making an absolute disposition of it to his wife. "He could only have the right to dispose of both houses and land in any way he pleased, only when there was not even one of the domestics surviving."

Chief Hama, by his linguist, whom I examined here on the 16th instant, gave practically the same answers.

The King of Anamaboe replies as follows (I am now substituting the real names for the fictitious ones used in my letter to the King):—

"The argument in favour of the children, viz. that the fellow-domestics who now represent Sarah have the same right as Sarah, is not quite correct or sound, for fellow-domestics cannot represent their master in such or same and equal position as to be capable of claiming the property of their fellow-domestics, at least the property acquired by themselves, and not descended from their master, as in this singular and rare case before you." I answer—1. Edward Jonah Fynn became entitled to the property of his sister and brother because he was of the same womb with them. 2. Not because he built the house without their assistance, though if they had given him assistance, it might have induced him to act otherwise, yet not necessarily so. 3. He could dispose of it as he had done. 4. If he said that he did not know or understand in his own right his telling them, that could not limit his interest." There is no question which calls for this answer, but I presume the King is referring to the message sent by Edward Jonah Fynn when about to build. " I think he only said that to encourage them, to assist them, or to avoid their groundless interference for the time being. I may add that, as Edward Jonah Fynn made a will and gave it to his wife, the children would not lay claim to it on the mere ground that they are fellow-domestics, and who never care to give assistance in the erection of a house by Edward Jonah Fynn. And the Emancipation has so affected such property of a slave, that Edward Jonah Fynn could dispose of it as he has done."

I am not quite sure whether this opinion of the King is not the outcome of a mixture of native and English law. I can well conceive cases in which the view thus expressed by the King would be more consistent with natural justice, equity, and good conscience. Such, for instance, when a domestic has severed his connection with the house of which he was a member, and after that had acquired wealth by his own individual exertion. In such a case, it would be unfair to control his power of disposition of his property. But the present case is not one of this character, and I must therefore decide it in accordance with native law, as expressed by the majority.

By that law, Edward Jonah Fynn had no more than a life interest in the land and houses, and therefore could not

have disposed of any of them by will, and the plaintiff
cannot be in a better position than he.   There will, therefore, be judgment for the defendants.   But I think this is a
case in which counsel was rightly and properly engaged,
and I allow him his costs.   Further, in view of the circumstances of the case, the rent of the shop will now be received
by *Susannah Kimfull*, representing the head of the family ;
the costs of counsel should be borne by the defendants.
And I order so accordingly, and with this exception each
party will pay its own costs.

MISCELLANEOUS CASES.

QUACOE KOOM *v.* OWEA AND KUDJOE TAINEE.

July 21, 1878.

Before MARSHALL, J.

Jurisdiction of Native Courts—Object of Supreme Court.

Plaintiff, of Mampon, in Denkera, claims property from
defendants.   It is at Sooberesoo, three days from Mampon.
It is called Sisa-Ansah.   I had four houses on it, broken
by the Asantis.   The land belonged to my predecessors.   I
succeeded them.

JUDGMENT.

This is a case which ought, in the first place, to have
been taken before the King of Mampon for his decision.
The Supreme Court is not intended to supersede the authority
of the kings and chiefs.   As this has not been done, I shall
uphold the opinion of the King given in the evidence of
his messenger, and give judgment that the land in dispute
belongs to the plaintiff, and the defendants are not to interfere with it, and defendant *Tainee* is to bear the costs of
this action.

QUABINA ABAKAN v. QUASIE ACKARSA.

July 23, 1878.

Before MARSHALL, J.

Trespass—land Abakaneckie, a short distance from Cape Coast, then in possession of plaintiff.   Chiefs find that the land belongs to the plaintiff.

The Court intimated that in these land cases the opinion of the assessors must be followed, unless there appears some injustice in it.

Judgment for plaintiff.

OPPON v. ACKINIE.

October 24, 1887.

Before HECTOR MACLEOD, C.J., SMALMAN SMITH, J., FRANCIS SMITH, J.

This is an appeal against a judgment of the Divisional Court of Cape Coast, dated February 14, 1887, confirming a judgment of the District Commissioner, Saltpond, ordering defendant *Ackinie* to pay damages to *Oppon* in the amount of £5, with 11s. costs.

Mr. *Eminsang*, with *Williams* and *Renner*, for appellant (*Ackinie*).

Oppon in person.

Judgment, October 24, 1887 :—

This is an appeal by the defendant *Ackinie* against a judgment of the Divisional Court of the Western Province, dated February 14, 1887, affirming a judgment of the District Commissioner of Saltpond, dated February 25, 1886, by which the defendant was ordered to pay to the plaintiff the sum of £5 as damages, with 11s. costs.

The facts of the case are practically not in dispute.   A person, named *Ghartey* (formerly one of the defendants in this action), charged another person, named *David Otchafoo*, before the defendant *Ackinie*, who is the King of Aikunfie, with receiving bribes.

According to the custom, in such matters a surety had to be found, and the plaintiff *Oppon*, one of *Ackinie's* own subjects, became surety for the payment of any costs to be found due by *Otchafoo*, in the matter of that complaint.

Otchafoo was found liable to costs.

If *Oppon* was dissatisfied with the decision, his remedy, according to one of the witnesses called on February 14 last, was to pay the costs and cause an appeal to be brought to the British Courts ; but *Oppon* refused to pay the costs, alleging that he was not satisfied with the decision of King *Ackinie*.

Thereupon *Ackinie* caused *Oppon* to be arrested and imprisoned in respect of the refusal to pay the costs.

The power of arrest and imprisonment under such circumstances has been exercised by the defendant and his predecessors as far back as the memory of living witnesses can carry us, as one of the royal prerogatives.

Upon these facts there arises a short but very important point in law. Important, because it affects the whole judicial powers of kings and chiefs throughout the Protected Territories. Short, because it is all summed up in this question : "Has the Supreme Court Ordinance, 1876, swept away the previously existing judicial powers of native kings and chiefs ? "

Before we proceed to discuss this question, we desire to make one preliminary observation, and it is so important that we shall direct it to be recorded in red ink.

We are not here engaged in any inquiry as to the extent of her Majesty's power and jurisdiction in and over the Protected Territories. We are only inquiring whether, through the medium of the Colonial Legislature, she has, in virtue of the power and jurisdiction vested in her, yet chosen to say that the judicial powers of native kings and chiefs shall no longer exist.

King *Ackinie* has, in the course of this case, had the benefit of nearly all the local legal talent. *Oppon* has had no such aid. Nevertheless, had BAILEY, C.J., still been alive, he would doubtless have given judgment in *Oppon's* favour. That is evident, from several cases decided by him in the Divisional Court of the Central Province. In none of these cases did the learned Chief Justice enter into any discussion upon the point, which one must suppose appeared to him so clear as to require no consideration.

We know, however, the reasons upon which he founded his judgments, and we think it only right that we should state them. He founded his opinion upon sects. 11 and 12 of the Supreme Court Ordinance, 1876. Regarding sect. 11, he would in substance say, if he were here to-day, "The Supreme Court Ordinance, sect. 11, vests all the jurisdiction of the High Court of Justice in England (Admiralty excepted) in the Supreme Court of the Colony. That being so, what jurisdiction the native chiefs formerly possessed, was from the date of the passing of that Ordinance extinguished."

Regarding sect. 12 he would doubtless say, "What jurisdiction, civil or criminal, was, or is not, exercisable by her Majesty in these territories? Absolutely none. All, then, is vested in the Supreme Court, and, according to the concluding words of the section, shall be exercised under and according to the provisions of the Ordinance and not otherwise." If *Oppon* had all the legal talent in the world to plead for him, we do not see how his case could be more powerfully stated.

But we think BAILEY, C.J., failed to apprehend the object and scope of this Ordinance. First, however, let us consider sects. 11 and 12 by themselves. While these sections contain words affirmative of the Supreme Court, we find in them no negative words, no words of conclusion, nothing to indicate that jurisdiction, other than her Majesty's, is to cease. We see no words that lead us to think it would be inconsistent with the object of the

Legislature that her Majesty's jurisdiction and the jurisdiction of the kings and chiefs should be co-existent. The civil and criminal jurisdiction of her Majesty exercisable in the Protected Territories at the commencement of the Ordinance, was one, to a great extent, occurrent with the jurisdiction exercisable by the native kings and chiefs; and that is, to our minds, a conclusive answer to the arguments which we have put into the mouth of BAILEY, C.J.

But we must not confine our attention to sects. 11 and 12 of this Ordinance. It is not by any means the only Ordinance that created a Supreme Court for the Gold Coast, and regulated its procedure. Various such Ordinances were passed from 1853 downwards, and we think we are right when we say that not one of such Ordinances referred to the Local Native Courts, yet these Native Courts exercised jurisdiction side by side with the Supreme Court so created.

The key to the successful interpretation of sects. 11 and 12 already mentioned is, we think, to be found in sect. 20 of the same Ordinance; from which it appears that, prior to this Ordinance of 1876, her Majesty had been exercising her jurisdiction by the help of a very confusing arrangement of Courts and magistrates. All these were to cease, and the one Supreme Court, whose powers and jurisdiction are described in sects. 11 and 12, took their place.

Two years later the Colonial Legislature passed an Ordinance (No. 8 of 1878) "to facilitate and regulate the exercise, in the Protected Territories, of certain powers and jurisdiction by native authorities." Can any one read that Ordinance, and particularly sects. 3, 4, 10, and 30 thereof, without coming to the conclusion that the jurisdiction of the kings and chiefs is there treated as existing, but requiring regulation? The Ordinance was confirmed by her Majesty though it was not thought expedient to proclaim any head chief's division under it.

In 1883 it was repealed, not because it did not speak the truth, but that an Ordinance more in harmony with the views of the Legislature for the time being, might take its place; and that successor is No. 5 of 1883. It also treats native tribunals as existing, but requiring regulation.

It might be observed of these two native jurisdiction Ordinances that, by mere recital, they could not restore what was taken away by the Supreme Court Ordinance of 1876. Perfectly true; but, when considering whether the Supreme Court Ordinance of 1876 did or did not take away jurisdiction from native tribunals, do not these native jurisdiction Ordinances give us considerable light?

Again, the point seems covered by authority. In the end of 1880, or beginning of 1881, the Divisional Court of the Central Province ordered *Quamin Fori*, King of Aquapim, to pay damages to one *Bruce*, as compensation for illegal arrest.

Bruce was charged with violating a girl in the bush, and *Quamin Fori* ordered his arrest. The Divisional Court was of opinion that *Quamin Fori* had used such violence in having *Bruce* brought before him that he must pay £30 damages and costs.

Upon the 1st of April, 1881, this judgment was reversed by the Full Court (MARSHALL, C.J., and J. W. SMITH, Ag. Judge), whose judgment says, "We are of opinion that the king, in all that was done, acted within the powers which have always been recognized and allowed to the Native Courts, unless those powers are taken away by the Governor; and that if he was in fault, it was in not proceeding further with the case, and inquiring more fully into the charge against *Bruce*."

As a criticism upon that judgment, it might be observed that it only recognized powers in kings and chiefs, which can be taken away by the Governor; and that, as the Governor has no power to take away inherent jurisdiction from a king, that cannot have been the jurisdiction recognized in *Quamin Fori's* case, and therefore his case cannot apply to the present one.

Without discussing whether a Governor has power to

take away inherent jurisdiction, and without pretending to understand what the Full Court meant by the words "unless those powers are taken away by the Governor," we cannot help regarding the suggested line of criticism as unworthy of comment.

Had it not been for the opinion of BAILEY, C.J., we would have entertained no doubt upon the question which we have discussed. Now that we have considered it from every possible point of view, we are clear that the Supreme Court Ordinance, 1876, has in no way impaired the judicial powers of native kings and chiefs, and, so far as we know, it has not been suggested that any other Ordinance has taken them away.

The defendant (appellant) in the present case has exercised a very ordinary judicial power, and therefore we think the judgment of the Court below ought to be reversed and judgment entered for the defendant *Ackinie*.

We are not inclined to give him costs, for the impression made upon our minds is that he had brought this action upon himself. It must be distinctly understood that there is to be no imprisonment without an adequate and regular supply of food, means of washing daily, and ample opportunities for obeying the calls of nature, being given to every prisoner.

EBBOE *v.* ABOMA.

April 19, 1844.

Plaintiff claims *from Aboma,* as representative of a deceased pawn, 3 ozs. 6 acks. of gold, subject to deduction of 1 oz. already paid by Mrs. F. Smith. Complaint dismissed, inasmuch as it appeared that plaintiff had done that which, by the native laws and customs, he had no right to do, namely, that he had pawned a person in pawn to him ; and, moreover, that when he was offered the balance of his claim against the deceased pawn, he had refused the same, wishing to keep up his claim against the family of the deceased.

QUASHI OTTOO *v.* ANOCHIE.

July 22, 1844.

Coram, MACLEAN.

Plaintiff claims from defendant the sum of 20 ozs. 4 acks., being a sum advanced by the plaintiff's uncle for the redemption of defendant's uncle.

Plaintiff states that while the Assins, to which tribe defendant belongs, remained under his (plaintiff's) immediate protection, he abstained from pressing this claim, but that the Lieutenant-Governor having recently declared the Assins entirely independent of him, and the whole of the Assins, including defendant, having solemnly sworn no longer to acknowledge *Ottoo* as their feudal superior, he now brings forward this claim in order to its being liquidated.

Judgment for plaintiff, 9 ozs.

AGAH AGUAH *v.* QUAMINA EFFEE.

May 8, 1844.

Witchcraft—Unlawfully charging.

Defendant accused of having charged plaintiff with practising witchcraft, and with having thereby caused the death of a child lately deceased, to the great annoyance and injury to plaintiff. Partially proved; defendant ordered to pay costs, and fined. Security, that neither he nor his family shall trouble plaintiff in future under a penalty of 4 ozs. of gold. Seckie and Appah, securities.

QUOW NYAKON *v.* KOFI SARR.

June 3, 1871.

Before CHALMERS, Judicial Assessor.

Liability of Principal to his Surety.

Chiefs : When palaver settled in the country, it is necessary for a man who is called on to find security, to find that security required. If he found security, the security would ask the man what he would give him for undertaking the whole result of the case. When that is arranged and the case is gone into, the security would be liable in the expenses and results of the case. And if there be debt to be paid by the party, the opposite parties would look to the security for payment of the debt and expenses. When case finished in one Court and the party who found the security was not satisfied and wished to go elsewhere, it would be necessary for the man who got the security to consult the surety and say he wished him to continue his suretyship, and, if he continued, he would still be liable in the second Court, otherwise he would not. The amount paid to the surety in return for his obligation depends on the nature of the case. The amount would be 2, 3, 4 ackies ; in fact, just matter of bargain.

JUDGMENT.

June 6, 1871.

Find that the defendant became security for the plaintiff in proceedings before Chief Amoah at his (plaintiff's) instance against Yow Accoffie ; and that the plaintiff is bound to reimburse the defendant for the expenses for which he became liable in these proceedings ; find that these expenses were of the amount of 12 ackies : further, the plaintiff engaged to pay $4\frac{1}{2}$ ackies to the defendant in consideration of his becoming security for him.

Judgment, therefore, for defendant, for $16\frac{1}{2}$ ackies. No costs.

SAMUEL FERGUSON *v.* JOS. TURTON.

March 18, 1872.

Before CHALMERS, Judicial Assessor.

*Current Account—Pass-book Debit and Credit Entries—Wrongful
Dismissal—Yearly Service—Allowance for Palm-oil Leakage.*

JUDGMENT.

The plaintiff entered in the employment of the defendants on January 1, 1871, under an agreement, in the
capacity of factor in charge of the factory at Saltpond.
He was supplied with goods and money by the defendants,
and his duty was to dispose of these to the best advantage,
receiving palm-oil and other produce in return. He continued in this employment till December 5, 1871, when he
was dismissed. During the currency of the employment,
accounts had been kept between the parties, but had not
been brought to any balance. On its termination, the
accounts were made up and balanced. The plaintiff being
dissatisfied with the result arrived at, now sues the
company for various items of credit to which he considers
he is entitled, amounting in aggregate to a sum of
£214 12s. These items it is necessary to consider
separately.

The first claim is for the value of 630 gallons of palm-
oil. The account between *Ferguson* and the company is
kept by means of a pass-book, on the credit side of which
entries are from time to time made by the company,
representing the various instalments of produce delivered
into the company's possession by *Ferguson* from the
factory. It appears that when the examination and
balance of the account were being made, the defendants
considered that *Ferguson* had received credit by these
entries for 630 gallons of oil more than he had transmitted to them, and, in order to correct the balance, they
debited him by cross entry with 630 gallons; this debit
Ferguson now seeks to expunge.

Amongst the books which it was *Ferguson's* duty to keep, was palm-oil book, and in this he should have entered all oil received by him into the factory, distinguishing what he received in the cause of his own transactions as a factor (for which alone he was entitled to receive credit), from that which he received for behoof of the company from persons who were indebted to them and which he held as custodian merely. The book ought also to show quantities of produce delivered by *Ferguson* into the possession of the company.

On examination, I find that the actual difference between the aggregate of the entries of the palm-oil with which the company have credited *Ferguson*, and the aggregate of the delivery items entered by him on his palm-oil book, is 609½ gallons of credit entries in excess of the delivery entries. It was explained by the witnesses that the credit entries were made after *Ferguson* had made shipments from the receipts given to him by the shipmaster and other person who received delivery from him for behoof of the company. The practice was that these receipts, together with all *Ferguson's* books, were sent monthly to the head establishment at Cape Coast, where the necessary entries were made, and as soon as that was done the books were returned into *Ferguson's* custody, the receipts being retained. It is impossible to check the items by comparison of the figures in the palm-oil book with the cash-book; the cash-book entries being frequently in lump sums, while the delivery entries are more detailed. Nor can I arrive at any satisfactory result by stating the delivery and credit entries in the form of a progressive account. I have endeavoured to do this, following the dates of shipments as shown in the oil-book and those of the credits as in the pass-book. As might be expected, the aggregate of the shipments is generally in advance of the credits, but sometimes, on the other hand, the credits are largely in advance of the shipments.

The rule of law which is applicable to the credit entries

made by the company in the pass-book is that these entries are evidence against the company in favour of *Ferguson*. But they are not conclusive; it may be shown by sufficient evidence that all or any of them are erroneous. If not thus shown to be erroneous they ought to stand good. Perhaps it may be supposed that *Ferguson's* entries in the oil-book should occupy a similar position as evidence against him to the effect of limiting the credits to which he may be entitled. To a certain extent they do bear this force, but not identically. There is the material difference that the effect of *Ferguson's* entries can only be negative, while the credit entries are positive. The same degree of inference is not to be drawn from the absence of an item in the oil-book to what belongs to the insertion by the company of a credit item in the pass-book.

The probability of the latter having been made erroneously, was considerably less than that of *Ferguson* having omitted to make an entry of oil to which he was entitled. Besides this, I am not quite satisfied, on the present evidence, that it was impossible for *Ferguson* to be entitled to any credit entry of oil not passing through the Saltpond factory. There is one item I observed in the pass-book which apparently did not pass through his hands or come from the Saltpond factory, and which nevertheless seems to be a legitimate credit entry. This is under date November: "291 gallons palm-oil from Mr. C. B. Acquah on your account—£21 16s. 6d." It is possible that other similar payments might be discovered as part of larger and lump payments, if the vouchers had been examined. It is therefore not enough that there should be an excess of the pass-book credits over the delivery credits claimed by *Ferguson* in the oil-book; the onus lies on the defendants to show specifically that there is error in the credits they have given.

The defendants have pointed to an entry of 608 gallons under date February 15, and again an identical entry under date April 11, and they contend that this should be held to be a double entry of the same consignment. There is but one entry in the oil-book of the shipment of a parcel of 608 gallons, but, as I have already noticed, the two sets of entries not being always counterparts of each other, there is not much to be inferred from this fact alone. Then the plaintiff has put in a memorandum dated March 31, 1871, showing 608 gallons purchased by him with cash as the return for £55, cash supplied to him by Mr. Capper. It appears to have been given with a view of showing *Ferguson* what was the balance of cash he owed on that transaction. From its date and the date of the letter transmitting it, it plainly belongs to the first parcel of 608 gallons, but standing by itself as it does in the present evidence, it throws no light on the second entry. Again, if I am correct as to the payment from Aĉquah, the amount over-credited on the Saltpond transactions would be the utmost only 318 gallons, and if I should disallow the 608 gallons, the credits would be short of the shipments. In these circumstances I have determined that the most equitable adjustment I can at present make is to direct the debt entry of 630 gallons to be struck out of the account, that being in any event erroneous. It follows that plaintiff's claim to have judgment for the value is superseded, leaving the proof still open as to the supposed over-credit of 609½ gallons.

The second item of demand is 1300 gallons, claimed to have been shipped by plaintiff, and for which he says he has received no credit. It is true that there is no credit entry of this particular item any more than there is of many other detailed items. But plaintiff has got full credit, as is shown by the aggregate results of the accounts which, in their present position, give him, as I have just stated, 609½ gallons more than there is any proof of his having shipped, except the company's own entries in his favour. This item is therefore disallowed.

The plaintiff next claims three months' salary in respect of his having been dismissed without notice.

Although there is not in the agreement any express stipulation as to the period of its endurance, yet being a contract for services to be rendered for yearly wages, it is impliedly a contract for a year; renewable, of course, by the consent, express or implied, of parties, but if not so renewed, coming to its natural termination at the end of one year from its commencement without notice. Plaintiff is consequently entitled to salary. from the date of his dismissal, viz. December 5 to the end of the year or December 31, unless his dismissal was justified. I consider that this is not established. Some improper message, or some message which was understood as improper, was sent by plaintiff, but it is not sufficiently instructed that this amounted to a cause of dismissal. Again, though it is said that there was dissatisfaction with the mode in which the plaintiff carried on his duties, it is not said that he would have been discharged for these faults; at least he was not so discharged. The actual and proximate cause of dismissal seems to have been that by his arrest and detention in Cape Coast plaintiff became for the time incapacitated for carrying on the charge of the factory. A disability such as this being merely temporary would not, any more than a temporary disability from sickness, authorize the employer to dismiss his servant. It is right to observe that in construing the agreement as for a year, I have done so in the absence of proof of any local custom in reference to trading agreements such as the present, which might attach to them a different significance.

* * * * *

Then there are three items of claim for oil used in filling up leakage, amounting together to 207 gallons used in filling up 112 puncheons. There was no agreement as to leakage. The evidence as to the practice is rather conflicting. While the defendants show that it has not been the practice of the African Merchant Company to allow their factors for leakage, there is evidence that it is the rule of the other firms to do so, and, of course, this general practice must regulate in the absence of stipulation. But there is not evidence of the extent of the leakage which is allowed, and it is certainly not to be supposed to be indefinite. The result which I arrive is that leakage should be allowed to the factor so far as inevitable, but not such as is the result of careless cooperage or other improper management. I regret there is little evidence as to what might be taken to be a reasonable average leakage allowance. As a mean I shall allow plaintiff to take credit for 84 gallons, being three-quarters of a gallon on each puncheon.

The next item of claim is for the value of a cask of tobacco seized by defendants when they took possession of the Saltpond store upon plaintiff's dismissal. They did so on the assumption that it was their own property, as they did not assume that the plaintiff had in their warehouse any goods for the purpose of trading on his own account, which it was not intended that he should do. It was undoubtedly within the spirit of his agreement, and more distinctly expressed, if need were, in his written instructions that he should not trade on his own account. Therefore I do not think that the defendants were in fault in taking the tobacco. Plaintiff should have accepted it when offered to be returned to him, and if the company have taken reasonable care of it in the mean time, it will be sufficient that they now restore it to the plaintiff.

The claim of the plaintiff having been so much reduced, his costs will be subject to modification.

Judgment for plaintiff, £20 19s. 4d.

ABADIE v. QUASIE OYAM.

April 26, 1872.

Before CHALMERS, Judicial Assessor.

For Contempt of King Moguah's Court, to whose Jurisdiction you are lawfully subject—Native King's Jurisdiction.

In this action the King of Edjumaku, prosecutor, prosecutes Oyam for having refused to attend his Court when summoned; and at last, when apprehended and brought there, having made his escape from the King's prison, to which he was committed on declining to make his defence. Oyam was a subject of King Moguah; the person with whom he had the dispute was also his subject; the matter of the dispute was of a nature which properly fell within the King's cognizance. There is no good reason alleged by the defendant for refusing to obey the summons, or for refusing to state his case; and if the matter (had) finished there, I should have given my decision against the defendant, and ordered him to pay satisfaction of sufficient amount to King Moguah.

But I find that on defendant's refusal to state his defence, King Moguah committed the defendant to prison. It does not appear to me that this was a proper step to have taken. It would have been sufficient if the King had proceeded to give judgment by default against the defendant. This being so, although I think it is right to decide in King Moguah's favour, because the defendant was clearly in the wrong in not promptly obeying his summons, I do not award more than a nominal fine on the defendant. He is fined 4 ackies; failing payment, he will be imprisoned with hard labour for fourteen days.

NOTE.—A king's subject, when summoned in a matter in which his King has full cognizance, should not refuse to attend. That is productive of much confusion. But he is not therefore bound to pay excessive expenses. If the decision is unsatisfactory, the party deeming himself aggrieved has an appeal to Cape Coast, and the expenses also should be subject to the appeal. What I have stated applies to the case of persons summoned by the King of their own district under whom they live; and I do not say anything at present as to persons summoned out of their district. It is a practice which prevails to considerable extent, but it seems to me to be abusive, and one about which the kings might do well to enter into some arrangement among themselves. This last remark does not apply to the present palaver heard by the King of Anamaboe, which was by arrangement, as it appears, with King Moguah.

D. P. C.

BEDDOOMASSOO *v.* JOHN BOSSOO.

August 3, 1844.

Abjuration—Calling Oath.

Defendant accused of going to the house where one of plaintiff's captains stopped, and calling down fetish to kill plaintiff, this being considered among the natives a serious and punishable offence.

Defendant guilty, and fined 4 acks, with costs.

QUACOE BUAFOO, OF AMANTIN *v.* ENIMIL, KING OF AMANTIN.

July 4, 1874.

Before MARSHALL, Judicial Assessor.

Jurisdiction of Kings—Liability for Results of Oaths.

JUDGMENT.

In this case, *Enimil*, King of Eastern Wassaw, is accused by *Quacoe Buafoo*, one of his blood relations, of cruelty and extortion exercised upon him and his nephew.

The defendant being summoned by me to answer this charge, promised by a letter, dated May 16, to do so in person, but asked for thirty days' time to put in an appearance. The thirty days elapsed without any further word from or of him. I again wrote and called upon him to keep his promise of appearing, but he has not done so. I therefore heard the case of the plaintiff in his absence, and now give judgment upon it.

From the evidence laid before me, it appears that the defendant accused the plaintiff of practising fetish against the late King, and by so doing causing his death. He also made defendant chargeable for an accusation of theft brought against plaintiff's late mother, which, according to plaintiff's evidence, was never proved against her, and further, accused plaintiff of absenting himself from the ceremony of defendant's being made King, when although, according to plaintiff, the reason for this was that he was too ill to attend. Defendant made these accusations against plaintiff the ground for laying upon him a fine so enormous that the chiefs interfered, and it was reduced to 15 pereguans 6 ackies. To raise this money plaintiff was forced to pawn six relatives and three slaves. In addition to this, defendant put plaintiff and his nephew, who had nothing to do with these matters, in cruel logs, and kept them so for five days and nights. For one day the nephew was kept with his hand chained to his foot. The defendant also swore his oath upon Adjuah Yarkoo, a wife of the plaintiff, driving her from her husband, forbidding her to give him food, and allowing any one to have connection with her. This last act is a great aggravation of the defendant's offence, and I wish to lose no opportunity of making it known that persons will be always held responsible for deeds committed under this pernicious practice of swearing oaths.

I have every wish and intention to uphold the authority of kings and chiefs when properly exercised, but it is my duty to protect the people against all cruelty and extortion practised upon them by their rulers.

The evidence in this case proves defendant to have used his power and position in exercising both cruelty and extortion upon the plaintiff and his family, bringing misery and ruin upon them, and causing nine members of it to be pawned. He has been guilty of breaking his word to this Court and of disobedience to its order, which is an offence which cannot be tolerated. The defendant was established on his stool by a proclamation of Governor Sir Garnet Wolseley, and after receiving large supplies of arms and ammunition he failed to give any assistance in the late war. And now he stands condemned of cruelty, extortion, and contempt of the highest native Court in the protectorate.

The Chief of Cape Coast, who sat in the case with me, informs me that extortion like this is constantly practised in Wassaw, and asked me to make a severe example of the defendant for this and for his disobedience to the Court, and also as a warning to other rulers.

The order of the Court is that the defendant is to refund to the plaintiff the 29 ozs. 5 ackies = £105 10s. 6d., which he extorted from him, and that he pay 3 ozs. to the plaintiff and 3 ozs. to plaintiff's nephew as compensation for the cruel and barbarous treatment they received, and also that he pay 1 oz. as compensation to Adjuah Yarkoo, besides the costs of this suit and maintenance for the plaintiff, his wife, and nephew, at the rate of 5s. a day for the three, commencing from April 28, until they are enabled to return to their home, and the defendant is warned against molesting them again.

Should defendant come to Cape Coast, he is not to be allowed to leave until this order is obeyed. A copy of this judgment will be sent to his Excellency Captain Strahan, that he may be acquainted with the behaviour of the defendant.

FULL COURT.

ALAPATIRA v. HALLIDAY; DAVIES, Trustee.*

Lagos, April 20, 1881.

Judgment by Mr. Justice MACLEOD :—

This case comes on appeal from the Divisional Court of the Eastern Province. The respondent, who in the Court below was plaintiff, got judgment in his favour for the amount sued for with costs, and from that judgment of July 9, 1880, the defendant now appeals.

The facts of the case are very simple. The cause of action was a balance of account amounting to £724 6s. 11d. for goods sold and delivered, alleged to have been due by the defendant to Mr. J. P. L. Davies in the month of January, 1876. Mr. J. P. L. Davies, however, was adjudicated a bankrupt on August 9, 1876, and the plaintiff in this case was the trustee appointed to take charge of his bankrupt estate.

* Callendar, Sykes, and Co. v. Colonial Secretary of Lagos and Davies ; Williams v. Davies (1891), Appeal Cases, 460 ; Wheeler's Privy Council Law, 868.

It was held by the Privy Council, in the Consolidated Appeals, that the Supreme Court of the Gold Coast Colony had no bankruptcy jurisdiction in 1877, and therefore could not act as an auxiliary to the English Court under sect: 74 of the Bankruptcy Act of 1869. *Held*, further, that the English Bankruptcy Act of 1869 applies to all her Majesty's dominions, and therefore that an adjudication under that Act operates to vest in the trustee in bankruptcy the bankrupt's title to real estate, situate in Lagos, subject to any requirements prescribed by the local law as to the conditions necessary to effect a transfer of real estate there situate. *Per the Court :* It would certainly be a matter for regret if it were found that a person in quiet possession of land could be expropriated by the State, and could not get the price of his land except by taking legal proceedings and paying the costs. Such miscarriages of justice have happened here in earlier times by the oversight of the Legislature ; but when notice was attracted to them, the law was put on a footing which effectually prevented their recurrence. Their lordships are glad to find that the law of Lagos is not such as to prevent justice being done in this respect.

The Colonial Secretary should be charged with the costs of the action and appeal in the colony.

On examination the defendant admitted that in the month of January, 1876, he did owe this sum to Mr. J. P. L. Davies, and further stated that since that time he had paid the whole debt either to Mr. J. P. L. Davies or his brother Mr. E. A. L. Davies. The plaintiff, however, contended that this was not a valid payment so far as he was concerned, because it was a payment made to the bankrupt by a person who at the time of that payment had notice of an act of bankruptcy committed by the bankrupt and available against him for adjudication. This contention of the plaintiff was supported by me in the Court below, and I see no reason now to change the view which I then formed. It is true that the defendant on examination denied all knowledge of such notice, and this point has been the mainstay of his counsel in the Appeal Court. But I am satisfied, on the evidence of Jacob Samuel Leigh, and his clerk John Payne Jackson, that a copy of notice marked D was served upon the defendant on the 1st of January, 1876. Mr. Leigh tells us that he caused one of these notices to be endorsed to the defendant, that he sent his clerk to deliver it, and that the clerk on his return reported to him that he had delivered it. The clerk himself, Mr. Jackson, corroborates this. He remembers addressing one of these notices to the defendant, and he handed it to the defendant himself. On that evidence I am satisfied that the service did actually take place as narrated to us by Mr. Leigh and Mr. Jackson. But what is the effect and value of this service? The notice is in English, and the defendant on whom it was served is a native. There are many things which must be considered in estimating the value of this service. Though the defendant can neither write nor read the English language, yet he is a native of superior intelligence. Ledger C shows that for five years the defendant carried on large business transactions with the bankrupt, and the first entry in the Ledger C shows a debit balance carried forward from Ledger B amounting to £293 8s. 11d.

The bankrupt is a man who carried on his business, so

far as it required to be written, in the English language, and in the course of the numerous and important transactions between the defendant and the bankrupt, many trade documents must have passed between them. We cannot ignore the custom of the traders in the country where we reside.

If a native trader receives a printed or written letter and does not keep an educated clerk of his own, he gets the letter interpreted to him. Unless he did so it would be impossible for him to carry on his trade. Now, I am not aware that the Bankruptcy Act has laid down any particular method of service; on the contrary, it only requires that the means of knowledge shall be placed in the possession of the party, and when that has been done the *onus* of proving want of notice lies upon the party in whose possession the means of knowledge are. Well, a copy of this notice D was put into the defendant's own hands by Mr. Jackson, just as any other trade document would have been handed to him, and from the moment that the means of knowledge were thus put into his power in the usual way, there fell upon the defendant an *onus* of proving actual want of notice, which he has not even attempted to discharge. He evidently preferred to rely upon a denial of the receipt of the copy of notice D. Then the terms of the notice are so simple, that one might almost suppose they had been framed with special regard to a savage and untutored mind. A reference to the technical terms of filing a petition, and an act of bankruptcy followed by an adjudication, was necessary in the notice; but in addition to that it conveys a very simple and telling warning to the defendant. It says in fact, "You owe Mr. Davies some money. Do not pay him. If you do pay him, you run the risk of having to pay over again the same amount." Far be it from me to say that I am satisfied that the defendant did actually pay this debt to the bankrupt or his brother. On the contrary, I have grave doubts respecting this alleged payment; but that point it is not necessary for me to express an opinion upon, as will appear further on. But at any rate the defendant alleges that he did so, and if he did, he has no one but himself to blame for his contemptuous disregard of the simple warning which is so clearly traced to his possession.

The only point which now remains for consideration is, whether notice D conveys notice of an act of bankruptcy available for adjudication. I am very clearly of opinion that it does.

In that notice Mr. Leigh, who lived in Lagos, intimates that he has been requested by Messrs. Callendar, Sykes and Mather of Manchester, to inform the defendant (by endorsation of defendant's name) that they have been compelled to file a petition in the London Bankruptcy Court, against Mr. J. P. L. Davies.

That intimation cannot refer to a petition of a later date than the last week of November, for the notice is dated December 31, 1875, and the information that a petition had been filed could not have been furnished to Mr. Leigh within a month after the actual filing. That circumstance brings the petition and the act of bankruptcy within the necessary relationship as to date.

That, then, is my view of the important items in this case, and it is unnecessary for me to determine whether the defendant actually paid the bankrupt the money for which he is sued in this action or not, as I am of opinion that it would not be a good payment as against the bankrupt's trustee.

These opinions force me to the conclusion that the decision of the Court below should be adhered to, and the appeal dismissed.

Judgment by Mr. Justice W. J. SMITH:—

The appellant in this case was sued by the trustee in bankruptcy of J. P. L. Davies for the sum of £724 6s. 11d., the balance of account for goods sold and delivered.

The defence raised, though informally, was a *bonâ fide*

payment to the bankrupt before adjudication, and without notice of an act of bankruptcy available for adjudication.

At the hearing neither the date of adjudication nor the date of payment to the bankrupt was proved, but we are entitled to assume, and, in my judgment, ought to assume that the payment was prior to the adjudication. There was no question raised as to the *bonâ fides* of the payment to the bankrupt, and the only question was as to the receipt by the appellant of notice of an act of bankruptcy available for adjudication. The Court below held that sufficient notice had been given to him, and judgment was accordingly against him.

The only question that we have to consider is that of the sufficiency of the notice. It is contained in the printed circular marked " D," dated December 31, 1875, and there is no doubt that a copy of this circular was served on the appellant, though he himself did not remember it. The appellant is a native trader who admittedly cannot read, and it is the respondent's contention that the mere handing of this printed circular to a man whom he knew could not read it, without translating it to him, and without one word of explanation as to what it was or what it meant, is a sufficient notice of an act of bankruptcy, so as to deprive this payment of the protection of sect. 94 of the Bankruptcy Act, 1869, sub-sect. 1. In this contention I am unable to concur. In my judgment the handing to a man a circular printed in a foreign tongue, without calling his attention to its contents, is not a good notice. It must not be forgotten, too, that the Bankruptcy Act is not in force in this colony, and I think some explanation should have been given of the meaning of this circular, that the English law had, through some act done by the bankrupt, vested the right to this money in another person. He would, of course, learn, if the notice had been read to him, that somebody was warning him not to pay money to his creditor, and that, in consequence of something that might happen, he might have to pay it again to some one in England ; but he would not understand, without explanation, how it was that money he owed to Davies in Lagos for goods supplied had become vested absolutely in somebody in England, or what right the person sending the notice had to give him the direction he did. It was argued that he should have obtained the assistance of somebody to translate and explain the circular to him; but I see no reason why the duty of having every printed circular that may be left at his house translated, should be cast upon him. And while we protect the interests of the creditors, we must also see that in a case where payment has been *bonâ fide* made to a bankrupt, in a country where the Bankruptcy Act is not in force and its provisions unheard of, that the notice of the act of bankruptcy and its consequences should be clearly brought home and explained to the person *bonâ fide* making such payment.

The agent of the trustee in bankruptcy might have done this by taking care that the clerk who took the notice should explain to the appellant its meaning and its effect, and so have placed the matter beyond all doubt. He has not done so, but has contented himself with sending round a printed circular to a man whom he knew could not read it; and for the reasons given above, I am of opinion that this is not a good notice.

I, therefore, think that the judgment of the Court below was wrong, and should be reversed.

Judgment by Chief Justice MARSHALL :—

In this case it is decreed in the Divisional Court that the appellant should pay to the respondent the sum of £724 6s. 11d., on the ground that, although he had already paid this amount to his creditor, Mr. J. P. L. Davies, he had done so wrongfully and knowing it to be wrong, as previous to that notice he had received notice in bankruptcy, which brought to his knowledge that such payment might be held void.

The main point which the Full Court has to deal with,

is whether this notice marked " D " sent to the appellant was a sufficient notice to render the appellant liable to pay again to Mr. Davies's trustee in bankruptcy the money which he had already paid to Mr. Davies.

In considering this point, I think we must bear in mind the peculiar state and position of this settlement.

The Supreme Court of the Gold Coast Colony has not had jurisdiction in bankruptcy conferred upon it, and the English Bankruptcy Laws are not in operation here, and are practically unknown to the native inhabitants. The protection and assistance given by these laws to persons unable to meet their liabilities are withheld from them, and therefore there is all the more reason for being very cautious and guarded in allowing native traders to become subject to the penalties of non-compliance with the provisions and enactments of these unknown laws.

I also think that in weighing the evidence given by the appellant at the hearing of the cause, we should bear in mind the disadvantage in which he was placed, and the great difficulty he must have been in to know what was the case he had to meet.

He does not understand English, and was unable, at the time, to obtain the services of any lawyer to advise or appear for him. On the other hand, the trustee in bankruptcy, armed with the rights and powers conferred upon him by the Court of Bankruptcy in England, was represented by the Queen's Advocate of the Colony. When the hearing came on, no one was called for the plaintiff to state and prove his case, but the defendant, the present appellant, was first called and examined. There is no mention of cross-examination by the Queen's Advocate, and he appears to have been examined as an adverse witness when giving his own evidence. No case had been brought forward for him to meet, and after he had given his own evidence, and been subjected to an adverse examination, two witnesses for the plaintiff *Halliday* were called to prove that the notice D had been served upon him.

It appears to me that the appellant was at a great disadvantage in making his defence, and it was only on the information that the Court below had taken official cognizance of a communication received from a Court of Bankruptcy in England that this Court, by allowing the respondent to put in the order of adjudication in bankruptcy, obtained evidence as to the date of the order of bankruptcy, and the right of *Halliday* to sue in this Court.

In considering the notice said to have been sent to the appellant, we have not, in my opinion, to decide whether it would be a good and sufficient notice in England, but whether it was for the appellant, a native trader in Lagos, who cannot read English.

He is a large trader, fully acquainted with all the ordinary routine of Lagos trade, but that does not include bankruptcy proceedings. Together with others of Mr. Davies's debtors he received a general circular, printed in English, which, if he could have read, or if it had been interpreted to him, could not, in my opinion, have been understood by him, and by very few persons in Lagos.

If Mr. Leigh had explained to him, or brought to his knowledge that a transfer of Mr. Davies's property to another person was about to be made by a Court in England, and that the transfer might date from that time and include his debt, the plaintiff *Halliday* might have had a good case against him.

I am of opinion that the notice given to the appellant was not a sufficient notice to make *Alapatira* liable to pay this debt to Mr. Davies's trustee in bankruptcy, as he has already paid it to Mr. Davies, and that the judgment of the Court below should be reversed with costs.

Judgment of the Court below reversed with costs, Mr. Justice McLeod dissenting.

Mr. *Moss*, agent and solicitor for the respondent, moved for leave to appeal to the Privy Council.

(Signed) J. MARSHALL, C.J.

FLETCHER v. SISARCON.

October 5, 1883.

Before MACLEOD, J.

Appeal—Right of Appellant—S.C.O. Order liii.

Plaintiff appears and asks leave to appeal. This application raises a nice little point, which I am glad to have the opportunity of considering and deciding.

A right of appeal is given to a defeated litigant when a decision is given which affects a civil right of £50 or upwards. If such defeated litigant has not otherwise a right of appeal, I do not think he can give himself such right by putting down a random sum in name of damage. He can only have such right of appeal when his claim can reasonably be held to be in respect of a civil right of £50 or upwards. In this action plaintiff claimed £100, but under the circumstances of this case I am very clearly of opinion that I have given no decision respecting a civil right which I can reasonably regard as amounting to £50, and I must therefore refuse leave to appeal.

SWANZY v. DE VEER AND VAN DER PUYE.

Before MACLEOD, J.

Supreme Court Ordinance Order xlvii., rule 17.

Application for warrant of attachment against the person of the defendants, returned from December 1, 1883.

JUDGMENT.

December 3, 1883.—Under the judgment in favour of the plaintiffs, dated August 4, 1883, neither a writ of *fi. fa.* nor judgment-debtor summons has been issued, and the judgment-creditors propose, as their first step under that judgment, to arrest the persons of the defendants, and with that object in view have made the present application.

Against the granting of this application there is a previous decision of this Divisional Court. In a similar application *in causa, Swanzy* v. *Madden,* upon December 23, 1882, I find it laid down by the learned Chief Justice BAILEY (1) that when a party obtains judgment he ought first to obtain a writ of *fi. fa.* if the judgment-debtor has property; (2) that if the judgment-creditor has no knowledge of any property belonging to the judgment-debtor, he must take out a judgment-debtor summons; and (3) that the judgment-debtor cannot be imprisoned unless he fails to appear or has misconducted himself. I regret to be under the necessity of expressing my inclination to think that each of those three propositions is bad in law. Let me examine them in detail.

First. It is said that if a judgment-debtor has property, his creditor knowing that fact must first take out a writ of *fi. fa.* Where is the authority for that bold assertion? I do not find it so laid down in the Supreme Court Ordinance, 1876; and, in passing, I may remark that if it were so, the Judge to whom the application for a writ against the person is made, would, in this particular case, have none of that discretion upon which the learned Chief Justice so strongly discourses. A contrary doctrine has been declared monstrous, but I must be strangely constituted, for I see no monstrosity, only common sense. I have said that I do not find it so laid down. On the contrary, I find a provision made for what is to happen when a debtor is imprisoned whose creditor is aware that he has property. That provision will be found in sect. 17, Order xlvii., Schedule ii., Supreme Court Ordinance, 1876, and the succeeding section provides that the mere issue of the writ against the person is not even temporarily to restrain writs against the property.

Second. It is said that if the judgment-creditor is not

in the knowledge of any property which his debtor has, he must take out a judgment-debtor summons before he can proceed further. Now, from what source is that dictum derived? I have searched through the Supreme Court Ordinance, 1876, and cannot find there any authority for it. It comes from the brain of the learned Chief Justice, and admirable as are the results when that brain is set to work upon materials existing outside it, yet I cannot recognize that brain itself as a fountain-head from which flows good law.

Third. It is said that the judgment-debtor cannot be imprisoned unless he fails to appear in answer to the summons, or misconducts himself. That is what the learned Chief Justice says. But the law says differently. Section 5, Order xlv., Schedule ii., Supreme Court Ordinance, 1876, says that a decree for money shall be enforced by the imprisonment of the party against whom the decree is made, etc.; while sect. 7 and following sections of Order xlvii., Schedule ii., Supreme Court Ordinance, 1876, provide in terms an additional imprisonment and punishment for those judgment-debtors who fail to appear or misconduct themselves in the terms of those sections, and expressly so as to state, that the imprisonment and punishment therein set forth are to be additional in the case of those who have already been imprisoned under sect. 5 of Order xlv.

If these doctrines enunciated in the case above mentioned had been promulgated by the authority of the Full Court, I would be bound by them, whatever I might think. But as they have been enunciated by a Court of co-ordinate jurisdiction, and as they are so manifestly opposed both to the letter and spirit of the law, I cannot act upon them.

On a review of the whole provisions of the Ordinance, I am satisfied that imprisonment was intended to be an effectual handle to make judgment-debtors (who in this colony have such facilities for concealing their property) disclose their property, and provision has been made in sects. 5 and 6 of the Order xlvi. to prevent this power being used oppressively.

Such was the practice which existed when I came to the colony, nearly four years ago. It was established by able and eminent judges, and I cannot be a party to its overthrow.

In this particular case, I think a warrant of attachment against the persons of the defendants and judgment-debtors admirably calculated to further the ends of justice, and I therefore grant the application and direct the registrar to issue the writ.

Mr. *Williams* asked leave to appeal, on the ground that an order has been given, and also on the ground that a decision has been given on the practice as to the issue of writs of execution.

Mr. *Richards* referred to Order liii.

By the Court: I do not think that this is a matter in which I shall give leave to appeal, and I have pointed out to Mr. *Williams* how he can bring the matter before the Full Court. I have not made an order between the parties. I have simply given an order to the registrar, and the parties are not supposed to be present, though, at my request, they have addressed an argument to me. I refuse leave to appeal.

EILOART *v.* BREW.

December 6, 1883.

Before HECTOR MACLEOD, J.

In this action I gave judgment for the plaintiff upon December 1, 1883.

The defendant has applied for leave to appeal, and I stayed execution until security had been found to the satisfaction of the Court.

Such security has now been found, and the plaintiff has made application to the registrar for the issue of a writ to attach the person of the defendant. The registrar has applied to me for directions.

In the case of *Swanzy* v. *De Veer and another*, I had, on December 3, 1883, under my consideration an application for the issue of a similar writ, and as I thought that a suitable case for the issue of such a writ, I ordered it to issue, although neither writ of *fi. fa.* nor judgment-debtor summons had been taken out.

The present application is made under very different circumstances, for in this case the defendant had mortgaged to the plaintiff certain property in security for the debt, and in exercise of the discretion which, I think, vested in me, I cannot order the issue of a writ to attach the person of the defendant until the plaintiff has done what he can under the judgment to realize the amount from, at least, that property of the defendant's property which has been specially set apart by the defendant for the plaintiff's security. I therefore direct the registrar not, meantime, to issue a writ to attach the person of the defendant.

SWANZY *v.* BREW AND BREW.

January 9, 1884.

Before HECTOR MACLEOD, J.

JUDGMENT.

I desire in this application to follow out the principles which I laid down for my own guidance in the case of *Swanzy* v. *De Veer and another*, upon December 3, 1883, and subsequently in the case of *Eiloart* v. *Brew*, upon December 6, 1883. The plaintiffs ask me to issue a warrant for the arrest of both defendants, but the defendant *J. H. Brew* has voluntarily disclosed in open Court the names of properties which he says will cover much more than the judgment debt, and he has stated his willingness to send a person with the bailiff to point out his properties. He was further asked to go into the box and make the same disclosure on oath, but this he refused to do. That was extremely unreasonable on his part, but at the same time perfectly competent, and the judgment-creditors can at any time get the disclosure upon oath by the issue of a judgment-debtor summons.

In respect of the voluntary disclosure and willingness to assist on the part of the defendant *J. H. Brew*, I am not inclined to order either of them to be arrested until the results of a writ of *fi. fa.* upon the motion of the plaintiffs have been ascertained by the judgment-creditors. I shall reserve consideration of the application for the warrant to arrest when that has been done.

SWANZY *v.* STANHOPE.

August 11, 1884.

Before MACLEOD, J.

Mercantile Custom—Purchase of Produce—Palm-Oil and Kernels.

Custom proved. C. W. Burnet:—

As a rule, kernels shipped out of these boxes turn out 40 lbs. to the box, after deduction of tare and draft. Oil from this coast, I have frequently known, turn out 296 gallons to the ton. If it turns out 305 gallons to the ton, I should not charge anything to the factor, but if more I should. A factor who does his work well ought to lose nothing if he is not charged anything up to 305 gallons to the ton.

Thomas Robert Gillet:—There is generally a very small deficiency in the weight as they turn out in England, after being calculated as shipped at 40 lbs. to the box. For example, the deficiency on 17 tons 19 cwts. was 7 cwt. and 3 lbs., that is, when calculated at 40 lbs. a box, and that I consider a fair deficiency; also 12 tons 10 cwts. 19 qrs. 12 lbs., there was a deficiency of 4 cwt. 2 qrs. 11 lbs. As a rule, I calculate 300 gallons of oil to the ton.

Tare is the weight of the cask or bag.

JUDGMENT.

The present claim for £41 5s. 11d. has been resisted as to items which may be divided into three groups.

First: In the account sued upon, the plaintiffs seek to charge the defendant with a sum of £8 8s. which they say he wrongly credited himself with during the first nine months of 1882, as subsistence at 2s. 6d. a day while travelling for the factory. (This is allowed to defendant.) Third: It was the duty of the defendant to ship to England for the plaintiffs kernels and oil. To save the defendant the trouble of weighing the kernels, and in accordance with the custom of the trade, the defendant bought the kernels in boxes which contained kernels, which, after reaching England, ought to weigh 40 lbs., and for each box stated to be shipped the defendant credited himself. When the turn-out of the kernels in England was very slightly in excess or very slightly in deficit of the estimated weight no notice was taken. But when any considerable surplus turned out the defendant got the benefit of it, and, after careful consideration, I am unable to see why he should not bear the loss arising from deficiencies. The same principles apply to the loss on palm-oil. Therefore, I think the plaintiffs ought to succeed on their claim for deficiency in kernels and oil, subject to a deduction in respect of the draft with which the defendant is charged, for some reason unknown. That deduction I assess at 4s. 9d. Accordingly, I give judgment for the plaintiffs.

DAVIS *v.* JONES.

December 18, 1884.

Before LESINGHAM BAILEY, C.J.

Slander—Proof of Special Damage.

Mr. *Renner* for plaintiff; Mr. *Niblett* for defendant.

I cannot help remarking that in a case of this kind, when there is no pretence, that the words declared are even actionable, unless the plaintiff has suffered special damage, and as there is not a tittle of evidence to show that such damage had been suffered by the plaintiff; I say, in such cases, I cannot help remarking that it would be far more decorous, if gentlemen of the Bar were to abstain from appearing in support of actions, which they must know are not maintainable for a moment.

I observe that various cases were cited by the counsel for the plaintiff in the cause before the District Commissioner, apparently with a view of imposing on his want of knowledge of law.

The District Commissioner's decision is altered, with costs.

EFFUA ANNOO *v.* ABBAGEE AND TWO OTHERS.

December 18, 1884.

Before BAILEY, C.J.

Action to claim Damages for Trespass on Land of Plaintiff's called Idan —Plea, Justification.

JUDGMENT.

There was a monkey who wanted to get some nuts that were hot and afire; he got a cat, and used her hands to pull the nuts out of the fire. The monkey got the nuts, and the cat burnt her fingers.

Anthony and the three chiefs are the monkeys, and you are the cats, and you have burnt your fingers to the extent of £1 each.

Judgment : £3 and costs—damages.

QUASIE v. ANSAFU.

July 11, 1885.

Before HECTOR MACLEOD, J.

Practice—Ejectment and Trespass—Sheriff's Sale—Certificate of Purchase.

JUDGMENT.

In this action the plaintiff claims £50 damages for trespass on land called Brahyun or Borahin. The previous actions regarding this land, of which there appear to have been several, were heard at Accra, and this one ought to have been taken there also; but as all the parties are here, I have heard the case, as the parties do not object. This is nominally an action for trespass, but ought to have been for ejectment, because the plaintiff has never been in possession of this land. He comes here as purchaser of the right, title, and interest of Quow Koon in this land Borahin, and sets forth that he is unable to get possession. He produces the proper certificate from the Court, and that undoubtedly entitles him to obtain actual possession of the right, title, and interest of Quow Koon in the land Borahin. He is unable to get possession, because *Ansafu* is in possession. The plaintiff has not even endeavoured to show that Quow Koon has any right, title, or interest in this land, and on plaintiff's own case I would not be able to eject the defendant. But defendant not only says this land is his, but produces a certified copy of a judgment of the Chief Justice, which sets out that, by virtue of previous decisions, this land Borahin is the property of *Ansafu.* I have narrated these facts to show that no injustice is done to the plaintiff when I dismiss this action with 20s. costs.

DES BORDES *v.* DES BORDES AND MENSAH.

January 23, 1884.

Before Mr. Justice MACLEOD.

This petition was resumed from yesterday, and the Divisional Court of Cape Coast now sat at Elmina for the purpose of delivering judgment in the presence of Mr. *Williams* for the petitioner, and respondent in person.

JUDGMENT.

MACLEOD, J. : This is a petition by *Elizabeth Des Bordes* for divorce from her husband, on the ground of adultery and cruelty.

The respondent in his answer admitted the adultery, and he also admits cruelty, which he has failed to justify, or to show that the petitioner brought it on herself by her own misconduct. I am therefore prepared to give a decree *nisi* for the dissolution of the marriage, provided such a marriage as this Court can recognize binds the parties to each other.

The marriage was, in 1878, solemnized in a Wesleyan chapel in Elmina by a Wesleyan minister, after publication of banns. The Wesleyan minister was not a clergyman of the Church of England. The Wesleyan chapel was not registered or licensed as a place where banns may be published or marriages solemnized. There was no registrar present at the marriage. It is therefore evident that if the Marriage Acts of England are in force in this colony, there is here no tie of marriage for me to dissolve. The Marriage Acts of England may be described as consisting of the 4th Geo. IV. c. 76; 6 & 7 Will. IV. c. 85, and the several amending statutes. The Supreme Court Ordinance, 1876, has rendered operative in this colony such statutes of general application as were in force in England upon July 24, 1874. I have therefore to consider whether the Marriage Acts of

England are statutes of general application in the sense of that Ordinance.

Now, what is meant by "statutes of general application"? That expression cannot mean statutes which apply to the whole United Kingdom, for this Court constantly enforces the provisions of statutes which do not apply to Scotland; neither can that expression mean those statutes which are printed under the designation "Public General Statutes," for statutes which apply to Scotland alone are among the "public general statutes;" neither does that expression include those statutes which apply to the whole of England, for the Full Court (sitting at Lagos) has decided that the Bankruptcy Acts of England are not operative here.

The Marriage Acts of England are of general application when compared with some statutes, and of particular application when compared with other statutes; and I am afraid I must designate those words "statutes of general application" as a slovenly expression, made use of by the Legislature of this colony to save itself the trouble of explicitly declaring what the actual law of the colony shall be.

I am not aware of anything in the Marriage Acts of England which makes them of more general application than the Bankruptcy Acts; it is my duty therefore to follow the Full Court (though I do not by any means say that I concur with the Full Court), and declare that the Marriage Acts of England are not operative within this colony. The same Ordinance to which I have already alluded, makes operative within this Colony the common law of England. There is no doubt as to what the common law of England was before the passing of the Marriage Acts to which I have referred. I have an epitome thereof set forth in the second edition of Macqueen on the "Law of Husband and Wife" at pages 4 and 5. It is there stated that, according to the common law of England, a private marriage, that is, a marriage not celebrated in *facie ecclesiæ*, was good only for certain limited purposes. It did not give the woman the right of a widow in respect to dower; it did not give the man the right of a husband in respect of the woman's property; it did not render the issue begotten legitimate; it did not impose upon the woman the disabilities of coverture, and it did not make the marriage of either of the parties (living with the other) with a third person void; but it had the following effects: (1) the parties could not release each other from the obligation; (2) either party could compel the other to solemnize the marriage in *facie ecclesiæ ;* (3) if either of the parties cohabited with another person, the parties might be proceeded against for adultery; and (4) if either of the parties afterwards married with another person, solemnizing such marriage in *facie ecclesiæ,* the same might be set aside even after cohabitation and after the birth of children. Such, then, was the common law of England before the passing of the Marriage Acts; but that is not the common law which the Ordinance of 1876 made operative within this colony. That Ordinance extends to this colony only, the common law which was in force in England until July 24, 1874. But at that date there was, on the subject of marriage, no common law operative in England, for it had all been swept away by statutes. This colony is therefore deprived (1) of the presently existing Marriage Acts of England, and (2) of the old common law.

Can the parties to this marriage, then, appeal to the native law and custom of their own country? Certainly not; for by the most unequivocal act of going to the white man's church to be married, they put native law and custom from them.

I am thus driven back to first principles. Marriage is a consensual contract capable of being completed by the parties without any interpositions of spiritual authority. The petitioner and the respondent have been joined together in the strictest society of life till death shall separate, and unlike other consensual contracts, this contract of marriage cannot be dissolved by the mere consent of parties. Why? simply on the ground of public policy. The colony is young, and it is the duty of the Court (as far as it comes within its province) to make the foundations of society strong. This attribute of marriage—its character of indissolubility—has not, so far as I know, been the creature of legislative enactment in any civilized nation. Just as a fire cannot fail to give heat, so a contract of cohabitation without the quality of indissolubility would not be marriage. If such be the law, and I cannot say that I have ever heard it so expounded before, I have here before me a marriage good by the law of the colony, and therefore good all the world over. Once thus established, the marriage and the parties hereto come under the operation of the divorce law of England, which by section 16 of the Supreme Court Ordinance, 1876, is made operative here. And as I find the adultery and the cruelty established, I give decree *nisi* with costs against the respondent.

APPENDIX.

——◆◇◆——

I.

Opinion on the native tenure on the Gold Coast, copied from a report published by the Gold Coast Government.

     *   *   *   *   *   *

2. The subject on which His Excellency requires to be informed is a large and comprehensive one, and having regard to the different customs that appear to obtain in different districts, nothing short of a Commission appointed for this purpose is likely to furnish full and satisfactory information. Such knowledge as I possess is derived from cases heard in the Courts, when native experts are called to expound the law; and even then the experts do not always agree. In fact, I have heard it stated on more than one occasion that pure native law is not always obtainable in the sea-coast towns, where the natives come in constant contact with European civilization. Still, on the main points, there appears to be a certain consensus of opinion, in the direction of which the decisions of the Court have generally proceeded.

3. Land in the colony is distinguished under the following heads :—Stool land, Family land, and Private land ; and under these designations all the land in the colony, save what the Government have from time to time taken for public purposes, has, according to native law, an owner.

4. By what means property attached to a king or chief's stool has been acquired is difficult to say, probably by conquest. A case occurred lately in the Court in which the King of James Town claimed a large tract of land on the other side of the River Densu as part of his stool property by right of conquest when the Accras and Akims fought against and drove away the Akwamus. In whatever way the property is acquired, it becomes attached to

the stool absolutely, the occupant thereof, during his life or good
behaviour, being considered the owner, but with no power of
alienating the property. Such property includes land cleared and
cultivated, waste and forest lands. Each subject of the king or
chief has a right to have allotted to him portion of the stool land
for cultivation. I understand that in some districts there are
what are known as town lands, though attached to a stool, that
is, land where no permission is required to be obtained to work
on, each of the inhabitants of the town having the right to take
possession of and cultivate any portion thereof so long as he does
not interfere with the right of a fellow-townsman. To natives,
other than subjects of the stool, permission may also be granted
to cultivate stool property ; but this permission is granted by the
king or chief with the concurrence of his headmen or councillors.
To obtain permission, rum or sometimes money is given, more or
less as the applicant is not or is subject of the stool, portion of
the produce of the land being from time to time given to the
king or chief, as the case may be. But this partial alienation
vests no right whatever in the cultivator of the soil beyond his
right of tilling the ground. No time is specified as to the duration of the grant ; but as soon as the grantee ceases to cultivate
the land, it reverts to the stool. Even during the period of
cultivation, should the grantee assert a title to the land in himself, he forfeits his right to continue the cultivation, and is at
once ejected from the land.

5. From the fact that property is a source of revenue to the
stool-holder, absolute alienation of stool land is rarely, in the
interior, made, and then under exceptional circumstances, such as
to raise money to pay a stool debt. In these cases the king and
his councillors or headmen are parties to the transaction. No
writing is necessary, and evidence of the transaction is orally
given. Some formalities to be gone through in order to vest the
land in the purchaser are required in some districts, but once the
land is acquired the purchaser takes it absolutely. In the sea-
coast towns, however, an absolute sale of stool property is of more
frequent occurrence, and takes place when the king and his
councillors desire to raise money for their own use. Stool
property may also be mortgaged by the concurrence of the king
or chief and his councillors. Tradition keeps this transaction
alive, and, at any distant period, it can be redeemed ; but till such
redemption takes place, the mortgagee or his representative is

practically the owner. Of late, however, in imitation of English law, sales and mortgages of stool property are done by deed. The leasing of timber and mining rights is of recent growth, and is now made by deed, which regulates the rights of the contracting parties. Such alienation is unknown to native law, but inasmuch as the leases are made with the concurrence of persons, who by native law are empowered to dispose of stool property, the question of the validity of any of these leases will only arise when a rival claimant to the land springs up, which is not unlikely to occur, owing to the absence of boundary marks between the forest land of one owner and another.

6. When, however, land is given for cultivation to a native, and he discovers gold, he is bound to report the same to the chief or king, and to share with him the find. The proportion that the king or chief is entitled to receive varies in different districts.

7. Land given for building purposes reverts to the grantor or his representative on the happening of one of the following conditions :—

(1) Where the building has fallen into ruins.

(2) Where the grantee disputes the title of the grantor. The grantee or his successor may, by keeping up the building and recognizing the right of the landlord, continue indefinitely in occupation. He pays a certain amount in money and rum for permission to build, but I am not aware that any rent is reserved. But land for building purposes is not, as a rule, granted to strangers.

8. Forest land is also reserved for cultivation, and is from time to time cleared for this purpose, as the cultivator is obliged to adopt the shifting system, no means of fertilizing the soil, beyond allowing it to lie fallow for some time, being known to the native. I am not aware of any permanent system of cultivation by natives.

9. Family property can be traced to individual ownership. A person being the absolute owner of land—that is, land that he has himself acquired—has every right to dispose of it, verbally or by writing, the latter mode formerly in one or two cases, but now frequently resorted to. Failing this, the land descends according to the native law of inheritance, and then becomes family property, and the mode of alienation is the same as that of the stool property of the chief or king. Family land may also

be acquired by purchase by the heads of the family, it being agreed at the time that the land is intended to be family property, and when it is desired to erect any building thereon, the members assist by labour or money, the labour being in some cases the carrying of swish balls from where made to the building, and this gives a vested interest in the house to the members so contributing labour or money.

10. Descent is traced through females. Property acquired by a man descends to his mother, then to his brothers and sisters by age. Failing this, to uncles and aunts, then to the eldest children of the eldest aunt, and so on. As males are preferred, a woman generally waives her right in favour of the next male successor, who is placed, with the consent of the family, on the stool, if any such exists, or otherwise takes charge of the property. The heir is superseded for just cause, such as drunkenness, extravagance, imbecility, &c.

11. The son, in the Fanti country, does not inherit his father's property, but his father may nominate him his heir, and may by gift, verbal or otherwise, give to him his acquired property. Children are not considered members of the father's family, as far as having any right to his property. They belong to the mother's family, and inherit from the mother's side. Failing all blood relatives, the domestics of the house succeed by age, I believe, males being also preferred to females.

12. With regard to family property, where there is a stool to which it is attached, I understand that the custom at Cape Coast, Elmina, and Chama is that the stool descends to the son, but the property of the stool descends as I have before mentioned. I have not, however, known a case involving these points decided by any of the Courts.

13. The property of a woman descends to her children, then to her brothers and sisters by the same mother, and then to the children of the sisters according to seniority.

14. In the Eastern Province the same rule of succession prevails, with this difference, that in some parts thereof, that is, Accra and east of it, children of legal marriage, that is, marriage according to native law, said to be known as the sixth-cloth marriage, sometimes inherit the property of their father in conjunction with the heir, and the property cannot be disposed of without the consent of the children. The mother, it is said, does not succeed to the property of her son, acquired or inherited ; but

I confess that I know of no decided case upholding this view, and I cannot explain the reason for this alleged custom.

15. As to the stool property of a king or chief, the succession is, in most cases, the same, but in the Eastern Province sons sometimes inherit the stool and property attached to it. A chief may, for good reason, be also set aside by his head chiefs or councillors. He himself may sever his connection with the stool, and thereby forfeit all right to the property by transferring his allegiance from his paramount king to another, and going through the custom of cutting the caul. Till this is done, he is said to have the *animus revertendi,* and may return and assume his position as a stool-holder. This custom obtains only in some parts of the Fanti country; but opinions differ thereon, some holding that without cutting the caul, the chief forfeits all the right to his stool and property, if he openly avows his intention of serving another king, and removes to, and takes up his residence in, the territory of the king to whom he has transferred his allegiance.

I have the honour to be, Sir,

Your obedient servant,

(Signed)   FRANCIS SMITH.

To this report is added a minute on land tenure by Mr. Justice Smith, dated May 22, 1891.

MR. JUSTICE SMITH, TO THE COLONIAL SECRETARY.

(Confidential M.P., 82/91.)

Lands, according to native law, are described as acquired, stool, and family, and their modes of alienation vary. As to acquired lands, the power of alienation by the owner is the same as of property acquired according to English law, viz. that they can be disposed of at the will of the owner, the only difference between the two being, in the modes of conveyance of stool lands, the holder of the stool exercises a power of alienation or concession, for purposes of habitation or cultivation, to subjects of his stool. In cases of alienation to strangers, whether of a limited or absolute character, that is, whether the property passes to the alienee for a time, reverting to the holder on the happening of certain events, or absolutely as a purchase, the concurrence of the head chiefs or councillors of his stool to such alienation is indispensable. The concession may be verbal or in writing. In either mode, whether the concurrence necessary to give validity to the transaction has been obtained will be matter of evidence. For a deed passing or dealing with stool property, and executed only by the stool-holder, may be valid, the deed being made with the consent and approval of the councillors or head chiefs, though not appearing as parties themselves to the deed; for it is only their concurrence that is necessary, the law imposing no necessity for the concurrence being given, or appearing, in writing. On the other hand, a deed purporting to comply with the requirements of native law may be worthless, for, as the councillors or head chiefs are illiterate, their names may be inserted therein without their concurrence.

With regard to family property the same law prevails, the head of the family, known as their heir or successor, with the elders of the family, taking the place of the stool-holder and his councillors or head chiefs.

(Intd.) F. S.

II.

SIR,—I have the honour to acknowledge the receipt of Circular No. 24/95, dated the 22nd ultimo, asking for a report upon the customs of the Non-Mohammedan African tribes in the Gold Coast Colony, in regard to the tenure of land.

2. The tribes referred to are numerous, and are spread over a large extent of territory; their customs frequently differing as much as their languages. When questioned as to their customs they are often suspicious and reticent, or misleading in their answers. In the courts the evidence of so-called experts generally differs remarkably, and usually according to the interest the witnesses have in the matter. The decisions of the Courts in these cases turning upon native customs are often leaps in the dark. There are, of course, no native records, and the generalities of casual European travellers are not, so far as I am able to judge, much to be relied upon. There is scarcely anything that can be laid down as absolutely of general application, and in the circumstances it is difficult, indeed it is impossible, to answer

satisfactorily the questions now put. However, I may say that from my seven years' connection with the place, from travelling in different parts of it, from inquiries made from time to time, and from matters in the Courts and appearing in papers submitted to me, I have formed certain general impressions in relation to the subject to be reported upon, which I will proceed to submit for what they may be worth.

3. It is considered by the natives that all lands, whether reclaimed or not, are attached to the stools of the different kings and chiefs, with the exception of the comparatively small portions detached in manner hereinafter mentioned. There is no land which is not or has not been so attached. The occupant for the time being of the stool, so long as he continues to occupy the same, is practically a trustee of the stool-lands for the common benefit of those under his authority. Generally, if a person wishes to have the occupancy of any land for cultivation or for building purposes, he applies to the stool-holder for an allotment thereof. The stool-holder consults with the minor chiefs, and if the proposal is agreed to, the applicant must provide the usual gifts—in many cases a sheep, some rum, a small sum of money, and some white baft for the Fetish. The boundaries of the land are defined, and the allottee is put in possession. In the bush the boundaries are generally fixed by particular trees, by natural features, such as rivers, streams, or hills, by ant-hills or mounds, a path being usually cut from point to point. The land so allotted is held during the pleasure of the stool-holder, though the tenant is rarely disturbed, provided that he furnishes to the stool-holder a fixed proportion of the produce, and, it may be, performs certain services. With regard to land for building purposes, it should be observed that the great majority of buildings so called are huts with thatched roofs and walls of bamboo or swish, or a combination of the two, readily constructed from materials at hand, and costing scarcely anything to speak of. It is not an uncommon thing to see these huts and even clusters of them entirely abandoned. In the native towns there are very few really substantial erections, and such as there are generally belong to the king or chief and some of the minor headmen. If a person wishes to acquire an allotment absolutely, he may do so much in the same way as he acquires the right of occupancy only. There is, however, a difference in the ceremony. This time a sheep is killed, and on the land the stool-holder and

the allottee take hold of a leaf of some kind and pull it asunder.
One name of this ceremony is "foyibah," and without it a
transfer would not be accomplished. It has been considered by
some of the natives that the land should not be parted with in
this way except in serious emergencies, such as the discharge of
stool debts which could not otherwise be paid; but nevertheless
the practice has gradually become more and more common. The
succession to the property acquired in manner last referred to
would be in accordance with the native custom, to be hereinafter
described. It has not, I think, been common amongst the
natives to make allotments of metalliferous land. They generally
have the right to win gold, out of which a certain proportion
goes to the stool-holder. As to forest land, much the same thing
applies—that is to say, a certain fixed tribute has to be paid out
of anything obtained therefrom. Of comparatively late years,
however, the custom has sprung up of granting long leases in
English form to natives as well as to Europeans, of mining and
timber lands, in consideration generally of a small premium, and
of a fairly high rent when full working operations commence,
and in some cases there is a proviso for re-entry if such working
operations are not commenced within a time limited. I do not
know that there are any lands properly describable as waste lands.
In some instances—not many, I think—there are lands allotted
to the people of particular places, and over these lands the stool-
holder has not the same rights as over land allotted to particular
persons; but I have no definite information as to the reasons for
and methods of allotment or the conditions thereof. Doubtless
they vary. Stool-holders again sometimes have private lands
previously detached from a stool, and coming to them by succession. These lands would not go with the stool in the event of
its going to some one who would not, according to native custom,
be the successor to such private lands. The rights of a paramount stool-holder over the minor kings and chiefs with regard
to consent, tribute, etc., in relation to land transactions vary, it
seems to me, and I am unable to do more than mention the fact
that rights of the kind exist. Besides the methods of detaching
lands from the stool by some such custom as that called
"foyibah," and the detachment in a way by allotment to communities, it has become a common custom to transfer land
absolutely for a consideration by conveyancing forms.

These conveyances are made at least as frequently to natives as to Europeans. Occasionally they are carefully drawn, but not as a general rule. They are generally held by the Courts to be valid instruments of title between natives, even if imperfect according to English law. The principal chiefs and headmen of the stool-holder in many cases sign as parties, or testify their consent by signing as witnesses, the document having first been interpreted to them. After execution the deed is stamped and registered, a list of these registered instruments being published from time to time in the *Gazette*. The same practice is followed with regard to leases for terms of years before referred to. Stamping is necessary for the purpose of putting such documents in evidence, if necessary. Registration is not compulsory, but as it gives priority and puts the transaction on record, documents are generally registered, and they cannot be registered without first being stamped. Of course there are no native records.

Mortgage, or rather pledge of land, is a transaction in the presence of witnesses, the possession of the land pledged being given to the lender of the money. The amount to be paid for redemption is ordinarily agreed upon, and as in the mean time the profits of the land go to the lender, the amount is often merely that of the advance, or that amount with a comparatively small addition. Tradition preserves these transactions, and redemption may take place generations afterwards by and from any successors in interest.

It may here be observed that there is no prescription by native law, and it has been held by the Courts that the statutes of limitation do not apply in matters between natives. There is also the mortgage in ordinary form, executed, stamped, and registered in the same manner as other documents relating to land. In the large coast towns the land has for the most part become detached from the stools, and is dealt with by natives and Europeans according to the methods and forms of English conveyancing. I think I have now disposed of the first four questions, and they have been dealt with together, because they seem to me so intimately connected as to make that the more convenient course.

4. Succession is traced through females, for reasons which it is not necessary here to state, but which are commonly understood. Property goes to the mother's sons, according to age; failing sons, to her daughters; failing these, to the mothers,

brothers, and sisters ; and these again failing, to the eldest child
of the eldest daughter, always according to age and to males
before females. Entire failure of heirs is extremely rare. There
is a difference between property acquired and property inherited.
The former can be disposed of out of the usual course of
succession ; the latter must go in course traced through the heirs
of the acquirer. Property acquired by a woman goes to her
children, and, failing those, in course as before mentioned.
Bastardy is a thing not considered or recognized. With regard
to inherited land, the heir becomes the head of the family, and
cannot alienate without the consent of the family ; and the
family, including the mother, has a claim upon him to look after
them to some extent. The heir has to pay half of the funeral
expenses, the other half being divided amongst the relations.
He has also to pay the debts of the deceased. Property given
can be disposed of out of ordinary course. A son cannot come
in for his father's property except by gift, and then the property
must have been acquired by the father. In a few places the
stool descends to the son, but not the property. The foregoing
is given only as a general idea. There are many differences in
the different parts of the country. One leading principle,
however, is fairly universal, that is to say, descent through
females.

5. Native rights and customs in reference to land and to
succession have constantly been subjects of litigation, and
almost as constantly have been recognized and upheld by the
Courts.

6. As to systems of cultivation, there is practically no permanent cultivation in the country. Plantains and cocoanut
trees are set and allowed to grow, and these plantations are, so
to speak, permanent, this being all there is of the kind. Such
system of cultivation as exists is shifting. The occupier of an
allotment cultivates part of it for two or three years, then
another part for about the same time, and so on, not returning
to the first part for at least six or seven years. When he first
begins to cultivate he burns the bush on the ground he intends
to work, clearing and enriching the soil, which becomes exhausted after two or three years, and the same process takes
place on the other portions. By the time the cultivator returns
to the first plot the bush has grown up again, and it is again
burned. The methods are most primitive, as also are the

implements—generally a cutlass and a hoe. The products are principally maize, yams, cassada, cocoa, groundnuts, and occasionally rice. So far as I know, there are no methods of fertilizing the soil or cultivating it other than those above described.

7. To obtain definite and accurate information on the different points referred to would necessitate the appointment of a Commission to take evidence in all parts of the country. The inquiry would take a long time, but if properly carried out the results would be most valuable, affording as they would a much surer foundation in dealing with native affairs than the slender and imperfect knowledge we now possess.

I have the honour to be, Sir,

Your obedient servant,

(Signed)   BRUCE HINDLE.

The Honourable the Colonial Secretary.
[195954.]

III.

FANTEE CHIEFS.

(Bond, 6th March, 1844.)

1. Whereas power and jurisdiction have been exercised for and on behalf of her Majesty the Queen of Great Britain and Ireland, within divers countries and places adjacent to her Majesty's forts and settlements on the Gold Coast, we, chiefs of countries and places so referred to, adjacent to the said forts and settlements, do hereby acknowledge that power and jurisdiction, and declare that the first objects of law are the protection of individuals and of property.

2. Human sacrifices and other barbarous customs, such as panyarring, are abominations and contrary to law.

3. Murders, robberies, and other crimes and offences, will be tried and inquired of before the Queen's judicial officers and the chiefs of the district, moulding the customs of the country to the general principles of British law.

Done at Cape Coast Castle before his Excellency the Lieutenant-Governor, on this 6th day of March, in the year of our Lord 1844.

Their

× Cudjoe Chibboe, King of Denkera ;

× Quashie Ottoo, Chief of Abrah ;

× Chibboe Coomah, Chief of Assin ;

× Gebre, Second Chief of Assin ;

× Quashie Ankah, Chief of Donadie ;

× Awoossie, Chief of Dominassie ;

(Signed) Quashie Ankah ;

× Amonoo, Chief of Annamaboe ;

× Joe Aggery, Chief of Cape Coast.

marks.

Witness my seal on the 6th day of March, 1844, and the 7th year of her Majesty's reign.

(Signed)   H. W. HILL, Lieutenant-Governor (L.S.).

Witnesses, and done in the presence of—

(Signed)   GEORGE MACLEAN, J.P., and Assessor (S.).

F. POGSON, 1st W. I. Regiment (S.), Commanding H.M. Troops.

S. BANNERMAN, Adjutant of Militia and Police (S.).

Blue book : Africa, Western Coast, p: 419.

IV.

MEMORANDUM EXPLANATORY OF "PANYARRING."

"Panyarring," or "kidnapping individuals," in order to obtain restitution of goods or money that has been unjustly withheld, is common amongst the Fantees on the Gold Coast.

If a resident of Anamaboe is indebted to a native of Cape Coast Town, and will not discharge the demand, or withholds property improperly, the first native of that place who may fall into the hands of the creditor is detained by him until the claim is settled or the property restored, which is often promptly acceded to, for the family of the man detained immediately compels the debtor to release their relation by discharging the debt. This is attended with considerable expense, and it frequently happened, during the existence of the Slave Trade conducted by the British, that a man so " panyarred " was sold and carried off the coast before it could be discovered what captain had made the purchase. In a case of this kind, it brought on a protracted and expensive palaver, and very frequently terminated in the sale of an entire family.—Blue Book: Africa, Western Coast, 1865, p. 437.

V.

LORD STANLEY TO LIEUTENANT-GOVERNOR HILL.

" Assessors Jurisdiction."

Downing Street, November 22, 1844.

SIR,—I have had under my consideration the correspondence noted in the accompanying schedule, and of which papers copies are herewith enclosed, and I have to acquaint you that upon the Report of the Law officers of the Crown, her Majesty has been pleased to pass an Order in Council, herewith enclosed, under the Acts 6 and ' Vict., cc. 13 and 94, appointing her Majesty's settlement of Cape Coast Castle as a place to which persons coming within the operation of the last-mentioned of those Acts may be sent for trial or punishment.

The Order, you will perceive, provides for two distinct classes of cases. The one, that of persons whom it may be deemed expedient to send from the neighbouring countries to be tried within her Majesty's settlement ; the other, that of persons who may have been tried in the neighbouring countries, but whom it is considered advisable to send into her Majesty's settlement for the purpose of undergoing their sentences.

As regards the first class of cases, you will of course bear in mind, that in any trial which takes place, the provisions of the 6 & 7 Vict., c. 94, applicable to that event, must be strictly observed ; and also, that as the jurisdiction for the trial of offenders sent under the provisions of the Act is given to the Supreme Court of the Colony only to which they are sent, that in the present state of the judicial institutions on the Gold Coast, such offenders would require to be forwarded thence to Sierra Leone for trial.

For practical purposes, therefore, as yet at all events, this power is not likely to be of any general utility. The powers, however, given under the second head will, I apprehend, greatly facilitate the working of the system which has grown up in our relations with the tribes surrounding the forts under your Government.

It being necessary to provide for the appointment of persons to be specially empowered to exercise the powers conferred by the different sections of the 6 & 7 Vict., c. 94, I send you additional instructions, under the sign manual, giving you the requisite authority, both to act yourself, and to nominate others for the same purpose, and I have, as you will perceive, taken the opportunity of providing for Mr. Maclean's absence or inability to discharge the duties of assessor to the sovereigns and chiefs of the neighbouring tribes, by making a fresh appointment to the office, including yourself and others with him, as such assessors, having power to act either jointly or severally.

Should Mr. Cloustun, the gentleman whom you have appointed, as reported in your despatch, No. 27 of June 16 last, to officiate for Mr. Maclean, not be already in the commission of the peace, or his name not stand first or second upon it, it will of course be necessary that a new commission should be issued.

I presume that the magistrates and gaoler at the gaol at Cape Coast Castle are already the persons to whom it appertains to carry into effect there any sentences which may have been passed by the Supreme Court at Sierra Leone.

Should that, however, be not the case, appointments to that effect ought forthwith to be made, and I have instructed the Governor of Sierra Leone accordingly, it being necessary, under the 5th section of the 6 and 7 Vict., c. 94, that the persons to give effect within any colony to sentences passed out of it, should be "magistrates, gaolers, or other officers to whom it may appertain, to give effect to any sentence passed by the Supreme Court, exercising criminal jurisdiction within such colony."

The royal instructions, you will perceive, also provide for the appointment of persons having the authority to exercise the powers given by the 6th section of the 6 and 7 Vict., c. 94, relative to the transportation of convicts; but you will clearly understand that, although it has been considered expedient to provide by the instrument the machinery necessary for bringing into operation all the powers conferred by the Act, yet that you, are not to consider yourself at liberty, in any case, to exercise or permit the exercise of that relative to transportation without special instructions from the Secretary of State.

Although likewise the instructions, as before observed, provide for the exercise of the office of assessor by several persons jointly, as well as by one person, you will not on that account make any alteration in the practice which has hitherto prevailed of leaving the duties to be executed by one person.

You will bear in mind that the power of the assessor, in his judicial capacity, is not derived from either the Acts of Parliament above referred to, or from the Order in Council; and further, that it cannot be exercised by him as such within her Majesty's dominions. It must be founded on the assent and concurrence of the sovereign power of the State within which it is exercised, either express, as in the case of the treaty transmitted by you in your private and confidential despatch of the 6th of March last, or implied from long usage, as in the case of the long and general acquiescence, which can be shown in many districts, in the authority hitherto exercised by Mr. Maclean.

You will understand that the system upon which Mr. Maclean has proceeded, in the exercise of judicial powers over the natives, is to be taken as the guide for the exercise of the powers of assessor for the future.

It consists, in fact, in combining with an impartial investigation of the cases brought before him, a mitigation of the severity of the sentences which in such cases would be awarded by native judges in the event of conviction. I need not therefore instruct you to caution the assessor of the necessity for a lenient exercise of the discretion entrusted to him; but in the event of his deeming capital punishment in any case inevitable, you will instruct him that the execution must be carried into effect by the native authorities, and take place in the country in which the offender is tried.

Having thus, as far as possible, brought the very peculiar case of the jurisdiction exercised among the tribes in the neighbourhood of the forts on the Gold Coast within the operation of the Acts of Parliament referred to in the commencement of this despatch, it only remains for me further to observe that I am not to be understood as affirming that the exercise of that jurisdiction is not capable of being justified and maintained independently of any such express sanction of the Legislature.

It is a jurisdiction which had its origin in a desire to mitigate, by the influence of Christianity and civilization, the effect of cruel and barbarous customs; it has been brought into operation upon a state of society, and under relations to savage tribes, necessitating a neglect of all technical rules and observances. In its effects, it has undeniably been the means of insuring justice, preventing cruelty, and promoting civilization; and I must guard myself against being supposed, because I endeavour to give it the aid of the forms I have adverted to, to assume that the general principles of the law of England are not comprehensive enough to allow for the necessities which such a state of circumstances as exist on the Gold Coast unavoidably creates, and to justify those measures by which such necessities, when created, can alone be adequately provided for.

I have, etc.,
(Signed) STANLEY.

Lieut.-Governor Hill, etc.

VI.

Draft of an Order of the Queen in Council for determining the mode of exercising the power and jurisdiction acquired by her Majesty within divers countries on the West Coast of Africa, near or adjacent to her Majesty's Gold Coast Colony.

At the Court at Osborne House, Isle of Wight, the 6th day of August, 1874.

Present: The Queen's Most Excellent Majesty; Lord President; Mr. Secretary Cross; Mr. Disraeli.

Whereas, by an Act made and passed in the session of Parliament, holden in the sixth and seventh years of her Majesty's reign, intituled "An Act to remove Doubts as to the Exercise of Power and Jurisdiction by her Majesty within divers countries and Places out of her Majesty's Dominions, and to render the same more effectual," it was, amongst other things, enacted that it should be lawful for her Majesty to hold, exercise, and enjoy any power or jurisdiction which her Majesty then had, or might at any time thereafter have, within any country or place out of her Majesty's dominions in the same, and as ample a manner as if her Majesty had acquired such power or jurisdiction by the cession or conquest of territory. And whereas by certain Letters

Patent, under the Great Seal of the United Kingdom of Great
Britain and Ireland, bearing date at Westminster, the 24th day
of July, 1874, in the thirty-eighth year of her Majesty's reign,
her Majesty's settlements on the Gold Coast and of Lagos were
constituted and erected into one colony, under the title of the
Gold Coast Colony, and a Legislative Council was appointed for
the same colony, with certain powers and authority to legislate
for the said colony, as by the said Letters Patent, reference being
had thereto, will more fully appear. And whereas her Majesty
hath acquired power and jurisdiction within divers countries on
the West Coast of Africa, near or adjacent to her Majesty's said
Gold Coast Colony, and it is expedient to determine the mode of
exercising such power and jurisdiction. Now, therefore, it is
hereby ordered, with the advice and consent of her Privy Council
as follows:—

1. It shall be lawful for the Legislative Council for the time
being of the said Gold Coast Colony by Ordinance or Ordinances,
to exercise and provide for giving effect to all such powers and
jurisdiction as her Majesty may, at any time before or after the
passing of this Order in Council, have acquired in the said
territories adjacent to the Gold Coast Colony.

2. The Governor for the time being of the said colony shall
have a negative voice in the passing of all such Ordinances as
aforesaid. And the right is hereby reserved to her Majesty, her
heirs and successors, to disallow any such Ordinances as aforesaid
in whole or in part, such disallowance being signified to the said
Governor through one of her Majesty's principal Secretaries of
State, and also to make and establish from time to time, with the
advice and consent of Parliament, or with the advice of her or
their Privy Council, all such laws or Ordinances as may to her
or them appear necessary for the exercise of such powers and
jurisdiction as aforesaid, as fully as if this Order in Council had
not been made.

3. In the making and establishing all such Ordinances, the
said Legislative Council shall conform to and observe all such
rules and regulations as may from time to time be appointed by
any instruction or instructions issued by her Majesty with the
advice of her Privy Council, and, until further directed, the
instructions in force for the time being as to Ordinances passed
by the said Legislative Council for the peace, order, and good
government of the said Gold Coast Colony shall, so far as they

may be applicable, be taken and deemed to be in force in respect
of Ordinances passed by the said Council by virtue of this Order
in Council.

4. In the construction of this Order in Council the term
"Governor" shall include the officer for the time being administering the government of the said Gold Coast Colony.

And the Right Honourable the Earl of Carnarvon, one of
her Majesty's principal Secretaries of State, is to give the
necessary directions herein accordingly.

(Signed) ARTHUR HELPS.

VII.

THE EARL OF CARNARVON TO GOVERNOR STRAHAN.

Downing Street, August 20, 1874.

SIR,—In my despatch of the 20th instant, I had the honour to
forward to you an order made by her Majesty in Council, which
delegates to the Legislature of the Gold Coast, the exercise by
ordinance or ordinances of such power and jurisdiction as her
Majesty has or may at any time have acquired in the territories
adjacent to the Gold Coast Colony.

2. The Legislature of the Gold Coast settlements has from
time to time enacted ordinances which were intended to take
effect beyond the local limits of the British settlements of the
Gold Coast. Doubts, however, have been entertained as to the
validity and force of such legislation, and in 1855 the law
officers reported that such assumption of authority was not
justified.

3. Her Majesty's Government, having decided to establish a
new colony and Legislative Council for the settlements of the
Gold Coast and Lagos, vesting in that Council the power to
legislate for the protected territories on the Gold Coast, the law
officers were requested to report upon the subject; and in
accordance with their opinion, of which I annex a copy for your
private information, the Order in Council already transmitted to
you was passed. By this Order the Local Legislature is (subject
to the conditions and reservations therein specified) clothed with
whatever legislative authority her Majesty has or may hereafter
claim to exercise on the Gold Coast.

4. This having been done, it becomes advisable to define as clearly as may be the extent of her Majesty's power and jurisdiction, so as to prevent misunderstandings in future, and to enable the Colonial Legislature to know on what subjects it may properly legislate.

5. I need not here examine in detail the origin and history of the peculiar jurisdiction exercised by this country in the protected territories of the Gold Coast. Carried to its highest development under Governor Maclean, its existence is first authoritatively recorded and recognized in the Report of the House of Commons Committee of 1842, which, in recommending the continuance of the system, suggested that it should be made the subject of distinct agreement with the native chiefs. That recommendation resulted in the negotiation with the native chiefs of the document called the Bond of the 6th of March, 1844, which is the only document purporting to define the extent of the Queen's jurisdiction on the Gold Coast in other than strictly political matters. But that definition, either from being an inadequate representation of the facts as they then existed, or from change of circumstances, no longer truly expresses what her Majesty's Government believe to be the extent and scope of her Majesty's power.

6. The Bond grants to her Majesty's officers the right to try and punish crimes and offences and to repress human sacrifices, panyarring, and other unlawful acts and barbarous customs. It is silent as to the Queen's right by her officers and delegates to collect customs, to administer civil justice, to legislate for the public health, to erect municipalities, to provide for education, to construct roads and regulate the industrial and social economy of the Protectorate. On all these matters, the Legislature or Government of the settlement has, with or without the co-operation of the native rulers, exercised authority to an extent which, strictly speaking, could only be justified on the assumption (the justice of which I am satisfied is not open to question) that these matters have by usage and by the sufferance and tacit assent of the natives fallen within the province of the Queen's authority.

7. The necessity of some more adequate definition of the Queen's authority that the obsolete Bond of 1844 being thus apparent, it remains to be considered whether that definition should take the form of a Bond to be negotiated with the chiefs,

as in 1844, or a Proclamation emanating from the sole authority of the Queen.

8. In 1844 the method of proceeding by negotiation was recommended by obvious considerations of prudence. But in the thirty years which have since elapsed, the power and resources of the British Government have been gradually increasing, until, by the recent victories of the British forces, they have been so strengthened and consolidated as to render an act of sovereign power, such as a Proclamation of the Queen, the only appropriate mode of proceeding for the attainment of the desired object. It may be added that there are many objections of policy to proceeding by way of negotiation. It is not for her Majesty to take as a grant what is already claimed and held as a right; whilst, looking to the number of petty chiefs on the coast, and the obscurity in which their relations with one another are involved, there would be some danger of not inviting the concurrence of chiefs who might afterwards allege, and with a certain show of reason, that their consent was as requisite as that of others whose co-operation had been asked and given. Besides this, the Government would be placed in a position of much embarrassment if any considerable body of chiefs refused their consent in part or in whole to the proposed treaty.

9. On the other hand, I should be anxious to avoid the risk, if any, attendant upon this manner of proceeding of alienating the feelings of the natives, and I am fully alive to the importance of their willing co-operation in the work of promoting the civilization and prosperity of the Protectorate. The nature of the proposed terms are such as, if not fully and clearly explained, might excite the alarm and aversion of the less intelligent rulers, whilst a too hasty assumption of authority might create a feeling of discontent, and possibly lead them to seek alliances beyond the Protectorate with tribes hostile to our power.

10. Before coming to any conclusion as to the best mode of procedure, I desire to know your opinion on a question which is, perhaps, as difficult as any that you may be called on to deal with, and one that demands the exercise of the most delicate tact and judgment. I enclose a draft of a Proclamation which I have caused to be prepared for consideration.

11. In defining the nature of the Queen's Protectorate on the Gold Coast, it may be well also to define and limit the local extent of that Protectorate.

12. What may be termed the natural boundaries of the Protectorate to the north and east are to a great extent marked out by the course of the Prah and the Volta, and the lagoon dividing Quittah from the sea ; but considerations connected with the protection of trade and the collection of revenue may compel your Government to plant establishments or exercise jurisdiction in parts of the Ahoonah country lying to the east of the Volta and behind the lagoon. The question of the northern limit of the Protectorate towards the Croboe and Aquamoo country will also call for careful examination in connection with the request of the Aquamoo people to be included in the Protectorate, recently reported by Dr. Gouldsbury, and it may be worthy of consideration whether some limitation should not be put on what are usually regarded as the boundaries of British jurisdiction in the little-known regions of the north-west.

13. Up to this point I have confined my observations to the Protectorate adjacent to the Gold Coast settlement ; but a further question of grave importance presses for consideration with reference to the boundaries of British territory and the British Protectorate at Lagos, for it will not have escaped your notice that the language of the Order in Council in effect delegates to the Local Legislature her Majesty's rights over both Protectorates. As bearing upon this point, I may refer you to Lord Kimberley's despatch of April 5, 1873, to Governor Keate.

14. You are well aware that the effect of including, under the same provisions and procedure, the area of country which has been called the Protectorate of Lagos, would have to be seriously considered as possibly involving us in difficulties with the neighbouring nations, which might prove deeply injurious to the prosperity of that settlement. The history of our relations with the protected territories of Lagos differs entirely from that of our relations with the protected territories on the Gold Coast. Her Majesty's Government have not assumed to so great an extent at Lagos as at the Gold Coast the direction of political and other affairs, and the Queen's forces have not at Lagos, as on the Gold Coast, been associated with the Native Powers in hostile alliances against a powerful common foe. For these reasons I am inclined to think that the Queen's authority as a protecting power need not, under present circumstances, be declared to extend to the Protectorate of Lagos, as proposed to be defined in the Draft Proclamation, although, of course, under our treaty

engagements, we must continue to exercise a control over the affairs of that part of the coast, and in some sense to discharge the functions of a protecting power.

15. I have to request your opinion and criticisms, together with those of Mr. Chalmers, on the Draft Proclamation, as well as on the form it should assume, and the territories to which it should be declared to extend. I shall be glad to receive your answer as soon as you feel yourself able to come to a conclusion on the various questions contained in this despatch.

16. If, contrary to my expectations, it should seem desirable to proceed by treaty engagements with the native chiefs, the Draft Proclamation, with due alterations of phrase, will probably suffice as a draft of the bond which those chiefs would be required to sign. But I have to request that you will apply to me confidentially for further instructions before taking any open action in the matter.

17. I need hardly add that, in the mean time, it will not be desirable for the Legislative Council, unless some very special emergency should arise, to attempt to exercise the powers vested in them by the recent Order in Council.

18. There remains the question of the existence of slavery within the range of the Queen's influence and authority. It is one surrounded by many and serious difficulties, but it is also one which affects, by its existence, not only the honour and traditional policy of this country, but the welfare and good government of the Gold Coast. It has ever, since I received the seals of this office, engaged my anxious attention, and though her Majesty's Government could not consent to have the decision of it forced upon them, and to be pledged to some precipitate and probably ill-considered course of action, they have at no time abandoned the hope and intention of extinguishing an evil which they have been compelled to tolerate, but in which they have never acquiesced. The time has now, in my opinion, arrived when at least the possibility of dealing with this important question may receive a careful and dispassionate consideration ; and I propose to address you in another despatch on this subject.

I have, etc.,
(Signed) CARNARVON.

VIII.

Draft of a Proclamation defining the nature and extent of the Queen's jurisdiction on the Gold Coast.

Victoria, by the grace of God of the United Kingdom of Great Britain and Ireland, Queen, Defender of the Faith, to all to whom these presents shall come, greeting :

Whereas, by an Act of Parliament made and passed in the session of Parliament holden in the sixth and seventh years of our reign, intituled " An Act to remove Doubts as to the Exercise of Power and Jurisdiction by her Majesty within divers countries and Places out of her Majesty's Dominions, and to render the same more effectual," it is, amongst other things, enacted that it is and shall be lawful for us to hold, exercise, and enjoy any power or jurisdiction which we now have, or may at any time hereafter have, within any country or place out of our dominions, in the same and as ample a manner as if we had acquired such power or jurisdiction by the cession or conquest of territory.

And whereas we have by grant, treaty, usage, sufferance, and other lawful means acquired, and do hold, exercise, and enjoy power and jurisdiction in divers countries on the West Coast of Africa, near or adjacent to our Gold Coast Colony :

And whereas by an Order made by us in Council, bearing date at Osborne House, on the 6th day of August, in the year of our Lord one thousand eight hundred and seventy-four, it was amongst other things ordered that it should be lawful for the Legislative Council of our said Gold Coast Colony for the time being by Ordinance or Ordinances to exercise and provide for giving effect to all such power and jurisdiction as we might at any time, either before or after the passing of the said Order in Council, have acquired in the said territories adjacent to the Gold Coast Colony :

And whereas the extent and nature of our power and jurisdiction, as now actually holden, exercised and employed by us in the said territories, have not been anywhere by us fully declared :

And whereas it is expedient for the guidance and information, as well as of the Legislature of our said Gold Coast Colony as for that of the native chiefs and rulers living under our protection in the said territories, that the nature of our power and jurisdiction, as well as their local limits, be declared by us. Therefore we do declare as follows :—

Our power and jurisdiction which we have acquired as aforesaid extends, amongst other things, to —

I. The preservation of the public peace and the protection of individuals and property.

II. The administration of civil and criminal justice, including :—

(1) The constitution and regulation of a Superior Court of Justice, such as that which has been hitherto known as the Judicial Assessor's Court, of District Magistrates' Courts, Native Courts, and such other Courts as it may from time to time be deemed expedient to create.

(2) The enactment of laws relating to crimes, wrongs personal rights, contracts, property rights, and fiduciary relations similar to those prevailing in our Gold Coast Colony, but framed with due regard to native law and customs where they are not repugnant to justice, equity, and good conscience.

(3) The determination of appeals from native tribunals to magistrates or to some Superior Court.

(4) The apprehension and trial of criminals and offenders of all kinds in any part of the said territories.

(5) The supervision and regulation of native prisons.

III. The extinction of human sacrifices, panyarring, judicial torture, and other immoral, barbarous, and cruel customs.

IV. The abolition of slave trading.

V. Measures with regard to domestic slavery and pawning.

VI. The protection and encouragement of trade and traders, including the construction, maintenance, and improvement of roads, paths, bridges, harbour works, waterways, telegraphs, and other public works which benefit trade and promote civilization.

VII. The maintenance of an armed police force for the preservation of internal order and the prevention of foreign aggression, and the organization of the military forces of the native rulers in alliance with her Majesty.

VIII. The settling by the authority of the Governor of our Gold Coast Colony of disputes arising between different chiefs and rulers in the said territories.

IX. The promotion of the public health, including the imposition, with the assent of the native chiefs, of sanitary rates in towns and villages.

X. The establishment of municipalities.

XI. Public education, including industrial and religious training.

XII. The raising of a revenue by licences and customs, and by such direct imposts as the native chiefs and rulers, or a major part of them, may agree to.

And further, We declare that the undermentioned territories are those within which at the present time we have power and jurisdiction as aforesaid.

(List of territories to be inserted by the local authorities in the first instance.)

IX.

British Charter, providing for the government of her Majesty's settlements on the Gold Coast and of Lagos; and constituting those settlements into a separate colony to be called the Gold Coast Colony, and providing for the government thereof. Westminster, July 24, 1874.

Victoria, by the grace of God of the United Kingdom of Great Britain and Ireland, Queen, Defender of the Faith, to all to whom these presents shall come, greeting.

1. Whereas, by certain Letters Patent under the Great Seal of Our United Kingdom of Great Britain and Ireland, bearing date at Westminster the 19th day of February, 1866, in the 29th year of our reign, provision was made for the government of our settlements on the West Coast of Africa, as therein is more particularly described:

And whereas by a Supplementary Commission under the Great Seal aforesaid, bearing date at Westminster the 8th day of November, 1872, in the 36th year of our reign, we did empower our Governor and Commander-in-Chief of our West Africa settlements to grant pardons to offenders in the manner and upon the terms therein mentioned:

And whereas, by our Commission under the Great Seal aforesaid, bearing date the 25th day of July, 1873, in the 37th year of our reign, we did constitute and appoint our trusty and well-beloved George Berkeley, Esquire (now Companion of our Most Distinguished Order of Saint Michael and Saint George), to be, during our will and pleasure, our Governor and Commander-in-Chief in and over our said West Africa settlements; and whereas it is expedient that provision should be made for the government of our Settlements on the Gold Coast and of Lagos, apart and separate from the government of our other settlements in the West Coast of Africa;

And whereas, by an Act made and passed in the 6th year of our reign (cap. 13), intituled " An Act to enable her Majesty to provide for the government of her Settlements upon the Coast of Africa and in the Falkland Islands," it was enacted that it should be lawful for us, by any Commission under the Greal Seal of our United Kingdom, or by any instructions under our sign-manual and signet accompanying and referred to in any such Commission, to delegate to any three or more persons within any of the settlements aforesaid, either in whole or in part, and subject to all such conditions, provisions, and limitations, as might be prescribed by any such commission or instructions, the power and authority to make and establish all such laws, institutions, and Ordinances, and to constitute such Courts and officers, and to make such provisions and regulations for the proceedings in such Courts, and for the administration of justice as might be necessary for the peace, order, and good government of our subjects and others within our then present or future settlements on the said coast.

Now know ye that we do by these our LETTERS PATENT, under the Great Seal aforesaid, declare our pleasure to be that our said Letters Patent of the 19th day of February, 1866, our said Supplementary Commission of the 8th day of November, 1872, and our said Commission of the 25th day of July, 1873, shall be, and they are hereby revoked so far as regards our said settlements on the Gold Coast and of Lagos, or any part or parts thereof; and we do further declare our pleasure to be that those settlements shall constitute, and they are hereby erected into a separate Colony under the title of the Gold Coast Colony.

2. And we do further declare our pleasure to be that our settlement on the Gold Coast shall, as heretofore, and until otherwise provided by us, comprise all places, settlements, and territories which may at any time belong to us in Western Africa between the 5th degree of west longitude and the 2nd degree of east longitude. And our settlement of Lagos shall, as heretofore, and until otherwise provided by us, comprise all places, settlements, and territories, which may at any time belong to us in Western Africa between the 2nd and 5th degrees of east longitude.

3. And we do further declare and appoint that the government of the said colony shall be administered by a Governor duly commissioned by us on that behalf.

4. And we do further declare our pleasure to be that there shall be within our said colony a Legislative Council, which shall consist of our said Governor for the time being, and of such other persons or officers, not being less than two in number, from each of our said settlements, as shall be named or designated by or by virtue of any instruction or instructions, or by any warrant or warrants to be by us for that purpose issued under our sign-manual and signet, and with the advice of our Privy Council; all of which persons or officers shall hold their places in the said Council during our pleasure.

5. And we do further, by this our Commission under the Great Seal of our United Kingdom aforesaid, delegate to the persons who within our said colony shall compose the Legislative Council thereof, full power and authority, subject always to such conditions, provisions, and limitations as may be presented by any Commission or instructions, to establish such Ordinances not being repugnant to the law of England, or to any order made or to be made by us with the advice of our Privy Council, and to establish such courts and officers, and to make such provisions and regulations for the proceedings in such Courts, and for the administration of justice, as may be necessary for the peace, order, and good government of such colony.

6. And we do further declare our pleasure to be that our said Governor shall have a negative voice in the passing of all such Ordinances aforesaid; and we do also hereby reserve to ourselves, our heirs and successors, our and their right and authority to disallow any such Ordinances as aforesaid, in the whole or in part, such allowance being from time to time signified to him through one of our principal Secretaries of State, and also to make and establish from time to time, with the advice and consent of Parliament, or with the advice of our and their Privy Council, all such laws or Ordinances as may to us or them appear necessary for the order, peace, and good government of our said colony as fully as if these presents had not been made. And we do further declare our pleasure to be that in the making and establishing of all such Ordinances, the said Legislative Council shall conform to and observe all such rules as may from time to time be directed or appointed by

any instruction or instructions issued by us with the advice of our Privy Council.

7. And we do further declare and establish that the laws now in force in our said colony shall continue in force as long and as far only as they are not repugnant to or repealed by any Ordinance passed by the Legislature of our said colony.

8. And we do further declare our pleasure to be that, for the purpose of advising our said Governor, there shall be for our said colony an Executive Council, which shall be composed of such persons and constituted in such manner as may be directed by any instructions which may from time to time be addressed to our said Governor by us under our sign-manual and signet, and all such persons shall hold their places in the said Council at our pleasure.

9. And we do further authorize and empower our said Governor to keep and use the public seal of our said colony for sealing all things whatsoever that shall pass the said seal, and we do direct that until a public seal shall be provided for our said colony, the public seal of our settlement on the Gold Coast shall be used as the public seal of our said colony for sealing all things whatsoever that shall pass the said seal.

10. And we do authorize and empower our said Governor to make and execute in our name and on our behalf, under the said public seal, grants and dispositions of any lands which may be lawfully granted or disposed of by us within our said colony, either in conformity with instructions under our sign-manual and signet, or in conformity with such regulations as are now in force, or may be made by him in that behalf, with the advice of our said Executive Council, and duly published in our said colony.

11. And we do further authorize and empower our said Governor to constitute and appoint all such Judges, Commissioners of Oyer and Terminer, Justices of the Peace, and other necessary officers and ministers as may lawfully be appointed by us, all of whom shall hold their offices during our pleasure.

12. And we do further authorize and empower our said Governor as he shall see occasion, in our name and on our behalf, when any crime has been committed within our said colony, or for which the offender may be tried therein, to grant a pardon to any accomplice, not being the actual perpetrator of such crime, who shall give such information and evidence as shall

lead to the apprehension and conviction of the principal offender ; and further to grant to any offender convicted of any crime in any Court, or before any Judge, Justice, or Magistrate within our said Colony, a pardon, either full or subject to lawful conditions, or any respite of the execution of the sentence of any ·such offender, for such period as to him may seem fit, and to resist any fines, penalties, or forfeitures which may become due and payable to us.

13. And we do further authorize and empower our said Governor, upon sufficient cause to him appearing, to suspend from the exercise of his office within our said colony any person exercising the same under or by virtue of any Commission or Warrant, granted or to be granted by us in our name or under our authority, which suspension shall continue and have effect only until our pleasure therein shall be known and signified to him. And we do hereby strictly require and.enjoin him, in proceeding to any such suspension, to observe the directions in that behalf given to him, by any instructions under our sign-manual and signet as may be hereafter addressed to our said Governor for the time being.

14. Our will and pleasure is, and we do hereby direct that, in the execution of this our Commission, and in the exercise of the command hereby vested in our Governor for the time being, he be resident in our settlement on the Gold Coast, or at such place or places in the territories adjacent thereto as may from time to time be appointed for the residence of our said Governor, except when the interests of our service may render his presence desirable in our settlement of Lagos.

15. And whereas it is necessary that provision be made for the execution of this our Commission in the event of the death or incapacity of our said Governor, or of his removal from his command, or of his absence from the limits of his said government : Now, therefore, we do further declare our pleasure to be that, in any such event as aforesaid, all and every the powers and authorities hereby vested in him shall be, and the same are hereby vested in such person as may be appointed by us and our sign-manual and signet, to be our Lieutenant-Governor of our said colony, or if there shall be no such Lieutenant-Governor therein, such person or persons as may be appointed by us under our sign-manual and signet to administer the government of our said colony, and in case there shall be no such person or persons

within our said colony so appointed by us, then is the person for the time being administering the government of our said settlement of Lagos, who shall for such time as he administers the government of our said colony, be called the Administrator of the Gold Coast Colony. Provided always, and we do further declare our pleasure, to be, that our Governor for the time being, during the period of his passage by sea from either of the settlements aforesaid to the other of the said settlements, or while visiting or residing at any place in any of the territories adjacent thereto, shall not, for any of the purposes aforesaid, be considered as being absent from the limits of his said command.

16. And we do further declare and direct that, during his absence from our said settlement on the Gold Coast, but while he is within the limits of his said command as aforesaid, our Governor may, if he think fit, appoint some person to act as his deputy in administering the government of our said Gold Coast settlement, upon such terms and conditions, and for such time, as he may think desirable for the good government of our said settlement; and all or such of the powers and authorities aforesaid as our said Governor in his discretion shall from time to time think it necessary or expedient to assign to such deputy shall, so far as the same shall be exercisable within such settlement, be vested in such deputy.

17. And we do further declare that so long as our said Governor, or (as the case may be) Lieutenant-Governor, or Administrator of the Gold Coast Colony, shall be absent from our settlement of Lagos, all and every the powers and authorities, except the powers of suspension and pardon, hereby vested in our said Governor, and so far as the same shall be exercisable within such settlement, shall be vested in such person within the same as may be appointed by us by warrant under our sign-manual and signet to administer the government thereof; and in case there shall not be within such settlement any such Administrator, then we declare that the said powers and authorities shall, in our said settlement of Lagos, be vested in such person, and upon such terms and conditions, and for such time, as our said Governor, Lieutenant-Governor, or Administrator of our Gold Coast Colony, as the case may be, shall provisionally from time to time appoint, subject to our approval. And we do further declare and provide that the officer for the time being administering the government of our said settlement of Lagos shall, in the discharge of such his

office, conform to and observe such instructions as shall, for that purpose, be addressed to him by our said Governor in the execution of this our Commission ; subject, nevertheless, to all such rules and regulations in that behalf as may from time to time be contained in any instructions under our sign-manual and signet, addressed to our Governor for the time being of our said Gold Coast Colony.

18. And we do further direct and enjoin that this our Commission shall be read and proclaimed within our said respective settlements on the Gold Coast and of Lagos, and that a transcript thereof shall be deposited and duly recorded in our said settlements, this our original Commission being preserved within our said settlement on the Gold Coast.

19. And we do hereby require and command all officers, civil and military, and all others the inhabitants of our said colony, to be obedient, aiding and assisting unto our said Governor for the time being, and to the officer appointed to administer the government of our settlement of Lagos, in the execution of this our Commission, and of the powers and authorities herein contained.

20. And we do hereby reserve to ourselves, our heirs and successors, full power and authority from time to time to revoke, alter, or amend this our Commission as to us or them shall seem meet.

In witness whereof we have caused these our Letters to be made patent. Witness ourself at Westminster, the 24th day of July, in the thirty-eighth year of our reign.

By warrant under the Queen's sign-manual.

C. ROMILLY.

X.

BRITISH LETTERS PATENT, constituting the office of Governor and Commander-in-Chief of the Gold Coast Colony, and providing for the government thereof. Westminster, January 13th, 1886.

Victoria, by the grace of God of the United Kingdom of Great Britain and Ireland, Queen, Defender of the Faith, Empress of India : To all to whom these presents shall come, greeting.

1. Whereas our Gold Coast Colony, as now constituted, comprises our settlements on the Gold Coast and at Lagos, lying

between the fifth degree of west longitude and the fifth degree of east longitude : And whereas by Letters Patent, under the Great Seal of our United Kingdom of Great Britain and Ireland, bearing date at Westminster the 22nd day of January, 1883, we did constitute the office of Governor and Commander-in-Chief of our Gold Coast Colony, and did provide for the government of our said colony : And whereas we are minded to separate the government of our settlement at Lagos from the government of our settlements on the Gold Coast, and to make further provision for the government of our said settlements on the Gold Coast : Now know ye that we do, by these presents, revoke and determine our said Letters Patent of the 22nd day of January, 1883, but without prejudice to anything lawfully done thereunder : And further know ye that we do, by these presents, order and declare that our Gold Coast Colony shall henceforth consist of our settlements on the Gold Coast as hereinafter described, and that there shall be a Governor and Commander-in-Chief in and over our Gold Coast Colony, and that appointments to the said office shall be made by Commission under our sign-manual and signet.

2. Our Gold Coast Colony (hereinafter called the colony) shall, until we shall otherwise provide, comprise all places, settlements, and territories, belonging to us on the Gold Coast in Western Africa between the fifth degree of west longitude and the second degree of east longitude.

3. We do hereby authorize, empower, and command our said Governor and Commander-in-Chief (hereinafter called the Governor) to do and execute all things that belong to his said office, according to the tenor of these our Letters Patent and of such Commission as may be issued to him under our sign-manual and signet, and according to such instructions as may from time to time be given to him under our sign-manual and signet, or by our order in our Privy Council, or by us through one of our principal Secretaries of State, and to such laws as are now or shall hereafter be in force in the colony.

4. And we do by these our Letters Patent declare our will and pleasure as follows :—

5. Every person appointed to fill the office of Governor shall, with all due solemnity, before entering on any of the duties of his office, cause the Commission appointing him to be Governor to be read and published at the seat of Government on the Gold Coast,

in the presence of the Chief Justice, or of some other judge in the Supreme Court, and of such members of the Executive Council of the colony as can conveniently attend, which being done, he shall then and there take before them the Oath of Allegiance, in the form provided by an Act passed in the session holden in the thirty-first and thirty-second years of our reign (cap. 72), intituled " An Act to amend the Law relating to Promissory Oaths," and likewise the usual oath for the due execution of the office of Governor, and for the due and impartial administration of justice, which oaths the said Chief Justice or judge, or, if they be unavoidably absent, the Senior Member of the Executive Council then present, is hereby required to administer.

6. Tho Governor shall keep and use the public seal of the colony, for sealing all things whatsoever that shall pass the said seal; and, until we shall otherwise direct, the public seal hitherto used for our Gold Coast Colony aforesaid shall be used as the public seal of the colony.

7. There shall be an Executive Council for the colony, and the said Council shall consist of such persons as we shall direct by instructions under our sign-manual and signet, and all such persons shall hold their places in the said Council during our pleasure.

8. There shall be a Legislative Council in the colony, and the said Council shall consist of the Governor and such persons, not being less than three at any time, as we shall direct by any instructions under our sign-manual and signet, and all such persons shall hold their places in the said Council during our pleasure.

9. In pursuance of the powers vested in us by an Act of the Imperial Parliament, passed in the sixth year of our reign (cap. 13), intituled " An Act to enable her Majesty to provide for the, Government of her Settlements upon the Coast of Africa and in the Falkland Islands," we do hereby commission the persons who shall from time to time compose the said Legislative Council, and we do hereby delegate to them full power and authority, subject always to any conditions, provisoes, and limitations prescribed by any instructions under our sign-manual and signet, to establish such Ordinances, not being repugnant to the law of England, and to constitute such courts and officers, and to make such pro-visions and regulations for the proceedings in such Courts, and for the administration of justice, as may be necessary for the

peace, order, and good government of the colony.   The Governor shall have a negative voice in the making and passing of all such Ordinances.

10. We do hereby reserve to ourselves, our heirs and successors, full power and authority, and our and their undoubted right to disallow any such Ordinances, and to signify such disallowance through one of our principal Secretaries of State. Every such disallowance shall take effect from the time when the same shall be promulgated by the Governor in the colony.

We do also reserve to ourselves, our heirs and successors, our and their undoubted right, with the advice of our or their Privy Council, from time to time to make all such laws or Ordinances as may appear to us or them necessary for the peace, order, and good government of the colony.

11. In the making of any Ordinances the Governor and the said Legislative Council shall conform to and observe all rules, regulations, and directions in that behalf contained in any instructions under our sign-manual and signet.

12. The Governor, in our name and on our behalf, may make and execute, under the public seal, grants and dispositions of any lands within the colony which may be lawfully granted or disposed of by us : Provided that every such grant or disposition be made in conformity either with some law in force in the colony, or with some instructions addressed to the Governor under our sign-manual and signet, or through one of our principal Secretaries of State, or with some regulation in force in the colony.

13. The Governor may constitute and appoint all such judges, Commissioners, Justices of the Peace, and other necessary officers and ministers, as may be lawfully constituted, or appointed by us, all of whom, unless otherwise provided by law, shall hold their offices during our pleasure.

14. The Governor may, upon sufficient cause to him appearing, suspend from the exercise of his office any person holding any office within the colony, whether appointed by virtue of any Commission or Warrant from us or in our name or by any other mode of appointment.   Every such suspension shall continue and have effect only until our pleasure therein shall be signified to the Governor.   In proceeding to any such suspension, the Governor is strictly to observe the directions in that behalf given to him by any instructions as aforesaid.

15. When any crime has been committed within the colony, or for which the offender may be tried therein, the Governor may, as he shall see occasion, in our name and on our behalf, grant a pardon to any accomplice in such crime who shall give such information as shall lead to the conviction of the principal offender, or of any one of such offenders, if more than one ; and further, may grant to any offender convicted in any Court, or before any judge or other magistrate, within the colony, a pardon, either free or subject to lawful conditions, or any remission of the sentence passed on such offender, or any respite of the execution of such sentence, for such period as the Governor thinks fit, and may remit any fines, penalties, or forfeitures due or accrued to us. Provided always, that the Governor shall in no case, except where the offence has been of a political nature unaccompanied by any other grave crime, make it a condition of any pardon or remission of sentence that the offender shall be banished from or shall absent himself or be removed from the colony.

16. Whenever the office of Governor is vacant or if the Governor become incapable or be absent from the colony, our Lieutenant-Governor of the colony, or if there be no such officer therein, then such person or persons as we may appoint under our sign-manual and signet, and in default of any such appointment the Senior Civil Member of the Executive Council, shall, during our pleasure, administer the government of the colony, first taking the oaths hereinbefore directed to be taken by the Governor and in the manner herein prescribed, which, being done, we do hereby authorize, empower, and command our Lieutenant-Governor, or any other such Administrator as aforesaid, to do and execute, during our pleasure, all things that belong to the office of Governor and Commander-in Chief, according to the tenor of these our Letters Patent, and according to our instructions as aforesaid, and the laws of the colony.

17. In the event of the Governor having occasion at any time to visit any territories adjacent to the colony, in pursuance of any instructions from us, or through one of our principal Secretaries of the State, he may by an instrument under the public seal of the colony appoint any person or persons to be his deputy or deputies within any part of the colony, and in that capacity to exercise, during his pleasure, such of the powers hereby vested in the Governor, except the powers of suspension

and pardon, as the Governor shall think fit to assign to him or them. The appointment of such deputy or deputies shall not affect the exercise by the Governor himself of any of his powers or authorities. Every such deputy shall, in the discharge of his office, conform to and observe all such instructions as the Governor shall address to him for his guidance.

18. And we do hereby require and command all our officers and ministers, civil and military, and all other the inhabitants of the colony, to be obedient, aiding and assisting unto the Governor and to such person or persons as may, from time to time, under the provisions of these our Letters Patent, administer the government of the colony.

19. In the construction of these our Letters Patent, the term "the Governor," unless inconsistent with the context, shall include every person for the time being administering the government of the colony.

20. And we do hereby reserve to ourselves, our heirs and successors, full power and authority from time to time to revoke, alter, or amend these our Letters Patent as to us or them shall seem fit.

21. And we do direct and enjoin that these our Letters Patent shall be read and proclaimed at such place or places within the colony as the Governor shall think fit.

In witness whereof we have caused these our Letters to be made patent. Witness ourself at Westminster, the 13th day of January, in the 49th year of our reign.

By warrant under Queen's sign-manual.

(Signed) MUIR MACKENZIE.

(Hertslet's "Commercial Treaties.")

XI.

Treaty of Friendship and Protection made at Prahsue this eighteenth day of October, one thousand eight hundred and ninety-five, between her Most Gracious Majesty Victoria, Queen of Great Britain and Ireland, Empress of India, etc., her heirs and successors, by her subject Captain Donald William Stewart, an officer in the Civil Service of the Gold Coast Colony, acting under instructions received from his Excellency William Edward

Maxwell, also a subject of her Majesty, Companion of the Most Distinguished Order of Saint Michael and Saint George, Governor and Commander-in-Chief of the Gold Coast Colony on the one part, and the king, chiefs, and principal headmen of the country of Adansi on the other part.

Whereas Kweku Inkansa, king of the country of Adansi, and the chiefs and principal headmen of that country, for and on behalf of themselves, their heirs, successors, and people, have presented to the Governor of the Gold Coast Colony a request that their country should be placed under the protection of Great Britain, and have agreed to enter into a treaty with her Majesty the Queen of Great Britain and Ireland, Empress of India, etc., her heirs and successors, by the said Captain Donald William Stewart, acting for that purpose for the said Governor.

Now, therefore, Kweku Inkansa, King of Adansi, and the chiefs and principal men of that country, whose names are hereinafter signed to this treaty, for themselves, their heirs, and successors, and the people of Adansi on the one part, and his Excellency William Edward Maxwell, Companion of the Most Distinguished Order of Saint Michael and Saint George, Governor and Commander-in-Chief of the Gold Coast Colony, a subject of and representing her Most Gracious Majesty Victoria, Queen of the United Kingdom of Great Britain and Ireland, Empress of India, etc., her heirs and successors, by Captain Donald William Stewart, a subject of her Majesty (acting for the Governor), on the other part, do hereby enter into this treaty containing the following Articles:—

ARTICLE I.

The king of the country of Adansi for himself and his lawful successors, together with the chiefs and principal men of the country of Adansi, whose names are hereinafter signed and seals affixed, for and on behalf of themselves and their successors, and people of Adansi, hereby place themselves under the protection of Great Britain, declaring that they have not entered into any treaty with any other foreign power.

ARTICLE II.

Her Majesty's subject, the Governor of the Gold Coast Colony, for and on behalf of her Majesty the Queen of Great

Britain and Ireland, Empress of India, etc., her heirs and successors, hereby takes the country of Adansi under the protection of Great Britain.

ARTICLE III.

It is hereby agreed that the king, chiefs, and principal men, together with the other people of Adansi, will not enter into any war or commit any act of aggression on any of the chiefs bordering on their country by which the trade of the country shall be interrupted, or the safety and prosperity of the subjects of her Majesty the Queen of England and Empress of India shall be lost, compromised, or endangered, and that the said king, chiefs, and principal men of Adansi hereby undertake to refer to the Governor of the Gold Coast Colony, acting on behalf of her Majesty, for friendly arbitration, any trade or other quarrels in which they may become involved before actually entering upon hostilities.

ARTICLE IV.

Should any difference or dispute accidentally arise between the King of Adansi and any of his chiefs and principal headmen, or between any of the chiefs and principal headmen, it shall be referred to the Governor of the Gold Coast Colony, or to the nearest British Authority, for the time being, whose decision shall be final and binding upon all parties concerned.

ARTICLE V.

British subjects shall have free access to all parts of Adansi, and shall have the right to build houses and possess property according to the law in force in the Gold Coast Colony; and they shall have full liberty to carry on such trade or manufacture as may be approved by any officer appointed for the purpose by her Majesty's Government, and should any difference arise between the aforesaid British subjects and the king, chiefs, and principal headmen of the country of Adansi as to the duties or customs to be paid to the said king, chiefs, or the principal headmen of the towns in that country by such British subjects, or as to any other matter, that the dispute shall be referred to the officer mentioned in Article IV., whose decision in the matter shall be binding and final, and that the king, chiefs, and principal headmen of Adansi will not extend the rights hereby guaranteed to British subjects to any other persons without the knowledge and consent of such officer.

ARTICLE VI.

In consideration of the protection guaranteed on the part of Great Britain to the king, chiefs, and principal headmen and people of Adansi, they hereby bind themselves, their heirs and successors, to keep their main roads in good order, that they will encourage trade and give facilities to traders, and will not cede their territory to, or accept a protectorate from, or enter into any agreement, arrangement, or treaty with, any other foreign power except through and with the consent of the Government of her Majesty the Queen-Empress.

ARTICLE VII.

The Government of her Majesty the Queen-Empress will not prevent the King of Adansi, or his chiefs, and principal headmen and their lawful successors from levying customary revenues appertaining to them according to the laws and customs of their country, nor in the administration thereof; and her Majesty's Government will respect the habits and customs of the country, but will not permit human sacrifices ; and slave dealing,* when brought to the notice of the Government, will be punished according to the laws of the Gold Coast.

ARTICLE VIII.

This treaty shall come into force from the date hereof, but power is expressly reserved to her Majesty the Queen-Empress to refuse to approve and ratify the same within one year from the date hereof. In witness whereof the parties to this treaty have hereunto set their hands and affixed their respective seals. Done in triplicate at Prahsue, in the country of Assin, this 18th

* Extract from report of Captain Stewart and Mr. Vroom, October 26, 1895.

" The treaty in triplicate we beg to attach. The Adansis objected very strongly to the clause in the treaty with reference to slave-dealing. However, notwithstanding that, they signed the treaty willingly."

day of November, in the year one thousand eight hundred and ninety-five, in the fifty-eighth year of the reign of her Majesty the Queen-Empress.

Names of signatories.   Their marks and seals :—

	Marks.	Seal.
1. Kweku Inkansa, King of Adansi	×	,,
2. Kofi Kwedu, War Chief of Adansi	×	,,
3. Kojo Gimma, Chief of Ayowasi	×	,,
4. Kweku Ashanti, Chief of Edubiasi	×	,,
5. Akwesi Fori, Chief of Dompoasi	×	,,
6. Kweku Afuakwa, Chief of Ekrofrome, represented by Yow Yamua	×	,,
7. Yaw Apia, Chief of Akrochire	×	,,
8. Kwabina Kwantabissa, Chief of Odumasi	×	,,
9. Kweku Wia, Chief of Kwisa	×	,,
10. Kwami Iduo, Chief of Brobidiasi	×	,,
11. Kwami Essifii, Chief of Abejimu	×	,,
12. Kwami Apeajo, represented by You Simpon, of Adomemu	×	,,
13. Kwabina Chiadi, Chief of Eginasi	×	,,
14. Kwesi Buabin, Chief of Medomma	×	,,
15. Kofi Ammua, represented by Se-Kojo of Kianbusu	×	,,

DONALD WILLIAM STEWART, Captain,
Travelling Commissioner, an officer in the Civil Service of the Gold Coast Colony, for and on behalf of William Edward Maxwell, Governor of the Gold Coast Colony.

(Seal) Signed, sealed, and delivered in our presence, the same having been first read over and interpreted to the king, chiefs, and people, who seemed perfectly to understand the meaning, conditions, and scope of the foregoing treaty.

HK. VROOM, District Commr.
J. H. CRAMER, Captain.
R. A. IRVINE, Captain.
M. HAWTREY, Captain.
K. F. T. BUEE, Ass. Col. Surgeon.

Blue Book [C. 7917], February, 1896.

XII.

Deed of Conveyance in the Fanti Language.

Ahyiemdzi-Wuma iyi wo-aye nu wo *Onumabu* wo busum o-tsiã *esiã* (June) ni dâ o-tsiã *10* wo afi 1903 numu A.B. onyi D.F. hon nyina wofi *Nkubem* wo *Isim* (Axim) afãm wo-gyina ma honara honhũ nna su wo-gyina ma hon ebusuĩa odzikor iyi wo-fre hon Atonfunu wo afã na onyi *Kofi Mensa* a wo-fi * *Sekunde* odzikor iyi wo-fre nu † Nya-Orito-iyi nusu wo afã.

Susuampa de Atonfunu wo nyi hon ebusuĩafu ‡ wo asiasi nyi numu adzi nyina wo-akyire mu wo he-iyi Na Susuampa de dam ebusuĩafu iyi numu etsitsir nyina wo-apini na wo nyi Nya-Orito-iyi akyi kyir de wo-riton asiasi nu na wo-edzi anu efua *abendaa anan* Na Susuampa de Nya-Orito-iyi oa-tsiw ni tsir Trama na wo-dzi asiasi nu ahye ni nsa na asiasi nu ni hyi wo-akyire na wo-etua kã wo adasifu anukwafu enim Na Susuampa de nkrofu emu-ebien nyina apini de wo-baye Ahyiemdzi-Wuma iyi edzi dza wo-aye iyi hũ adansi ama esu o-ahye Nya-Orito-iyi ni tum owo asiasi iyi du nu mã Sa-ntir-a nkiyi Ahyiemdzi wuma iyi dzi dasi de onam pini-a wo-abodzin nu na su onam Trama dwua sura oa tsiw na su abendaa anan a Nya-Orito-iyi etua ama Atonfunu nyi hon ebusuĩafu mu etsitsir nu mma Atonfunu wo-nam iyi du wo-pini de hon nsa akã Hon Atonfunu wo-nam Ahyiemdzi-wuma iyi du hyira asiasi nu nyi numu adzi nyina du ma Nya-Orito-iyi onyi obiara o-nam nu du asiasi iyi boko ni nsa mu nu na asiasi nu onu iyi ebusuĩafu Asiasi-a o-da *Mfuma* kwan nu nkyen na ni tsintsin ye anamon § *aha-esiã* (160) na ni teter ye anamon *ahaasã eduesiã* (360) na ni hyĩ nyi *Mfuma Kwan Kwesi Kuma n'asiasi Emisa baka* de mbre wo-akyirew nu yie wo nfopin a owo iyi mu nu Na Atonfunu de mbre wo-akã nu dadã nu wo-pini na wo-dzi asiasi nu onyi numu ndzinua nyi tûm nyi ahû-womu a hon nyinara nkurkur nyi hon ebusuĩafu wowo wo du na onyi biribiara wo-piri nu wo mu ankurankur nyi ebusuĩafu nu nyinara wo dzi ma Nya-orito-iyi na onyi obiara o-nam nu du asiasi iyi beye nu dzi nu afibõ kepim de asiasi nu nyi nu mu nyi nu hũ adzinyina o-ye Nya-Orito-iyi na obiara o-nam nu du asiasi

---

* If more than one purchaser, substitute " o-fi," for " wo-fi."

† " Hon Nympa-Worito-iyi " for " nu Nya-Orito-iyi."

‡ If the land belongs to a clan, then write " Ebusuĩa."

§ Or fathoms, *abasamu.*

beye nu dzi nu kurakura de ATONFUNU hon ebusuĩafu biara o-
mpaa hon hũ egō o-ntũtũ hon anamon mu wo hũ o-npiripiri hũ
onnyi du tûm o-nbisa hon h asem biara Na asiasi nu odzikor iyi
owo ho de mbre hen man iyi mu asiasi hũ aman-mbra nu kyire
nu ara Na ATONFUNU wo-nam iyi du nyi NYA-ORITO-IYI onyi
obiara o-nam nu du asiasi iyi beye nu dzi nu kyikyir de hon na
hon ebusuĩafu sesie wowo hũ kwan nyi tûm de wo-ton asiasi nu
de mbre wo-akā dadā nu esu de asiasi nu o-da ho totoritō de
mbatahũ biara onyi hũ nna hon ebusuĩafu nu hon mu obiara o-
nkaye biribiara a o-bama oton a wo-aton asiasi nu anā mbre wo-
aye nu iyi wo-etsia aman-mbra Nna su NYA-ORITO-IYI onyi obiara
o-nam nu du asiasi iyi beye nu dzi nu wowo de wo-fa asiasi nu
mu adzi nyina wo-tsina du kōm na ofir nde o-dzi-kor iyi wo-gye
nu mu asrandzi nu mu mfasu nyinara wo-dzi ma hon de Atonfunu anā obiara nsiw hon kwan o-ntũtũ hon anamon mu o-nbisa
hon hũ asi anā mpiripiri hũ Na su Atonfunu de mbre wo-akā nu
dadā nu wo ni hon ebusuĩafu nyinara ofir nde dzikor iyi se Nya-
Orito-iyi ana obiara o-nam nu du asiasi iyi beye nu dzi hwihwe na
se o-tua kā a wo-beye biribiara ana wo-bakyirew wuma biara a o-
bama Nya-Orito-iyi onyi damu nyimpa iyi hon tûm wo asiasi nu
mu esi pi de mbre o-hyā de wo-ye nu Na iyi nu hũ dasihye nna
nkrofu emu-ebien iyi wo-dzi hon nsa onyi hon daagyii ahye asi
wo dā onyi afi a wo-akyirew dadā nu.

Asiasi nu hũ nfonin iyi.

*   *   *   *   *   *

Nsem a o-wo wuma iyi mu wo-kinkan na wo-kyire ⎫ A.B.
  asi kyire nkrofu iyi wo hon kasda mu ma wo- ⎪ D.F.
  tsi asi kotō nu nna wo-dzi hon nsa hye asi na ⎬ Kofi
  wo-dzi daagyii si du wo adasifu iyi hen Enim. ⎭ Mensa.

Akwesi Danfu,
Efua Inkosu.

INDEX.

THE END.